The Asian Gang

Ethnicity, Identity, Masculinity

Claire E. Alexander

BERG

Oxford • New York

First published in 2000 by
Berg
Editorial offices:
150 Cowley Road, Oxford, OX4 1JJ, UK
838 Broadway, Third Floor, New York, NY 10003-4812, USA

© Claire E. Alexander 2000

Berg is an imprint of Oxford International Publishers Ltd.

Library of Congress Cataloging-in-Publication Data
A catalogue record for this book is available from the Library of Congress.

British Library Cataloguing-in-Publication Data
A catalogue record for this book is available from the British Library.

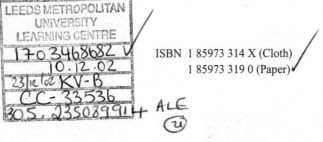
ISBN 1 85973 314 X (Cloth)
1 85973 319 0 (Paper)

Typeset by JS Typesetting, Wellingborough, Northants.
Printed in the United Kingdom by Biddles Ltd, Guildford and King's Lynn.

For my families – old and new

Contents

Acknowledgements

The Asian Gang began as a three-year postdoctoral study on Muslim youth identities funded by the British Academy and based at the Open University. I am grateful for both institutions for their support and for allowing me the time and space to conduct such an in-depth study. I especially benefited from the wisdom and patient guidance of Professor Stuart Hall over those years and since. The writing of the work mainly took place during my time at Southampton University and was finished at South Bank University. I would like to thank colleagues at both places for their support, most especially Professor John Solomos, who gave me advice on publishing, feedback on earlier drafts and listened to my occasional rants with good humour.

I am grateful to Berg publishers and particularly Kathryn Earle, for taking a chance on the manuscript at a time when monographs are unfashionable and Asian youth still considered a marginal topic. I would also like to thank their reader for the comments offered on the manuscript.

Thanks also to Suki Dhanda for providing a stunning photograph for the book cover.

Many friends and colleagues have been roped into commenting on the formulation and drafts of the book, and I would like to take this chance to thank them for their time, effort and generosity. In particular, I would like to thank Ko Banerjea for taking time out from buying '80s vinyl to offer detailed comments and for the many hours of conversation over oceans of tea from which I learned much (but for which he refuses to be held responsible). I have also benefited from the insights and sympathetic critiques of Brian Alleyne, Les Back, Wendy Bottero, Barnor Hesse, Kate Reed, Tracey Reynolds, Brett St. Louis and Ossie Stuart. Thanks are due also to many colleagues at Southampton and South Bank, including Caroline Knowles, Susan Halford, Mel Semple, Paul Bridgen, Harry Goulbourne, Lisa Schuster and Shaminder Takhar. I would also like to thank Ash and Sanjay Sharma and Virinder Kalra, as well as others in the *TranslAsia* project, for providing me with a stimulating intellectual environment with which to engage and think through the work.

Da Asian Gang (as it has become popularly known amongst my friends – thanks Ryan) has been an all-consuming passion for nearly five years.

Acknowledgements

My friends and family have stood by me through a number of personal and professional changes, and I would not have made it without them. I thank my parents for tolerating with equanimity what must have been some trying times and for having, as Hanif put it, 'brought me up very well'. Special thanks are due to my mother who transcribed my interviews for me. Thanks and love also to my new families in India and in London, especially Shanaz, Shahena (who sat with two dictionaries to read the book and kept asking why I didn't write it more clearly) and Kudheza (for all those cups of tea). I would also like to thank AnnMarie Sylvester-Charles, Clare Twigger-Ross, Huma Rizvi, Simone Abrams, Simon Heighes, Mark Larrimore, Emma Truman, Rachel Wicaksono, Ruth Quinn, Yunas Samad and Mariam Khan for always being there or at the end of a 'phone.

The study would not have been possible without the assistance of many people, including the Youth Service and the SAYO project office and I am grateful for all their help. Thanks to Dave, Hyacinth and Roger for giving me my second home, a desk and a computer. Thanks too to all the people who took part in interviews and discussions as part of the study – Julia, Shopna, Majid, Amitabh and Michael. Love and thanks to my friends and co-workers over the past years – to Yasmin, Sher Khan, Silver, Farhan and Hashim without whom the study would never have happened.

Last and most, I send my love and gratitude to the young men of the SAYO project, who have transformed my life in many ways: to 'the older lot', Shahin, Humzah, S. Ahmed, Zohar, Khalid and Shakiel who have been a source of strength and support; and to 'the little ones', Hanif, Ifti, Jamal, Sayeed, Ismat, Mohammed, Faruk, Enam and Shafiq, who have sometimes driven me to the point of distraction but who have always been a source of joy and laughter and love. To Shahin, Humzah, Khalid and Hanif, who read every word in the following pages, I send special thanks. Thanks are also due to the many young men who make fleeting appearances in the text but whom I have come to know and respect over the past years, especially Mustafa, Salman, Liaquot, Jahedul, Ashraf and Malik. Thank you for trusting me enough to open up your lives and for bearing with me – I hope the book comes close to repaying that trust.

Preface

In the early weeks of 2000, a young Bengali man appeared in a local Crown Court charged with grievous bodily harm. The prosecution case was straightforward: that the previous summer he and a friend had attacked another young man, also Bengali, and attempted to rob him. Later that day, when the victim and four friends saw the two young men on the road, they stopped their car to talk to them. The victim and two friends got out of the car but on approaching the other two young men, the defendant pulled a knife and stabbed the victim twice – once in the lung and once on the shoulder – before running away. An ambulance was called and the victim was in hospital for a week, needing forty six stitches in his lung and two in his shoulder. The defence case was also straightforward: the defendant had been the subject of abuse earlier in the day due to a long-standing feud between himself and a friend of the victim; that the victim and his friends were a 'gang' seeking revenge on an outsider; that *they* had brought the knife and had stabbed the defendant first in the leg; and that he had acted in self defence.

The victim and his friends were all in Court to give testimony: that they had no intention to harm the young man; that they were on their way to see his parents; that they carried no weapons and that they were concerned only to sort out the earlier incident with a young man whom they had known for years and regarded almost as a younger brother. The police evidence was clear: they had been called to the site of the stabbing of the victim; his was the only blood present at the scene; they had been called twenty minutes later to the defendant's aid, where they found a bandage with the victim's blood on the floor and a jacket belonging to the defendant's friend covered with the defendant's blood hidden in a nearby skip; there was a trail of blood leading from that area to the defendant's home. There was no knife. The police argued that the evidence showed that the defendant had been stabbed by his friend in the leg to give credence to his claim of self-defence. On his arrest, the defendant lied about his name and age and refused to give any account of the incident. The registrar from the hospital, who had treated the victim's wound, told the Court that the knife had entered the lung twice and had been inserted with considerable force. On the last day, the defendant took the stand – he was the only defence witness, his friend could not be found. He admitted to smashing a bottle over the victim's head earlier in the day; claimed that he had been too afraid to tell the police his real name and age for fear of reprisals; that he had wrested the knife from the victim after he had been stabbed in the leg; that he had not meant to hurt him; that he had acted in self-defence.

After two and a half hours, the verdict was returned: the defendant was not guilty.

Watching the proceedings, sometimes from inside the courtroom, sometimes from outside, through the glass door panel, where I was keeping the victim and his friends company, I wondered how the jury – two Asian, two black, eight white – would make sense of the jumble of facts and assertions before them. For me, knowing the history leading up to the stabbing, knowing the young men involved – the victim and his friends well, the defendant slightly – and knowing that the defendant had a history of violence and criminal behaviour, it seemed (and still seems) incomprehensible that the verdict could be other than guilty. In the absence of this knowledge, the jury was faced with six unknown Asian young men, with two diametrically opposed versions of events; one version backed up with police and medical testimony and the other with a convenient explanatory framework – 'the Gang'.

The symbol of 'the Gang' in framing these events was a compelling one on a number of levels; one that was established by the defence barrister from the outset as providing a common-sense set of under-standings and justifications that stood, even in the face of the evidence, and emerged triumphant. Within the setting that perhaps most of all symbolizes British institutional power – the judicial system – the notion of 'the Gang' served to position *all* the Bengali young men present as alien and implicitly deviant, as outside the realms of law and citizenship, beyond understanding and – as it turned out – beyond its protection. 'The Gang' thus broke down any distinction between victim and perpetrator to cast *all* the young men as villains, a situation in which none could be innocent and all were equally guilty. 'The Gang' also worked to eradicate the specificities of the incident, its history, its personalities, its con-sequences, and replace them with a catch-all fantasy of feuds and revenge, through which acts of extreme violence become naturalized and dismissed as simply part of the script. The substitution of a set of ready-made pathologies for explanation served to silence or render suspect alternative accounts, erasing cultural, historical and individual specificities in favour of a racialized all-purpose framework, in which the young men were

viewed as all the same, all as bad as each other, and all equally to blame
for what had happened. 'The Gang' was, then, explanation and justification for the events: that one young man nearly died was, simply, his
own fault. One of those things that comes with the territory of 'the Gang'.
One group of unknown Asians against another group of unknown Asians;
a self-contained, internal dispute that had gone out of hand with no-one
(or everyone) responsible, nothing to be done and no-one to really care.

'The Gang' exists more as an idea than a reality – a mode of interpretation rather than an object, more fiction than fact. It becomes self-
generating, self-fulfiling and axiomatic, impossible to disprove and
imbued with the residual power of common-sense 'Truth'. It is this
common-sense truth that transforms five Bengali young men who grew
up together, went to the same school and live on the same estate into a
vengeful hit squad, an unprovoked attack into a turf war and its victim
into a mere casualty of that war. However, as the Court verdict made
painfully clear, the concept has more than explanatory power, becoming
a concrete reality with embodied consequences – something the victim
and his friends have to live with. Not that *that* was a surprise for the
young men involved. Living with 'the Gang' was something they did on
an everyday basis.

'The Asian Gang' in particular has gained currency in recent years as
a commonsense fiction of life. Media reports have gleefully announced
the arrival of this new 'folk devil' on the urban landscape and academia
has followed in the wake of tales of burgeoning 'Asian' criminality and
civil unrest. 'The Asian Gang' shares with its more embracing generic
counterpart the assertions of threat, of anger, of alienation, of violence,
but it also carries its own culturally specific twists – of culture conflict,
religious antipathy, of alienness and unknowability, of introspective, intra-
ethnic hatred. A menace to society, but *theirs* not ours – for now at least.

'The Asian Gang' marks a re-imagination of Asian communities in
Britain around the nexus of gender, generation and class. The gaze is
now on a reinvented 'Other' – young, male, working class, or underclass
– increasingly fused with the spectre of religious 'Fundamentalism'. Asian
youth identities are increasingly unimaginable in any other terms,
characterised by unremitting negativity and multiple pathologies. The
space for alternative imagination is increasingly surveyed, patrolled,
legislated and censored. Stories and identities framed in black and white
– literally and figuratively – heroes and villains, mainly villains.

The Asian Gang is an account of this story, of this folk devil, if not in
glorious technicolour then at least in shades of grey. Taking as its starting
point the emergence of 'the Asian Gang' in the media, the book charts

the academic underpinnings of this latest moral panic around the formation of Muslim identities, with its triple pathologization of 'race', gender and youth. While the past decade has seen the reconfiguration of the race relations landscape around issues of religion and the reification of cultural 'difference', it has also placed Muslim young men in the spotlight as the epitome of crisis and cultural atrophy. By making explicit the common themes and assumptions underlying this 'crisis', the book aims to challenge the common-sense foundation of 'The Asian Gang', and point towards a re-imagination of identities focused on process, context and negotiation. At the same time, the book insists on the constitutive, if not definitive, role of dominant representations in the formation of identities. Identities are created, resisted and negotiated in the encounter between structure and agency, 'Other' and self, representation and a more complex reality.

Although such claims are easily and fashionably made, they too often remain at the level of assertion rather than exploration. *The Asian Gang*, like my earlier work, *The Art of Being Black* (1996) is an attempt to flesh out theoretical abstracts through ethnographic research. Both are concerned with the creation of raced identities amongst young men, both focus on change, contestation and ambivalence, and on the tension between external definition and self-invention. Where the earlier work saw this encounter as a creative space – perhaps a 'third space' – the present work sees it more as an engagement, inescapable and ongoing, fraught with danger and contradiction. Less a dramatic play than a struggle for the right to exist, literally and conceptually, outside of the logic of 'the Gang'. Like *The Art of Being Black*, the present work focuses on internal definitions, on moments that exist apart from the dominant paradigm, away from the 'Othering' gaze. It focuses on understandings that are made invisible in the reductive objectification of 'the Gang', or that are rendered deviant through its lens. However, these alternative identities are placed in relation to dominant constructions, contested and constrained – but never quite contained; what I always envision as the play between a dancer and his (in this case) shadow.

The study aims to paint an in-depth and intimate portrait of a small group of young men over an extended period of time – to date four-and-a-half years and counting. Based in and around an Asian youth project in South London, the book explores the formation of peer group and community identities set against the backdrop of national and local mythologies of 'the Asian Gang'. The emphasis throughout is on change and constraint, on fragmentation and solidarity, on boundaries imagined and re-imagined, on creativity and survival. Like the previous work, the focus is on process, which renders authenticist and essentialist accounts of Muslim youth identity untenable, yet still allows for the imagination of community, for loyalty and for friendship. The aim is not to turn villains into heroes – though I suspect most people still prefer their stories in black and white – still less into victims; but to argue for the recognition of complexity in the living through of identities, not just at the level of empirical lip-service and theoretical posturing but in flesh and blood.

The search for flesh-and-blood theorisation has led me to explore a more open, dialogic approach to the study and the process of writing. Rather than privileging the myth of ethnographic experience as 'Truth', I have attempted to highlight the interaction of researcher and subjects in the production of a highly situated knowledge. The result is an explicitly partial and personal account of a set of encounters located within a particular space and time – what I have chosen to label 'fiction'. While resisting claims to 'Truth' or 'the real' in this portrait, the aim has not been to abdicate responsibility to the wider context of racialized representation, inequality and violence that frames 'the Asian Gang', but to insist on the implication of research and writing within this framing and the necessary contestation of the mono-dimensional caricatures and too easy solutions on offer. Just as 'the Asian Gang' is not an ideologically neutral empirical reality, nor can *The Asian Gang* allow itself to be separated from this wider web of signification and struggle.

The Asian Gang, then, is a set of stories within a larger narrative – stories that are not reducible to that narrative nor apart from it. It is a study of social processes writ small, but it is also a story about people, who live and breathe – and bleed – outside of these moments, outside of these pages and beyond the limits of 'the Asian Gang'.

Introduction

Details have emerged this week about a recent flare up between black and Asian youths at the Thomas More School . . .

Police had to call on support from the Territorial Support Group to deal with the tension that erupted last month.

Superintendent Daniel Hirons told the Police and Community Consultative Group that a fight broke out between black and Asian pupils in the school canteen.

Police returned to the school later that day, but the pupils went home without any incident. The following day, a black youth was attacked by fourteen Asian youngsters and sustained a fractured elbow and a bump on his head.

Police patrols were stepped up and were called to deal with several stand offs between youths on the nearby Stoneleigh Estate.

Things came to a head when officers patrolling Abbey Street came across youths making petrol bombs – with six already prepared.

Police called in the TSG to ensure a large presence to deter any more trouble, particularly when large groups of youths were seen roaming the estate.

Superintendent Hirons told the SPCCG: 'We must get the message across to young people that they should not be taking the law in to their own hands.

They risk damaging the quality of life for everyone where they live if they continue to behave in this way.' (Local Press Report, Summer 1996)

At 7.30 p.m, Friday 25 October 1996, the lights went up on the stage at the Clifton Community Centre, South London. To the sound of Josh Winks' techno-track, *A Higher State of Consciousness*, ten young men walked into the spotlight and introduced themselves. They were Stoneleigh Asian Youth Organization[1]: this was *Style and Culture '96*.

Taking place as part of a wider series of events to celebrate Black History Month, *Style and Culture '96* was a fashion show and cultural display by a group of predominantly Bangladeshi young men. The models were all aged 14–15 years old, members of a project for Asian young men based in a South London borough. With the support of three semi-professional Asian models, their full-time youth worker, Yasmin Ullah and her staff team (including myself), these young men took control of the lighting, music and stage management, helped choreograph the walks, modelled and compered the show. The clothes were a combination of the group's own designer labels, and traditional and designer Asian wear donated by stores in Brick Lane and Green Street. The result of over six months of research and preparation, and two months of practice, nervousness and foot-faltering, confusion and increasing self-confidence, the fashion show lasted an hour and a half, enacting a dramatic mixture of routines to an audience of jubilant and noisy, if slightly astonished, brothers and sisters, youth and community workers, friends and neighbours. *Style and Culture '96* was, in every sense, a 'community' event. And it was a triumph.

A week or so later, I found myself on a housing estate in East London, at 7.30 in the morning, in the cold and rain, dressed for summer, on the set of a new British film. I was there with Yasmin, who had been contacted at the youth club by a casting agency in desperate search of Asian extras, particularly women, for an unspecified project. The film, it transpired later, was a 'love story/thriller', about a teenage girl who joins 'a gang', but then falls in love with a teacher and runs away to Yorkshire with him. The intricacies of the plot eluded me but my role, as I shivered in the requested 'traditional *costume*' was obviously to provide background ethnic colour – literally and figuratively – for one of the gang scenes. In search of an authentic inner-city environment, which fully reflected the depravity of youth gang sub-culture, the film crew chose to locate in a condemned, though still inhabited, block on one of the poorest housing estates in London. Even this was obviously, however, not quite 'authentic' enough, so the crew had imported three 'yoof' skateboarders from a public school in Hampshire and a burned-out estate car for added atmosphere. It was a strange feeling, being transformed from an anthropologist with a morning to spare and her own 'costume', to a marker for inner-city deprivation; an experience I, perhaps rather naively, had not expected and not one with which I was entirely happy. The film did not seem to draw much support from the crowd of Bengali young men who gathered around, either, watching with a mixture of bemusement and vocal derision as their homes and lives were transformed into gangland fantasy.

What struck me more forcibly was the continuity between this fantasy masquerading as cutting-edge reality and the current popular and media obsession with inner-city youth. Amongst the clamour of anger, accusation and recrimination that characterizes the recent series of moral panics over youth gangs, girl gangs, Triads, bullying, exclusions, violence against teachers and failing schools, events such as *Style and Culture '96* become something of a sideshow. Or perhaps more accurately, are rendered simply invisible, supplanted by a series of snapshots and soundbites characterized by an unremitting negativity that requires only a burned-out car in the foreground to ensure its authenticity.

What my stint as an Asian extra also made me acutely, and rather painfully, aware of was the way in which markers of 'race' have become – or perhaps I mean remained – a symbol for all of these concerns. Indeed, it could be argued that the phantasm of 'race' is what binds these new moral panics together, and provides the continuity with their earlier incarnations. 'Race' has become so completely synonymous with ideas of moral and social decline as to become invisible; an absent-presence, the power of which is so much assumed that it no longer needs to be overtly articulated. The silent racialization of images of urbanization, poverty, and particularly of 'problem' youth, acts as unquestioned cause and sufficient explanation – a necessary marker of contemporary life and more so of contemporary social breakdown. Rather than a participant in a multi-cultural, multi-racial landscape, I had become instead a representation of all that was wrong with it, an easy but potent signifier of urban decay, social anomie and cultural atrophy. I had become a folk-devil.

A couple of weeks later still, an article in the London *Evening Standard* formally proclaimed the arrival of this new folk-devil – 'Asian Teenage Gangs Terrorising London' (13 November 1996). Here are all the hallmarks of 'authentic' gangland London – youths wielding weapons, alienated from their families, their community and British society, locked into a cycle of meaningless violence, low self-esteem and self-destruction. Headteacher Michael Marland thus warns of 'a new underclass of illiterates, who have acquired a habit of violence', creating what the article describes as an 'almost apocalyptic vision of unrest'. And if the talk of 'nihilistic . . . violence' echoes a Powellian 'rivers-of-blood' style philosophy, then it also plays silently into the same images of racial and cultural conflict.

The evocation of racialized representations of Asian youth, and particularly of Asian young men, has served both to focus media and public attention on this new 'problem' group and obscure a wider, more complex understanding of youth identities and identifications. Images of hooded young men on council estates have fed on well-established tropes of racial alienation and cultural difference to create a potent symbol of disorder that seemingly requires no further explanation – 'race' has become a substitute for analysis.

The same processes are at work in the opening article, taken from a local newspaper. The article concerns a series of encounters between some black young men and some of the Bengali young men from the SAYO project, which took place over several weeks a few months prior to the

– 3 –

fashion show. The actual details of these encounters will be considered in a later chapter. What is of interest here is the way in which notions of 'race' and 'difference' are inscribed in the article and used as an implicit rationale for the events.

'Race' is used overtly throughout the piece only as a form of group label; it is significant that it is the 'racial' identifications 'black' and 'Asian' that form the primary identification for the two groups, which were in reality formed around a relatively narrow subset of friends from school and the local area. In addition to these labels, however, 'race' is articulated through a series of racialized codes focused on disorder and lawlessness. Emotive and meaning-laden language such as 'flare up', 'tension', 'stand offs', 'erupted', conjure up a vision of urban unrest, a vision consolidated through the image of 'large groups of youths roaming the estate', petrol bombs at hand and only held in check through the intervention of the Territorial Support Group. And if this sounds like the Bradford riots, it wasn't – it was a series of loosely connected, sporadic and small-scale, admittedly sometimes violent, but intensely personal and personality-led, fights between a very specific group of fourteen- and fifteen-year-old young men.

The effect of this silent racialization is to render obsolete any more complex or alternative explanation for these events. No reason or context for the fights is given in the article nor, in its own terms is it deemed necessary: the spectre of 'race' with its implications of absolute and hostile difference, conflict and 'nihilistic . . . violence' is left to speak for itself – at once cause, effect and justification.

Of Youth and the New Asian Folk-devil: The Rise of 'the Asian Gang'

What both the local newspaper report and the *Evening Standard* article reflect is a growing concern with the 'problem' of Asian youth – and more specifically, with the 'problem' of *Muslim young men*. If they share the same well-established tropes of racial alienation and social breakdown that created, and continue to create, moral panics over Rastafarian drug dealers, black rioters, muggers and Yardies (Hall 1978; CCCS 1982; Gilroy 1987; Alexander 1996), what they also reflect is a new cultural formation.

It is revealing, and perhaps more than a little ironic, that these same shared markers were until comparatively recently used as a form of distinction between the African-Caribbean and Asian communities. Where the former were racked with tales of culture conflict, generation gap, lack of parental control, alienation and despair, Britain's Asian communities were held to be, by contrast, holistic and coherent, alien and incomprehensible perhaps, but peaceable, law-abiding, successful and – the odd scare about illegal immigration aside – largely unproblematic (Benson, 1996).[2] A *Guardian* article (13 September 1991) states:

> There is worse poverty today in some Asian communities. But very poor Asians, however desperate their material plight, have a sense of their own worth; they connect to a tradition, a history and a culture.

Indeed, it is in this very coherence – the assumption of absolute and unchanging difference – that both the strength and the weakness of Asian communities and cultures is held to reside. As an article in the *Daily Mail* (28 July 1993), intriguingly titled 'Can Asians Recivilise our Inner Cities?' argues:

> One does not encounter among them [Asian communities] that moral, spiritual and cultural vacuum in which so many of the native young now live. Indeed, the very closeness of Asian families often gives rise to terrible and tragic problems when parents seek to keep alive the traditions that they remember from their upbringing in India and Pakistan while their children, *surrounded by a different culture,* seek to enjoy the *freedoms of British youth.* [emphasis added].

Leaving aside here the opposition of 'native young' and implicitly alien Asian families, not to mention the questionable freedoms of British youth, the article displays a more profound ambiguity about the Asian presence in Britain. On the one hand, the invocation of strong cultural values and traditions are seen as a positive contribution to society, overtly challenging wider social decay, whereas on the other, they are seen as constituting a source of internal oppression for the young. The coalescence of strength and oppression has been most noticeably focused in relation to Asian young women, where public concerns particularly over arranged marriage systems have served as a critique of an assumed patriarchal absolutism (CCCS, 1982: 75). It is worth noting that although concerns over African-Caribbean communities have been primarily fixated on black young men, Asian young men have been largely invisible until three or four years ago, the presumed beneficiaries of a rigid system of male hierarchy and privilege.

However, written into this attribution of cultural homogeneity and particularity are the seeds of its inevitable atrophy, a sense of cultural displacement and anachronism, which has been easily reinvented as contemporary assertions of 'nihilistic ... violence' amongst Asian communities.

* * *

On the wall of the office of SAYO there is a poster, one of a series entitled 'Common assumptions and stereotypes about the Asian community'. The poster is a cartoon, depicting two Asian men, one with goatee beard and Muslim headwear telling the other, 'I suppose with you being Gujerati and me being Bangladeshi and being born and brought up 4500 miles apart, you can forgive them for thinking we're the same'. In the wake of the *Satanic Verses* furore and the Gulf War, this perception of homogeneity has undergone something of a sea change (Samad, 1996). The attention generated by these events has had two broad effects; firstly, it has led to a division in the perception of previously undistinguished Asian communities (Modood, 1992) and secondly, it has brought the issue of youth to the foreground.

Although in some quarters this change has been welcomed as liberating and a belated recognition of the diversity of Asian cultures (Modood, 1992), it has also created a perceptual split along religio-cultural lines, which has more damaging implications. Attention has thus become focused on religious difference, which has in turn become a marker for differential social success or failure. Tariq Modood, for example, has contrasted Indian 'achievers' with the disadvantaged 'believers' (1992: 43), an emergent Muslim Pakistani and Bangladeshi 'underclass' given its most notorious embodiment in the 1993 *Panorama* documentary *Purdah in the Underclass*.

The reification of Islam as one of the key markers of difference in contemporary British racial discourse has proved pervasive and politically potent, providing the impetus for renewed public debates around immigration, integration and the requirements of citizenship. Voicing these concerns in the aftermath of the Rushdie affair, John Patten was quoted in the *Times*:

> The last few months have been difficult ones for British Muslims. The issue of race relations has been thrown into sharp relief and all of us have had to think deeply ... about what it means to be British, and particularly about what it means to be a British Muslim. (5 July 1989, in Solomos, 1993: 224)

Increasingly it seems that what it means to be a British Muslim is definably solely in terms of negativity, deprivation, disadvantage and alienation. It is worth noting here that the term 'Asian' in relation to negative images and stereotypes has become synonymous with Muslim communities, again drawing on the notion of an emergent Pakistani and Bangladeshi underclass. An *Independent* article of July 1995, warning of an 'Asian crime "timebomb"' suggests, 'that the country is on the verge of an outbreak of disorder caused by Asians'. Recent Home Office research pins this to 'A demographic timebomb of Pakistani and Bangladeshi youths [which] is likely to explode and could shatter the belief that Asians are more law-abiding than white or black people'.[3] As an inevitable corollary to this, images of cultural dysfunction have grown apace, most notably in regard to young men, who were at the visual and perceptual front-line of both the anti-Rushdie protests and the demonstrations against the Gulf War.

In the wake of angry demonstrations in Tower Hamlets following the racial attack on Quddus Ali in September 1993, Vivek Chaudhary points to the 'discovery' of Asian youth:

> The press claim to have discovered something new – that Asians are at last fighting back. But active resistance has been an integral part of the history of our community . . . from Southall to Smethwick, from Bradford to Brick Lane . . . the rolecall of resistance is endless, (*Guardian*, 16 September 1993)

Through the lens of the media, however, 'resistance' has become increasingly synonymous with criminality and upheaval, with the breakdown of perceived traditional values and the growth of a pathologized culture of alienation and confusion. As part of this, representations of 'the Asian community' have moved from a concern with a uniformly victim status to that of perpetrator – a reinvention of passive recipient to active combatant which has simultaneously, and significantly, transformed the gendered markers of imagined Asian identities. Concerns have thus increasingly focused on the public activities of young men – the youth in the streets (Keitha, 1995) – rather than the more domestic, 'private' concerns of young women.

An *Independent* article (20 April 1992) captures the beginning of this transformation. Its author writes:

> The East End is fast becoming a neighbourhood of ghettos, a breeding ground of intolerance and violent frustrations . . . Racial violence has been increasing for several years, but *the Asian gangs are a new phenomenon*, and the increasing frequency of their confrontations is a sign, many fear, of things to come. (emphasis added)

The links between 'race', violence, urban decay, ghetto life, the underclass, poverty and criminality are made explicitly here. On the one hand the article asserts socio-economic justifications, 'The new East End is, like its predecessors, a product of poverty', while simultaneously conjuring images of racial/ethnic specificity on the other – these are, as the title of the piece makes clear, 'new rivalries'. Integral to both is the construction of 'the Asian Gang', with its inevitable links with notions of tribalism, violence and criminality, 'Every estate has its gang . . . They fight to protect not only their territory but their rights to steal.'

Two years later, the transformation seems complete. A *Sunday Times* feature of 21 August 1994, a week after the death of Richard Everitt in Camden, for example, reports that sixty per cent of racial attacks in Oldham are perpetrated by Asians on whites. Leaving aside tangible problems in the reporting and registering of what constitutes a 'racial attack', the article is significant in its representation of Asian youths as newly active, and newly threatening, agents in the public arena. Again, racialized images are at the forefront of the piece, notably making a direct comparison with African-American gang subculture, with all its implications of extreme violence, nihilism and danger:

> The gangs, predominantly youngsters from Bangladeshi families, take their inspiration from Afro-American culture. Mimicking gangs in L.A., they wear hooded jackets and baggy jeans and listen to rap and ragga music. An increase in drug taking and dealing among young Asians has happened in tandem.

Besides criminalizing by association a large section of contemporary mainstream youth culture and style in an extraordinary manner, the article draws on the assumptions of Asian cultural particularity discussed earlier as the most salient – not to mention the most readily available – explanation. Hitherto holistic cultures are thus portrayed as breaking down in the face of implicitly superior Western values and freedoms, playing into familiar tropes of cultural difference and inevitable tensions. The same article reports:

> Police and community groups are increasingly alarmed by an upsurge in inner-city violence, led by *traditionally well-behaved* Asian youths. Detectives blame the disturbing rise in crime on the disintegration of family life in Asian homes as children refuse to obey their elders. (emphasis added)

The ongoing criminalization of Asian youth, and especially Muslim youth, can be traced in recent years to two significant events – the murder of Richard Everitt in 1994, and the 'riots' in Bradford in the following year.

Introduction

Richard Everitt was stabbed and killed in South Camden in August 1994, by a group of Asian young men, one of whom, Badrul Miah, is now serving a life sentence for murder.[4] The attack was understood and represented in the media as a motiveless racial attack in an area that has become notorious for high levels of racist incidents and tensions between the white and predominantly Bangladeshi communities. Significantly, it is the same area that the *Evening Standard* article represents two years later as the crucible of 'nihilistic intra-Bangladeshi violence', and the coverage of the Everitt murder contains all the seeds of this later portrayal. The explanations for the attack in the broadsheet newspapers are a compelling mixture of culture clash, inter-generational conflict and social and economic breakdown, with a strong emphasis on a 'between two cultures' identity crisis amongst Bengali young men. These young men are constructed as caught between an oppressive and rigid parental culture at home and a ghettoized subculture of poverty outside, with its incumbent implications of youth deviance, criminality and violence.

Several months prior to the Everitt incident, the *Sunday Telegraph* reported on the high incidence of violence between black and Asian pupils in South Camden schools, pointing to tensions between the now more successful African-Caribbean community and the less successful Bengali community. The article notes 'In response, the Bangladeshis have formed *vigilante gangs to protect their own*' (emphasis added), continuing ominously, 'Members of the "Drummond Street" gang are known for their proficiency in martial arts' (20 April 1994). Later articles, in the wake of Everitt's death, build up a more dramatic picture of these Bengali 'gangs'[5] – the Drummond Street Posse, the Brick Lane Gang, the Chalk Farm Posse – asserting 'Young Bangladeshis are acquiring many of the characteristics of a common inner-city youth culture' (*Telegraph* 21/8/ 1994).

A letter to the *Observer* newspaper from Jonathan Stanley, an officer for Camden's Race Equality Unit fleshes out this picture:

The first generation of Bengalis born in the area are now reaching adulthood. Their formative influences largely coincided with those which shaped the values of their white peers: television, school, poor quality housing, inner-city streets, long term unemployment. It is unsurprising that they are prepared to react to violence in the same way as their white counterparts. (19 August 1994)

In a twist on the 'culture-of-poverty' thesis, an article in the *Daily Mail*, entitled 'youths combine *the worst of both worlds*' (16 August 1994), blames this crisis on racism, which causes Asian young men to deny their cultural identity and turn instead to a pathologized youth culture:[6]

> The unremitting propoganda of English culture deriding the Asian one has produced a generation of Asian youth combining the worst of the Western model – disrespectful of authority, nihilistic, violent . . . The result has been a crisis of Asian culture where the authority of the old has all but collapsed.

The duality of this representation, between the image of the Asian 'alien' on the one hand and marauding youth gangs on the other, marks out the creation of the Asian youth folk devil. The tension between 'race' and 'class' explanations are a constant feature of media accounts and their conflation provides a powerful icon for a plethora of social problems and dangers, real or imagined.

The same mixture of cultural crisis and class conflict is found in coverage of the so-called 'Bradford riots', which took place over two nights in June 1995. The disturbances were directly triggered by police reaction to a complaint about Asian youths playing football in the streets, during which the officers involved were said to have mistreated two Asian women (*Independent* 12/13 June 1995). However, the events were held to be more widely significant as signaling a crisis in the community. Where Bradford had been in the spotlight several years earlier, during the *Satanic Verses* furore, when it was portrayed as reactionary and anachronistic, the community now appeared in the throes of cultural and social break-down. Or as one article put it, 'a picture began to emerge yesterday of a community struggling to come to terms with itself and *modern* Britain' (*Independent*, 12 June1995, emphasis added).

The image of a backward, tradition-bound culture struggling in the face of progressive Western values provides the parameters within which theories of generation gap and culture conflict are forged. The *Independent*, for example, reports, 'Senior police last night blamed a generation gap in the Asian community, saying that young people were alienated from their parents and cultural leaders' (12 June 1995). Another article, on the same day, states that in addition to issues of police harassment and high levels of unemployment, 'Another important factor is the breakdown of the influence of the family and community as many third and fourth generation British Asians have adopted Western values and aspirations' (Bennetto, 1995). The disturbances thus become both effect and symbol of youth alienation and a racialized cultural incompatibility – a situation made more overtly threatening with the overarching spectre of religious fundamentalism, a legacy of the *Satanic Verses* affair. Yasmin Alabhai Brown reports:

The result is unexplored territory for young Asians – adrift from the values of their elders, immersed in an Islam which is essentially a reaction, out of step with the liberal values of secular society and yet enamoured of its amoral materialism, while being denied the means to fulfill the modern dream. (*Independent*, 13 June 1995)

What is conveniently lost within this discourse is any sense of alternative explanation. As happened in the wake of the riots in Brixton and elsewhere in the 1980s, notions of identity crisis serve as an effective disavowal of responsibility and an emblem of innocence. As Norman Bettison, Assistant Chief Constable of West Yorkshire Police altruistically asserts, 'The police is *simply* the anvil on which the youth is beating out its frustration and anger' (*Independent,* 12 June 1995, emphasis added). Similarly, *The Times* argues of the events leading up to the confrontation:

Although it was a mundane police task, it quickly led to disturbances, fuelled by *festering tensions* among British-born Asians and reflecting a *generation gap* within the Asian community. (12 June 1995, emphasis added)

The article continues:

All these factors have created a widening gulf between British-born Asians and their elders, for whom their way of life, with their interest in *Bhangra* music and contemporary fashion, is *alien.* (12 June1995, emphasis added)

It is a short conceptual step to the representation of 'nihilistic . . . violence' and of 'vicious schoolboy tribal wars' in the *Evening Standard* article referred to earlier. The article replays all the hallmarks of cultural dysfunction – of meaningless expressions of frustration by uncontrollable and unemployable young men of 'poor peasant stock', whose parents are illiterate, who live in overcrowded and substandard housing (presumably by choice – cf. CCCS, 1982) and whose command of English is poor. The article asserts:

The evidence is clear that Bangladeshi youth are turning violently against each other – almost as if their prowess in a brawl and their collective strength offer the only prospect of status and self-esteem. (13 November 1996)

Here too is the evocation of inner-city/ghetto youth subculture – of gangs like the Drummond Street Posse, or the Lisson Green Posse, of territory and turf wars, of knives, knuckle dusters, belts and baseball bats, of Lucozade bottles and anonymous teenage boys with covered faces and macho poses recounting tales of former victories and future challenges.

And if all this scene seems to need is a burned-out estate car and a couple of skateboarders to make it complete, then perhaps this ought to give us pause for thought.

Imagining 'the Asian Gang': Ethnicity, Masculinity and the Problem of Black Youth

It would perhaps provide a little comfort – to academics at least – to hold up 'the Asian Gang' as simply the latest example of media mythmaking and popular panic. Nevertheless, the creation of 'the Asian Gang' outlined above draws upon and reinscribes a number of well established tropes of racialized identities that have assumed the status of 'common sense' as much in academic understandings as in the more fertile ground of media and popular imagination. 'The Asian Gang' then brings together conventional academic wisdom around what it means to be 'black'[7] and young and male to legitimate the formation of this new folk devil. Although, as usual, academia has been a little slow in jumping on this particular bandwagon – though the signs are that this is about to change (Goodey, 1999; Macey, 1999) – it has in one sense laid the crucial foundations for this new creation; Dr. Frankenstein to the monster, as it were. Though perhaps few would claim parentage of this particular invention, it is nevertheless true that the portrait sketched above rehearses truisms that now stand as Truths – self evident and incontrovertible – as often found in contemporary sociology as in its more popular incarnations.

The thumbnail sketch drawn above centres its arguments on three interwoven strands: ethnicity, masculinity and youth. Each of these facets is posited in and of itself as constituting a problem – the coalescence of all three leads to prophecies of social doom. Each facet also has a well-established status *as problem* within the social sciences; while not wishing to rehearse the history and breadth of this scholarship here, I want to draw out some broad themes that reflect on the imagination of 'the Asian Gang' and that act as the conceptual baseline for the present study. Though they are here considered as largely distinct strands, these three dominant themes are in reality intricately enmeshed and mutually corroborative; some of these coalitions will hopefully become apparent and can be re-read into the imagination of 'the Asian Gang'.

Ethnicity

As Sue Benson has convincingly argued (1996), studies of Asian communities in Britain have been largely dominated by an anthropological gaze, which has constructed these groups as homogeneous, bounded and autonomous entities (Shaw, 1988; Werbner, 1990, Ballard, 1994). Attracted by the supposed culture-rich/culture-bound nature of Asian collective identity, the emphasis has been on 'difference', which has placed diverse Asian groups as the cultural 'Other'. This has focused attention on Asian 'ethnicity' as the primary marker of self-definition and of boundary maintenance (Barth, 1969), in which culture is transfixed and reified as the only authentic form of identity creation and solidarity. This in turn has had two significant effects: firstly, it has denied the structural positioning of Asian communities within a racialized discourse of inequality and oppression; and secondly, it has paved the way for the fragmentation of Asian identity around the notion of multiculturalism and the celebration of 'difference' (Benson, 1996; Eade, 1996).

The celebration of 'difference' has led to the increasing fragmentation of Britain's Asian communities, proliferating a range of separate and bounded 'ethnic bubbles' (Gates, 1992) in which the emphasis has been on 'culture' as the primary source of collective identification; what Modood refers to as 'one's mode of being' (1992: 55). The central symbol of this multi-culturalist rainbow vision is 'community', in which individual subjectivity blends seamlessly with collective ideals of culture, ethnicity and belonging, and in which there is seemingly little room for contact or change, and less for conflict or confusion. The ethnicity-as-cultural-tapestry approach presupposes the existence of internal homogeneity and external difference, in which boundaries are absolute and uncontested, yet which fit neatly and exactly within the framework of the British nation. As I have argued elsewhere (Alexander, 1998), however, the assertion of 'difference' has brought unintended consequences, not least in the reinscription of Asian identities as implacably alien and unassimilable – as outside the nation. The emergence, in particular, of Muslim sensibilities in the aftermath of the *Satanic Verses* affair, the Gulf War and the Bradford riots has not only championed the cause of diversity but also reformulated the boundaries of British citizenship and nationhood along religio-cultural lines. Rather than dealing the intended death blow to dualistic anti-racist perspectives, the result has been to replace black/white divisions with one of British/Muslim, with Muslims placed as the new social and cultural pariahs – and increasingly as the new objects of desire for academic research.

The comparatively recent focus on religious identifications amongst Britain's ethnic minority communities has resulted in some ambiguous manifestations. Where in 1996 Benson could, with some justice, caricature research on race and ethnicity along the 'Asians have culture; West Indians have problems' dichotomy (Banks, 1996), the appearance of religion centre stage has muddied the picture, with 'Asians' being divided along a non-Muslim/Muslim culture/problem axis and African-Caribbeans falling out of the picture altogether. Where ethnicity theorists have largely decided to treat religion as synonymous with ethnicity, and continued to write about 'Sikhs', 'Muslims' and 'Hindus' as distinct *cultural* communities (Baumann, 1996), or have privileged one or other dimension (Modood (1992, 1997), for example, writes about 'Muslims', while Werbner and Anwar's 1991 collection privileges 'ethnic' groups), others have seized on the problematic and problem-oriented dimension of emergent religious identities. Across Europe, and across the social and political sciences, the rush to categorize, analyse, interpret and understand these 'Muslim voices' has led to what Glavanis (1998) has termed a 'neo-Orientalist' perspective. In Britain, concerns over Islamophobia (Runnymede Trust, 1997), or alternatively, religious fundamentalism have concurred in the positioning of Islam at the centre of political and academic discourse as Public Enemy Number One – Britain's Most Unwanted, as it were.

The interest in religious identities, and particularly in Muslim identities, has a number of important consequences for the study of Asian youth, and particularly the imagination of 'the Asian Gang'. Firstly, it has precipitated the focus on youth as the adherents of the new 'fundamentalism', and has given new life to the 'culture conflict' theory of Britain's black communities. Jacobson, for example, has written (1997) of the distinction between 'ethnicity' and 'religion' amongst young British Pakistanis, in which the former is associated with the traditional and tradition-bound cultures of their parents and rejected, whereas religion is embraced as an 'alternative' self-definition tying the individual into a global, culture-free identity (cf. also Gardner and Shakur, 1994). Secondly, this new religious identification is most usually understood as the manifestation of this culture conflict, representing a defensive and usually hostile reaction to racism with which the parental culture is unable to fully contend. Like Rastafari before it, Islam thus stands as a psychological barricade behind which Pakistani and Bangladeshi young people (usually young men) can hide their lack of self esteem and proclaim a fictional strength through the imagination of the *umma* (Gardner and Shakur, 1994; Jacobson, 1997; Macey, 1999).[8] Thirdly, and integral to this depiction, is the increased concern about 'the Muslim underclass', which places Pakistani and Bangladeshi communities at the top of a reformulated hierarchy of oppression, notably vis-à-vis other South Asian groups (Modood, 1992; Modood et al., 1997); focusing, in Modood's evocative phrase, on the material and cultural distinction between the 'achievers' and the 'believers' (1992: 43). This has further marginalized Muslim youth as the unwilling and resentful heirs of a culture of disadvantage, and as the perpetrators of a burgeoning 'Asian' criminality (Modood et al., 1997; Webster, 1997).

The focus on Islamicization has, moreover, underscored the longer standing sense of threat posed by 'the enemy within' (Gilroy, 1987; Saeed, Blain & Forbes, 1999; Halliday, 1999). In this sense, the emergence of Islamophobia, or anti-Muslimism (Halliday, 1999) is less a new phenomenon than a translation of earlier concerns around the presence of black communities in Britain or Europe. The current academic fascination with Islam/Islamophobia/Fundamentalism has, however, served to dislocate Muslims from this broader (if not longer) history of black/Asian struggle (Brah, 1996), and concentrated more on the authenticity debate than its implications for the structural positioning of Muslim groups within a racialized discourse. What the focus on religion shares with its precursors is the evocation of fixed boundaries and absolute identities, in which religion, ethnicity and culture are naturalized and essentialized, and become, in effect, synonymous with 'race' (Gilroy, 1992). Muslims have then, ironically, become the new 'black', with all the associations of cultural alienation, deprivation and danger that come with this position.

Masculinity

One crucial by-product of the resurgent interest in Muslim identities, particularly in relation to the imagination of 'the Asian Gang' is the re-gendering of Asian identities. Largely because of the anthropological monopoly on Britain's 'ethnic' (as opposed to 'racial') minorities, with its unfaltering assertion of bounded and internally homogeneous cultures, Asian communities in Britain were considered as previously unthreatening, law abiding and unproblematic[9] – a portrait that erased the role of both racial inequality and violence, and resistance in the formation of community identities (Brah, 1996; Sivanandan, 1981/2). The only critique of this perspective came from black feminists, concerned with the role and experience of Asian women within these struggles (Wilson, 1978; Brah, 1996). At the same time, however, it was upon assumed gender relations that the few moral panics about Asian communities were hung,

The Asian Gang

notably, and most sensationally, concerns over arranged marriages for young women. Where Britain's African-Caribbean communities were constructed as male – with the incumbent associations with threat and violence (Alexander, 1996) – Asian communities were largely imagined as female, with the resulting focus on the gendered and sexualized arenas of family and marriage (CCCS, 1982), most notoriously around immigration legislation and virginity testing.

As argued above, recent years have seen the regendering of Asian communities as much in the academic imagination as in the media and in the popular imagination. The shift, then, has been from a focus on 'women' as the subjects of study towards 'gender relations', in which women are positioned as the objects of control and legislation. Glavanis has argued (1998) that gender relations play a central part in Orientalist and neo-Orientalist perspectives on Asian cultures, especially in the representation of the inherently patriarchal and sexist nature of Muslim societies (Sahgal and Yuval-Davis, 1992). Where, until recently, these concerns remained largely 'private', invisible and unremarked, concerns over Muslim young men and 'the Asian Gang' have cast the spotlight on the public performance of masculinities. This has signalled a shift in the perception of Asian masculinities, traditionally visioned as passive and hyper-feminized, towards an association with violence and a highly visible hyper-masculinity (Alexander, forthcoming).

Asian men are comparative latecomers to the race to 'unwrap' masculinity (Chapman and Rutherford, 1988). It can be argued that the field of masculinity studies has always been concerned with the problematization of masculine identities, and that Asian men are simply the latest inheritors of a tradition that almost instinctually positions them as 'problem'. The breakdown of perceived patriarchal authority, notably in the arenas of family and employment, have led to the redefinition of masculinity, most potently captured in the notion of 'masculinities in crisis'. The position of working-class young men is particularly fraught:

> Male redundancy has created cultures of prolonged adolescence in which young male identities remain locked into the locality of estate, shops and school . . . Violence, criminality, drug taking and alcohol consumption become the means to gaining prestige for a masculine identity bereft of any social value. (Rutherford, 1988: 7)

The foundation for gang mythmaking is already present here, and the association of masculinity-in-crisis, criminality and working-class youth is crucial. For Muslim young men, the correlation of ethnicity/religion with perceived underclass status is an additional nail in the coffin; a series of associations clearly traceable in the media representations discussed above. This already tenuous stance is undermined further, however, by the racialization of Asian masculinities, which places them as triply in crisis, triply deviant, and triply dangerous. As I have argued elsewhere (Alexander, 1996; forthcoming) the equation of black male identities solely with 'race' has served to focus concerns on violence, criminality and control, inscribing a hyper-visibility of black masculinity, which disguises a more profound invisibility (West, 1993). Black masculinities are then positioned uncritically as 'subordinated' to hegemonic ideals (Connell, 1987; 1995), as always already flawed and inevitably failing (hooks, 1992). Violence, criminality and hyper-sexuality are posited as the alternatives to the fulfilment of patriarchal responsibilities and control, to 'real' male power. It is no accident, then, that the representation of 'the Asian Gang' above should draw explicit comparisons with African-American 'gang' subculture, with its associations with ghettos, drugs, black-on-black violence and 'nihilism' (West, 1994). It is interesting, moreover, that the concern over 'Islamic fundamentalism' is usually understood as a *male* issue and interpreted as a reaction to racial hostility and loss of patriarchal authority, a way of gaining self-esteem and a sense of individual and group control.[10]

Goodey (1999), for example, has recently argued that 'Islamophobia' can be seen as a reaction of white male hegemony against 'new-found' assertiveness on the part of Asian young men. The move from 'victim' to 'aggressor' has served to homogenize and demonize Asian men externally, but it also, according to Goodey, works internally to threaten Asian young men by promoting intra-group tensions and fear. Goodey conflates this new assertive form of male identity unproblematically with the expression of violence and with 'fundamentalist' Islam, and places these young men as oppositional to dominant white society. She thus cites Webster (1997) who posits a range of Asian male identifications from conformist, ethnic brokers and experimenters to vigilantes and Islamists (again the typology is reminiscent of Pryce's 1979 work on African-Caribbean young men), stating 'vigilantes and Islamists are more predictive of aggressive behaviour and a negative public image' (Goodey, 1999). Recognizing in part the role of representation in the re-imagination of Asian identities, Goodey ultimately rests the blame on the actions of Asian young men themselves, moving from 'image' to reality without noticing, and privileging the white hegemonic gaze as interpreter and legislator:

The interest and apparent 'problem' with Asian youth, for the white majority, arise when an image has been drastically changes from 'passive' to 'aggressive' in combination with the recent ascendancy of Islamophobia on the world stage. The development of a 'tough' identity of and by Asian youth may assign them a degree of power where there previously existed a sense of powerlessness, but in the eyes of the white population, this can pose a threat against their order and against them. Nowhere is this more the case than when Asian youth are aggressive, violent and apparently racist towards the white population. (Goodey, 1999)

Macey similarly equates Pakistani male identity in Bradford as emerging out of a 'culture of poverty', adopting a 'gangsta fashion ... of disenchanted urban American youth gangs' (Taj, 1996, cited in Macey, 1999), and centred on a lifestyle of drug dependency, violent crime and prostitution – a portrait almost identical to the media images outlined above. For Macey, however, this new male identity cannot fully be explained by deprivation and exclusion; it has a cultural twist that is aimed at the oppression of Pakistani women and that, by implication, delegit-imizes any political claims – an assertion of misogyny that perhaps echoes the concerns over black cultural misogyny and homophobia in the United States. Macey blames this new, 'Islamic' identity for exacerbating racial exclusion and increasing generational and gender hostility (Macey, 1999: 852); for promoting 'public disorder' and violence, and excusing private harassment and violence against Asian women. However it is explained, excused or demonized, it seems all are agreed on one thing – Asian men are out of control and in trouble.

Youth

Implicit, though often unstated, in the problem-oriented approach to both ethnic/religious identities and masculinities is generation; that is, that the groups most often positioned as 'in crisis' are young people, particularly, of course, young men (who are largely synonymous with the term 'youth'). Although the category 'youth' has been a popular focus of study since the 1950s, particularly the notion of subcultures and resistance through rituals, black youth have largely been absent from this canon, perhaps because of the complicating and seemingly constraining factor of 'race'. Where it has been present, black youth style and expressive cultures have been positioned as defensive, negative and oppositional, with an emphasis on authenticity and exclusion (Hebdige, 1976; Cashmore, 1979). By extension, black youth have been perceived as outside mainstream society, and hostile towards it, defined through what might currently be termed 'social exclusion' and marginalization. Asian young people have, until very recently (Sharma, Hutnyk and Sharma, 1996) been completely invisible, except as perhaps reluctant brides and runaways. Asian young men have simply never featured.

As Giroux (1996) has argued, the category 'youth' itself denotes a specific set of associations focused on crisis, making the seamless association of deviance, violence and threat.[11] He cites Hebdige:

> In our society, youth is present only when its presence is a problem. More precisely, the category 'youth' gets mobilised in official documentary discourse, in concerned or outraged editorials or features, or in the supposedly disinterested tracts emanating from the social sciences at those times when young people make their presence felt by going 'out of bounds', by resisting through rituals, dressing strangely, striking bizarre attitudes, breaking rules, breaking bottles, windows, heads, issuing challenges to the law. (in Giroux, 1996: 3)

The 'rebel without a cause' naturalization of youth resistance has been more recently re-problematized through economic and social structuring, which has left large sections of young people – male and female – at the margins of work and social participation, extending the transition to adulthood and throwing up new challenges, particularly in the formation of working-class masculine identities (cf. Rutherford, 1988).

While it could be argued that the category of youth is in transition, both extending its boundaries and diversifying internally, with an emphasis on youth style and consumption patterns (Giroux, 1996), the representations of black youth have proved remarkably resilient to change. Black youth have remained then the epitome of oppositional youth culture, defined through disadvantage and alienation. Black youth masculinities, even more so than their white working-class counterparts, have been cast through the appeal to peer group as the last remaining source of security and self-esteem, what Mac An Ghaill refers to as 'the building of a defensive culture of masculine survival against social marginalization' (Mac An Ghaill, 1994: 187). Importantly, Giroux has noted that where white male youth identities are read against a wider backdrop of structural and economic changes, black male identities are seen as hermetically sealed, self-referential and destructive, a product of a 'culture of poverty' (Giroux, 1996). Explanations for black youth behaviour are thus placed on black communities themselves rather than wider forces – a culturalist, blaming-the-victim perspective that is clearly discernible in the media accounts of 'the Asian Gang', and also in the account of black masculinity discussed above. At the same time, black youth are seen as turning against the culture of their parents, precipitating a 'culture conflict' or 'generation gap', which is often lived through as gendered hostility. Mac An Ghaill (1996: 191) brings this cauldron of pathologies together in his account of African-Caribbean young men:

> For young black men's racially subordinated masculinity there are potential intergenerational tensions . . . one way of attempting to resolve these tensions was to displace onto their mothers and sisters their experiences of social inferiority as men in the wider society.

There are tangible echoes here with the account offered by Macey (1999) and also with Goodey's account of emergent youth masculinities (1999). Although many studies of Asian communities tend to reify community, and render youth invisible (Werbner, 1990), where they do appear, usually as an afterthought (Shaw, 1988; 1994), generation is experienced as conflict and as threat (Anwar, 1994), a product of cultural overdetermination, on the one hand, and failing masculinities on the other.[12]

The primary source of black youth identities, almost by default, becomes the peer group – the repository of self-esteem, security and status. Which brings us rather neatly back to the association of youth cultures with deviance, and slides easily into the evocation of 'the Gang'.

The idea of 'the Gang' is, in many ways, the archetype of the inter-section of all these dimensions – 'race'/ethnicity, masculinity and youth – the ultimate symbol of crisis, deviance and threat. Klein (1995), for example, has noted in his description of *The American Street Gang*, that 'gang' identity is largely defined as black, male youth. He argues that 'gangs' tend to be self identified groups of ethnically/racially homo-geneous, almost exclusively African-American or Hispanic, men with an average age of twenty years. In addition, they are urban, territorially based and with an involvement in criminal activity and a strong association with violence (although Klein does not see this latter attribute as a defining characteristic). Although the British history of 'gang' activity traditionally differs, with its somewhat romanticized notion of East End villains, it can be argued that, as with the concept of 'mugging' before it (Hall et al., 1978), the notion of 'Gang' has been re-inflected through this American discourse, to present the idea of 'the Gang' as an already raced entity, standing for the dangerous 'Other' in contemporary British society. Although little, or no, research work has been carried out on 'gangs' in Britain in recent years, the term is used widely and uncritically in relation to black and Asian youth identities, and increasingly to denote any group of black and Asian young men. The term works not only to naturalize and criminalize group identities, but it also serves as a substitute for analysis, particularly where ethnicity or 'race' is privileged as the primary group marker and offered as a self-explanatory motivation for conflict (Keitha, 1995) or control.

(Mis)Representing Asian youth: Invisibility and the Iconoclasm of Style and Culture

Ironically, in the blinding glare of recent media and academic reimagination, Asian youth have been rendered effectively 'invisible', which Cornel West, in another context, has described as, 'the relative lack of [cultural and political] power to present themselves and others as complex human beings and thereby to contest the bombardment of negative, degrading stereotypes' (West, 1993: 210). The adherence to an unflinching cultural absolutism has led to the reification of racial/ethnic identities as mono-dimensional icons, which carries with it the belief in absolute choices 'between' cultures, experiencing the characterization of change as distortion and the emergence of new syncretic forms of identification as a loss of authenticity. The creation of a folk devil demands simplicity at the expense of any recognition of humanity, with all the complexity, contradiction and uncertainty that this entails.

What I am not asserting is a rose-tinted, Pollyanna style approach to youth – inner-city, Asian, Bengali or otherwise. For many of Britain's Bengali and Pakistani communities there are very real problems of unemployment, overcrowded and substandard housing, exclusions from school and racial harassment. There is violence too, but these conflicts often carry with them a complex local history and set of understandings that should not be simply dismissed as a catharsis for the culturally dispossessed. To imagine, however, that these problems can adequately account for the lives and experiences of an individual or an entire community is to project a set of cultural pathologies that brings us back to the realms of unreconstructed ghetto fantasies.

Of course, neither the desire nor the capacity to define a community or a generation in exclusively negative terms necessarily makes it so; nor does it come close to exhausting the creativity and potential of most young people. And it was in this resilience that, for me, the real significance of *Style and Culture '96* lay. The young men involved were, on one level, the same youths whose lives have been too easily reduced to caricature and dismissed; they have been uniformly labelled as gang members, criminals and bullies, defined as disruptive, suspended from school, targeted by police, and regarded with an uncomprehending horror by some older members of their community. When they walked on stage, it was in the face of an almost blanket negativity, an expectation of failure of which they were all too aware.

Yet these are the same young men who are now three-quarters of the way through their Duke of Edinburgh's bronze award; who pored over books about Bangladeshi history, religion and language for their cultural display; who practised routines for nearly two months; and who turned up on the day with white boxer shorts, a neat row of shirts fresh from the dry cleaners and – the biggest sacrifice of all – no hair gel. And if at times none of them felt they would make it, the motivation to show what they were capable of, given the chance, overrode everything else. On the night they were foot-perfect, acne-free and, when they walked on in traditional Bengali dress, they brought the house down.

For Stoneleigh Asian Youth Organisation, *Style and Culture '96* issued a challenge – to see them for whom they are and what they could achieve; to look beyond easy images and convenient stereotypes to see the real, and complex, picture. The show demonstrated at once a knowledge and celebration of the culture of their parents, acknowledged its continuity and, perhaps more importantly, enacted its changes. It refused easy categorization and played out the paradoxes of being young and male and Bengali and Muslim and British without apology, without problematization, and with Definite Attitude. It was not about one evening, or about an award, but about their lives. It was about 'culture' but not an imagined culture that could be neatly labelled and pathologized. It was a vibrant fusion of tradition and change, of Bollywood remixes and jungle music, of *kabbulis* and Moschino jeans, of Islam and dry slope ski-ing, football and hairgel.

For me, *Style and Culture '96* captured the energy, creativity and imagination of Bengali youth expression as it is lived, in all its contradictions and frustrations and strengths and joys. It was a dramatic and positive enactment of potentialities, of cultural syncretism and of emergent identities amongst this group of Bengali young men, their friends and families and their communities, both local and 'imagined' (Anderson, 1993). It was with this potentiality, this syncretism and these hybridized identities that the present study is concerned. Focusing on a small group of Bengali young men, the study hopes to explore the fissures and fusions of emergent youth identities. In counterposing the fashion show with media representations of Asian youth as a means of introduction, I have hoped to draw attention to one of the dominant themes of the work – the ongoing, constitutive and often creative tension between external imaging and internal identification. The aim is not simply to replace 'false' representations with 'true' pictures, but to unravel the complex interplay of elements in the articulation of identities.

The work thus hopes to challenge monodimensional, essentialist accounts of Asian youth identities, and 'identity crisis' through an exploration of their more fluid and dynamic performances, transgressions and negotiations. However, this is not to insert in this space a perhaps more fashionable, but no less simplistic, account of a celebratory hybrid culture, captured in the notion of 'the new Asian cool' – a free-for-all One-World mixture of Talvin Singh, bindis and henna tattoos (Banerjea, forthcoming). It is rather to argue for a more nuanced, local and histor-ically situated account of identity formation, which encapsulates often contradictory processes of continuity and change, constraint and agency, solidarity and diffusion, representation and re-imagination.

To this end, I have chosen to present this work as an in-depth, textured and highly personal account, which explores the process of identity formation at a level of analysis usually overlooked – or considered theoretically questionable, if not actually morally reprehensible – by academic research. This is not to make claims for the authenticity of experience over theoretical abstraction, but to assert the significance of time- and place-specific research, which acknowledges the contours of the research encounter and the located and embedded nature of identity construction. In focusing on 'the Asian Gang' – or perhaps more accur-ately '*not* the Asian Gang' – the aim is to disentangle some of the processes at work in creating the mythology of 'the Gang', the role of these representations in interpreting and constraining Asian youth identities and experiences, and the challenges or alternatives pursued – or not – by these young men at a particular time and place in their lives. Chapter Two describes the process of research, the frictions and transitions of the research encounter, the role of innocence and subjectivity in the study, and its status as 'fiction'. Chapter Three paints in the background and setting of the study, exploring the nexus of 'deprivation' and 'threat' which marks out the creation of 'the Muslim Underclass' and its relation to the history of the Stoneleigh Estate and the SAYO project. Chapter Four returns to the events of 1996, referred to in the opening extract, and explores the role of racialized representations in the mythmaking around 'the Asian Gang', its local incarnation and its contested history. Chapters Five and Six explore the performance of masculinity in these encounters; firstly, in the formation of peer group identities and friendship, and secondly, in the re-imagination of community through notions of authority, hierarchy and respect between 'brothers'. Chapter Six also explores the articulation of age, gender and sexuality in the relationship with 'sisters'. The conclusion reflects on the process of research and of 'writing fiction', and re-examines understandings of 'ethnicity', 'identity', 'masculinity' and 'the Gang' in the light of the present work.

A Note on Terminology

Although this study is entitled *The Asian Gang*, the subjects of the study are all Bengali young men. The term Bengali, rather than Bangladeshi, Muslim, Asian or British Asian, is used throughout the work in reference to the young men since this was the label most used by themselves. Although most did describe themselves as 'Muslim' this tended to be in more specific circumstances, when discussing religion or the representation of Islam in the media. 'Black', 'Asian', 'Muslim' or 'Bangladeshi' are terms used more as generic labels in relation to external constructions of identity, other academic work in the field, or as a convenient shorthand in referring to more inclusive formations of identity, or a particular structural positioning.

Notes

1 All place and personal names have been changed to maintain confidentiality and anonymity
2 The notion of Asian communities as 'unproblematic' refers here to the commonsense perception of Asian communities as unthreatening to the public sphere. It is true, however, that Asian (especially Muslim) cultures have always been perceived as outside, and opposed to, the values of Britishness, with the persistence of demonologies around illegal immigration, domestic violence and deviant sexualities. There is, in addition, a 'hidden history' of fears around the activities of Asian youth/communities which are more generally subsumed into the discussions of black (African-Caribbean) youth and resistance/ criminality, and are thereby rendered invisible (but cf. Sharma, Hutnyk and Sharma, 1996; Bains, 1988).
3 In the following account, it should be noted that 'Asian' usually refers exclusively to Muslim groups.
4 Ko Banerjea has pointed out to me that the conviction of Badrul Miah is regarded by many as 'unsafe' and that it was acknowledged by the

sentencing judge that Miah was being left to shoulder the blame for those (unknown) individuals who had actually carried out the attack. The newly formed notion of 'joint enterprise' was used by the prosecution to secure the conviction – a manipulation of the British legal system that suggests an urgent desire to contain the Asian threat – by any means necessary. This can also be seen to relate to the construction of Asian communities as outside the normal imagination of Britishness (and British justice). An instructive contrast might be drawn with the handling of the Stephen Lawrence case and the resistance to any legal innovation (or action) to deal with his murderers.

5 An *Independent* headline (dated 1 November 1995) after the sentencing of Badrul Miah reads '*Gang leader* gets life for killing boy' (my emphasis). The article goes on to describe Miah as 'leader of a ten strong Asian *mob*.'

6 Here, as throughout, interesting comparisons can be drawn with the demonization of African-Caribbean youth

7 Although currently rather unfashionable, the following section uses the label 'black' to refer to both African and Asian descent young people. While noting Modood's (1992) critique of the term in relation to Asian groups, it is used to denote the process of racialization at work in the construction of African-Caribbean and Asian youth identities. The argument marks differences where appropriate.

8 It is significant, I think, that 'Asian gangs' are most usually conceptualized around religion, either Muslim (Pakistani or Bangladeshi) or Sikh.

9 The same reservations are made here as in note 2 above.

10 Again, comparisons can be made with the interpretation of black subcultures such as Rastafari which have been (mis)understood as a reaction to social marginality and the lack of self esteem, cf. Mac An Ghaill (1994)

11 It is true, of course, that subcultural theory has its origins in the sociology of deviance and criminology (cf. Cohen, 1955; Downes, 1966 etc.)

12 Cf. Alexander (1998, forthcoming) for a fuller discussion of these issues.

Methodology

Several months into my fieldwork, the SAYO project was contacted by a researcher from the Home Office. An earnest thirty-something white woman subsequently arrived at the club during one evening session, with a general – and to me, untenably broad – brief to investigate the transmission and enactment of racist ideas and behaviour in the area. Covering everything from racial attacks to over-suspicious shopkeepers, the researcher wanted to interview the young men of the project about their experiences as the victims of racism. As had happened with me previously, Yasmin stopped the club activities, introduced the researcher and explained the study, asking for volunteers to be interviewed that evening. The senior members of the project refused outright, muttering sardonic asides about their immigration status and the need to check their passports. The junior members, however, were persuaded by Yasmin to take part in a recorded group discussion with the researcher. The group retired upstairs for over an hour, where they recounted stories of attacks and fights, abuse and discrimination. As the discussion continued, however, and spurred on by the Home Office researcher's expressions of sympathetic outrage, the young men began to elaborate on these events, until imagination finally took over altogether. Tales of abductions from nearby subways by sex-starved perverts regaled the horrified researcher, much to the young men's increasing delight, until Yasmin finally called a halt. The Home Office researcher remained unaware of her role as audience and dupe in this performance until Yasmin enlightened her as she left the project later that evening.

For me, myself in the process of establishing tentative relationships with the young men of the project at this time, the experience constituted something of a cautionary tale. It fed my already well-rooted misgivings about the possibility – not to mention the wisdom – of achieving constructive relationships within formal research parameters and the significance of such research to those on whom it is based and for whose benefit, presumably, it is carried out. While the young men's obvious duplicity made me laugh, I felt at the same time a sympathetic complicity with the researcher's undoubted good intentions and a sneaking paranoia about the outcome of my own fledgling research activities. In the same moment wondering if I would share the Home Office researcher's fate, soothing my fears with the – with hindsight, rather desperate – conviction that my research differed so greatly from hers as to bear only passing resemblance, and resolving that I, at least, would not be so easily misled when the time came, the experience proved both a revelatory and a salutary one. Personal anxieties aside, however, this encounter between researcher and researched – and the perhaps more telling silence of the un- and non-researched – has more wide-reaching implications for the process and progress of discovery.

Perhaps the most significant dimension of this encounter was the presumption of 'innocence' (Van Maanen, 1995) on the part of the Home Office researcher. Occupying a stance of disinterested goodwill and beguiled by the language of good intentions, this 'innocence' served to mask the unequal and objectifying perceptual gulf between researcher and researched. This was most clearly apparent in the stark contrast between the institutional position of the researcher, as the embodiment of the Home Office with all its implications of state authority and control, and the young men who formed the object (and most definitely not the subjects) of the study. This position of control defined the parameters of the research, clearly positioning the young men in a uni-dimensional role as the 'victims' of racism and defining out, either by intention or by default, any alternative representations. A consequence of this dominance was the denial of agency to the young men by both the researcher herself and in the boundaries of the research subject, carrying with it the implicit and unquestioned assumption that the researched submit as of (her) right rather than (their) will. The refusal of the senior members to participate in the interviews, presumably because they were aware of and uncomfortable with the power dynamics of the research relationship, is rendered invisible in this encounter. What a position of 'innocence' most lacks in its championing of disinterested intervention is the recognition of the profoundly interactive and complicit nature of any encounter between not only unequal players – researcher and researched – but also between individuals *as* individuals. The absence of self awareness on the one hand and the denial of humanity on the other leads to a perceptual myopia in which much understanding becomes superfluous or is simply lost. The monologic nature of the research process silences voices that may contest and disrupt the dominant object-ive, and becomes deaf to the cross-currents of character, emotion and humour (Rosaldo, 1996). 'Innocence' does not allow for challenge, for refusal or for the high spirits of young men with an all-too-clear understanding of their function as folk devil and a talent for caricature.

In recounting this story, the aim is not simply to posit guilt in the place of 'innocence', nor to claim a position of privileged knowledge for myself. While I could share the young men's joke, I was also inescapably part of it, both outside the research encounter and implicated within it. If the nature of research is, perhaps inescapably, monologic, hierarchical and objectifying, if its truths are always 'partial' (Clifford, 1986) and if its claims to 'innocence' are convenient fictions, what follows is an attempt to make visible these processes and these relationships as they were established, developed, translated and disrupted. More than this, however, I want to explore the dialogues, the interaction and the humanity of this fieldwork, recognizing the agency of the young men I worked with, and the profoundly personal weaving of our relationships. The account which follows is my own unashamedly subjective understanding of this process: it makes no claims to 'innocence'.

Tales of Experience . . .

My initial introduction to the SAYO project was not an auspicious one, although with the benefit of two-years' hindsight, it is almost impossible to recall the feelings of complete alien-ness and hopelessness my first few months engendered in me. I found the project after a number of 'phone calls to the local youth services and organizations in the area where I lived, all of which pointed me to the only two Asian youth projects in the borough – one for young women and one for young men. My reasons for wanting a fieldwork site near to where I lived were largely personal – as a newcomer to this part of London, and a rather nervous driver, I did not want to face the additional stresses of a long drive across London to work. More than this, however, I wanted to avoid areas that had already been extensively researched, and in which the atmosphere was more politically laden and tense; and I wanted to be within easy reach of the young people with whom I was hoping to work. My previous fieldwork, with mainly African-Caribbean young men (Alexander, 1996), had clearly demonstrated to me both the disadvantages of living at a distance, which too greatly restricted and formalized any interaction, and the – admittedly sometimes fraught – advantages of a more informal, up-close and personal approach.

Access to both projects was negotiated through the local area worker, Julia, who had worked in the Abbey Street neighbourhood for fifteen years. Although my explanation of the research project was probably rather vague and garbled – something about the misrepresentation of Asian youth and a desire to get a more well rounded picture – Julia introduced me to the workers-in-charge of both the young men's and the young women's groups, Hassan and Shopna. Having given them the same rather garbled explanation, both agreed that I should attend the projects and just see how it went.

In retrospect, I think that all three workers gave their support at this stage on the basis of trust rather than knowledge. Since I had little idea what to expect and still less about what I would finally focus on, it was simply impossible to give a comprehensive and persuasive account of myself or my intended work. Although I talked to them about my previous study, I think that ultimately the decision was made on an altogether more personal basis. Certainly, both Hassan and Shopna supported me, at least partially, on the basis of my being Asian and our shared concern with the experiences and representations of Asian young people. Julia, for her part, saw my role as a way of learning more about the young people, particularly the young men, she had seen grow up but felt she knew so little about; she also clearly felt that my being Asian would facilitate this process.

I myself was less certain of this 'advantage' and less confident about my role as a 'native' researcher, and although my initial access was agreed on it remained very much on a sink or swim basis. The young people would either accept me, or they would not – that was up to them and to me. I initially felt more positive about the young women's group, which ran in the local Thomas More school at lunchtimes. Although I do not personally subscribe to the universal woman myth, I did hope that a combination of perceived ethnicity and gender would provide some basis for mutual understanding with the young women. Unfortunately the only response I initially provoked was a bemused curiosity, and our relationship never really developed beyond this. This was partly due to the confines of the project, which ran rather erratically and never managed to attract a core group from one session to the next, and to the cultural constraints associated with women's work in the area, but was also, I suspect, largely to do with its rather authoritarian internal structure. Its youth worker, Shopna, actively sought to create a familial atmosphere in which age, status and authority are inextricably interwoven. The young women were encouraged to call her *apa* (older sister), a term of respect that gave, at the same time, an aura of security and respectability and a morass of unstated restrictions on the forms of interaction that could take place. The formality of these interactions constructed palpable barriers and silences which seemed at odds with the confidence and whispered conversations of the young women, but which I was unable to penetrate. Ironically, it was the combination of ethnicity, gender and age, rather than my expressed role as researcher, that placed me as the object of a guarded and polite suspicion – it separated me and placed careful boundaries around me. Periods of staff shortage or illness, Shopna's visits to Bangladesh, closure during Ramadan, all conspired to disrupt and finally disband the group which has, with the exception of a two-week summer programme that year, simply never revived in any consistent or accessible form. Although I have come to know several young women from the area in the eighteen months since this summer project, this has largely been through my work with their brothers, and has been too haphazard, too limited and perhaps too easily identifiable to form part of the present study.

The young men's project promised less and my initial feelings of self doubt and nervousness were fuelled by what were hardly flattering accounts of its members. The project itself has a complex and combative ten-year history, which will be considered in the next chapter; its current members, mainly aged sixteen to twenty-two, have similarly attracted a reputation as troublemakers and rebels. First Julia and then Hassan issued solemn assurances of the problematic character of both group and members – the young men were, I was told, out of control, irreligious, unemployed and probably unemployable, failed at school, into drugs and crime and violence, and generally spent their days on a wall next to the shops in Abbey Street, to the shame of their families and the local community. And of course, they were sexist, had persecuted Shopna throughout the time she worked with them and had even finally physically assaulted her – so there was no guarantee of how they might respond to me, a woman researcher, Asian or otherwise. Although I tried to maintain an air of polite and detached scepticism – not wanting to buy into someone else's folk devil – it was several weeks before I could summon up the courage to attend the project sessions. During my first visit, Hassan turned off the music and introduced me to the ten or twelve young men present. I explained what I was hoping to do and was greeted with shrugged shoulders and a blanket indifference, before they all returned to their pool or table tennis games and their own conversations. Over the following sessions, I spoke to curious youth workers, who identified the group's 'leaders' and told me something of their history. I could not bring myself to speak to the young men, feeling generally self-conscious and embarrassed, as well as a little intimidated – an anthropological sore thumb, and a female one at that. Partly I could see no reason why they would want to talk to me, a total stranger, and partly, I could not think of anything sensible to ask; more than this, the whole environment was new and strange and made no sense to me.

My anxieties over the research project and my ability to carry it out were not eased by the almost tangible tension in the project between the members and the youth workers, particularly with Hassan. There were constant arguments and minor confrontations over the music being too loud, or smoking in the club or in front of Hassan, or damage to equipment or to furniture or to the building. Towards the end of one evening session, a major dispute erupted between Hassan and the project members over a pane of glass in the front door, which had been smashed. As the argument became heated, Hassan approached the young men shouting, 'I am at university and I am studying for a degree in law, so don't treat me like a fool'. One look at the faces of the young men persuaded me to leave the project quickly. The next day I telephoned Julia, who told me that soon after I had left one of the members had punched Hassan and fractured his jaw – the project was now closed until a new worker could be appointed and new arrangements made.

These new arrangements actually took over three months, during which time the young men underwent courses on conflict management, while I went to the young women's group (when it ran) and waited for the club to reopen. Although the Hassan incident had, perhaps strangely, not convinced me of the folly of continuing with the group, the newness of my (non)contact with the young men meant it was impossible for me to progress with the fieldwork during this period. In the absence of any alternative plan, I simply waited.

The project finally reopened in July 1995, with a new full-time youth worker, Yasmin, a Bengali woman in her late twenties. Given the recent history of the group, I was a little surprised that the post had been given to a young woman, although Julia assured me that Yasmin was hardly the personification of a (stereo)typical Bengali woman. She was, moreover, the unanimous choice of the Project's members, who had taken full part in the selection process. My continued access to the project had to be negotiated afresh with Yasmin, who sounded less than thrilled at the prospect, but agreed to meet with me. Yasmin was, I confess, not at all what I had expected – smaller and younger looking, but with an air of implacable confidence, energy and determination. And very blunt. My access to the project was fine with her but had to be cleared again with the members and could be withdrawn at any time if she or any of the project members felt uncomfortable with my presence. My reintroduction gave me a strange sense of *deja vu*: the members looked at me as if they had never seen me before, shrugged their shoulders again and, with the exception of one young man who wanted to know if I could get him on television, turned back to their activities.

Nevertheless, it was with the arrival of Yasmin that my fieldwork-proper began, the short time with Hassan and my longer trials with the young women's group constituting more of a false start than a beginning. Yasmin, it transpired, already knew a number of the older members through her husband, who had worked with them the previous summer, and through informal networks and mutual contacts between the Abbey Street area and North London, where Yasmin had grown up and still lived. A combination of this, the increased resourcing and more effective management of the club and Yasmin's strictly up-front, open and non-hierarchical approach lessened tensions within the project with remarkable speed. The same could not be said of me, and several months passed while I hovered, nervous and embarrassed, in the background. An occasional smile and an even more occasional greeting was the only interaction I had with the members for this time, and I despaired of ever establishing more meaningful contact or coming closer to understanding anything. Yasmin, however, had other ideas and persuaded me, encouraged me and often bludgeoned me into a more active role. I started working as a volunteer youth worker, which brought me into direct contact with the project's members on a regular basis. I signed them in, took care of the pool list (always a rather contentious position to occupy), served them drinks and chocolate from the canteen, played cards and slowly started conversations. During this period, I got to know, at least by name, around fifteen young men, aged seventeen to twenty-two, who used the club regularly and on whom I decided to focus the study.

Unfortunately, also around this time, two changes occurred which proved this decision rather premature. Firstly, Yasmin decided to split the project's sessions between junior and senior members. This meant that Monday evenings would be reserved for under sixteens and Friday evenings for over sixteens, with mixed sessions on Wednesday evenings and Saturday mornings. Although this was initially an unpopular move with the senior members, it did result in a shift in focus of the club's activities towards the younger group. Released from the watchful gaze of their older brothers and their friends, the junior group, then aged thirteen to fifteen years old, gradually emerged from the project's margins to become the main users. They took part in all the activities and excursions, formed the core of the new football team and, as their confidence increased, began to dominate even club-based activities. This was facilitated by what appeared to be a split in the senior group, which resulted in a number of the older members ceasing to use the project on any regular basis. The reasons for the split are unclear, but seem to stem from a combination of work and college commitments amongst some of them and the enactment of long-standing, but formerly latent, tensions in the wake of an incident on Abbey Street during the summer. The details of this incident will be considered in a later chapter, but involved an attack on the teenage sisters of one of the project's senior members, Humzah, by a group of white men and women, during which a number of the group were said to have stood by and done nothing.

Whatever the reasons, the group I was hoping to base the study on splintered and shrank before my eyes, a situation made even more impossible by a second incident that took place shortly before Christmas. One Friday evening, Yasmin telephoned me to tell me not to come in because she was too short-staffed to open the club and had to cancel the evening's senior session. Although she waited to explain the situation to the members, two of the young men, S. Ahmed and Liaquot, reacted badly to the news, becoming verbally abusive and throwing stones at the club building, shattering several windows. As a result of this, Yasmin closed the senior sessions for eight weeks, reopening in early February 1996. She also placed a six-month ban on S. Ahmed and Liaquot, and although the majority of senior members agreed with the justice of the decision, many of them also stayed away from the project for this period – a gesture of friendship, if not of solidarity.

The net result of what seemed to me at the time like a series of personal catastrophes was that my original fieldwork plans went up in smoke, and the younger group moved to centre stage. My frustration at being unable to control events, just when I had started to relax and enjoy the youth group, was matched by a set of new anxieties over what I would do next. The junior members seemed so young, and even more unreachable, I could not imagine how we would ever find mutual ground or under-standing. Being thirty and a woman, and a stranger and a merely phenotypical Asian seemed insurmountable obstacles and fourteen-year-old Bengali boys seemed as far away from my own experience as it was possible to get.

There were, however, two breakthroughs in our relationship – or rather in my understanding of our relationship. In January 1996, I travelled to India with an Open University/BBC production team to make a pro-gramme on satellite TV. I was away for two weeks, and when I returned to the club Faruk, one of the youngest members, approached me – 'Claire, where have you been?' Telling him about the trip, I added, 'Why, Faruk, did you miss me?' 'Yes' he responded bluntly, and strode back across the room, leaving me feeling astonished and deeply touched. Shortly afterwards, several of the junior members travelled with Yasmin, Sher

Khan (a volunteer at the project) and myself to Manchester on a two-day residential trip to an Asian youth project. On the way up, one of the young men, Enam, amused himself by gently pulling my hair and cheating me at Blackjack. Over the next two days as we fought over washing up, went on fairground rides, played cards, went bowling, cooked breakfast and met new people, the group established an easy informality which drew me in without conscious effort on my part and largely without my even realizing it. Somewhere along the way, I later realized, I had become a significant figure in the life of the project and its members; while I still felt like an intruder, they had grown used to me, accepted me and established relationships of their own.

Over the next few months, which were difficult ones for the younger members of the project, these relationships grew stronger and more individual. The months between Christmas and the summer of 1996 were dominated by a series of conflicts involving the junior group. Battles with the local school over exclusions and suspensions, a number of fights between the Bengali young men and a group of African-Caribbean young men from the area, increased activity by the police (it was at this time that the opening article in Chapter 1 appeared) and a number of arrests for alleged offences from shoplifting to mugging led to high levels of tension within the project. The SAYO project suddenly found itself at the centre of a huge institutional row between the youth service and the school administration, in which accusations of racism, the incitement of the young people and general malpractice on the part of the project flew fast and furious. Yasmin and Amitabh,[1] the local racial harassment monitoring officer, were targeted the main culprits in this furore, some of the details of which will be considered in later chapters. Perhaps hardly surprisingly, the school administration were less than thrilled at my presence and a number of accusations were also levelled in my direction – 'that so-called Dr Alexander' as one Head of Year put it.

This situation of conflict served to galvanize the members and staff of the project into a powerful sense of mutual support, understanding and trust. Assured that Yasmin and myself were prepared to stand by them – warts and all – welded bonds that provided a strong and enduring basis for the relationship with the younger members. My focus, both ethnographic and personal, shifted naturally to these events and these relationships and became inseparable from them. As the situation eased and the tension disappeared, the mutual trust, respect and affection remained intact.

My new-found ease and familiarity with the junior group also facilitated my relationships with the senior members. As they drifted back into the club after some time and we talked about what was happening and about the project and about my research and about themselves, their hopes and problems and aspirations, my latent feelings of intimidation largely disappeared. Which is not to say that everything went completely smoothly, and with some notable exceptions, my relationships with the senior members have been marked by greater distance and formality. Some of the reasons for this will be considered in the next section.

I finally began my interviews in September 1996, over eighteen months from the time I first entered the project. Having decided to make the junior members the main focus of the study, most of the interviews were conducted with this group, involving informal discussions around family, friends, school, religion and gender. I also interviewed young men from the senior group (which actually contains two distinct sets of friends), as well as youth and community workers associated with the project. The interviews lasted between one hour and five-and-a-half hours, and took place in the club building, at the young men's homes and, on one occasion, at my home. Although much of the interviews covered areas, events and attitudes I already knew well by this time, I also learned a surprising amount about the young men themselves, their histories and their more private thoughts – not all of which appear in the present study. Most were open and forthright to a degree that surprised me, even in the light of our long-standing friendships; and they trusted me enough to tell me when they did not want to discuss something. The young men themselves were, I think, surprised at the things I wanted to know: the interviews were not, several told me afterwards, what they had expected – they were more personal, less clearly focused on particular issues and problems and often asked about things they simply took for granted. They were, I think, more about *them* than they had imagined. As one of the young men's older brother rather caustically remarked after one interview: 'You mean you're going to write a book about what *they* say to you?'

... and of 'Innocence'

In August and September 1996, accompanied by Yasmin and her two daughters, I travelled to India to visit family. For several weeks after our return, I was met with the same question from colleagues, friends and the project members – did I get married while I was away, or had my marriage been arranged? At first I was puzzled, then amused, by the assumption – even by those who should have known me better – that the trip must have something to do with marriage, that any other rationale was more- or-less unthinkable. Later I realized that the question reflected not only a culturally based supposition – that a trip 'home' would inevitably be concerned with this matter – but also a more general set of ideas about me personally, my role and status, my gender, age and sexuality. As a single woman in my early thirties, my marriage was assumed to be not only imminent and desirable, but my primary concern – and theirs. Several months later, Hashim, one of my co-workers at the project, accosted me to find out when my marriage was taking place, why I had kept it such a secret and why he had not been invited. Unconvinced by my protestations of ignorance on the matter, he insisted that 'everyone' knew I was getting ready to marry a mysterious but eminently suitable man from India, whom I had met during my summer visit. Hashim was not prepared to tell me where he had heard this information, although he claimed it was from someone who had met me on a few occasions. The project members I asked had not heard the rumour, so it seemed it had been generated by people I either barely knew, or had never met. Until this moment, the thought that my existence, my life or my holiday – let alone my marriage – was a subject of public interest, discussion and speculation had never occurred to me. On reflection, however, it made perfect – if uncomfortable – sense: as a young(ish) woman in almost daily contact with a large proportion of the young men in a small and closely knit community, I was bound to be a focus of curiosity. More than this, as an Asian young woman, my background, origins, age, appearance, education, employment, marital status and other vital statistics were of inescapable significance. My marriage became the symbol of all these concerns; a means of analysing, locating and, to an extent, policing me and my relationships within the community.

What surprised, and disturbed, me about the rumour was that it seemed to be circulating amongst people with whom I had little or no contact. Although aware, in a vague critically self-reflexive way, of the complexities of my burgeoning relationships with the young men, I was still unprepared for the wider set of relationships within which I found myself working. Far from the ethnographic invisibility I had somehow imagined myself cloaked in, I was, in fact, acutely visible to people I had barely realized even existed – and visible in a very personal way.

In many ways, this perspective does not form part of the present study, except inasmuch as it is here acknowledged. It did not impact on my research activities in any direct form, nor did it seem to effect my relationships with the project members who form the core of the study. However, it is a significant gaze, in that it challenges notions of invisibility and places my immediate relationships in a wider context of 'family' and 'community' than is perhaps apparent in what follows. It demonstrates the partial nature of my own ethnographic and personal gaze and highlights the often hidden, or silenced, mutuality of the research encounter. As a researcher, I was not a cipher – in fact, I became significant in ways I could not foresee and cannot, even now, fully quantify.

The same can be said of my relationships with the young men of the project. What is of particular significance here are the ways in which what I had initially seen as barriers became part of our interactions as they developed; the incorporation, negotiation or transcendence of structures of age, gender, ethnicity, class, sexuality on both sides of our ongoing dialogue. More than this, as my fieldwork progressed, the significance of individual personalities increased, establishing varying degrees of familiarity and affection, which are written inescapably into the present work.

On the morning of Eid Ul Adha 1996, arriving to pick up one of the young men's sisters from their house, I bumped into a group of the senior members walking through the Stoneleigh estate. As I got out of my car – tripping rather inelegantly on the folds of my new *lehnga* suit – the young men smiled and murmured obligatory compliments on how beautiful I looked. One of them, Shahin, turned to me: 'So, Claire, is this the *lehnga* you bought in Leicester?' It was, but the question took me by surprise; the outfit had been bought during a residential trip with the junior members, one of whom was Shahin's youngest brother, Hanif. That Hanif had gone home and reported the visit in such detail, and that my clothing purchase was of any interest to either of them, was something I had not expected. Though Yasmin and I spent many hours talking about the young men, it had never really occurred to me that they might do the same with us. When we met Shahin's mother several months later, she told Yasmin that she felt like she already knew us because her sons talked about us constantly, and she welcomed us as daughters.

Acknowledging the hierarchical and structured nature of the research encounter requires that these personal relationships also be taken into account – that the artificial and objectifying distancing of the ethnographic gaze is fractured, cross-cut and riven by complex and shifting sets of understandings, emotions, proximities and preferences (Rosaldo, 1996; Clifford, 1986; 1988). Within the framework of my fieldwork experience outlined above, what follows is an attempt to unravel some of these subjectivities.

Perhaps the most crucial relationship of the fieldwork was my friendship with Yasmin. Although she was, I think, initially reluctant about my presence as a researcher in the project – understandably so, especially during her first few months – it was she who encouraged me to become more actively engaged with the members and the project's activities. During the first year of the study, and even until today, Yasmin was my first and main guide and interpreter (both figuratively and often literally since I do not speak Bengali), a source of support, a sounding board, an intermediary – and, on occasion, a mediator – my first means of contact with the project members, an advisor, a co-worker and a friend. After the first few months our friendship moved beyond the confines of the project, establishing a close personal relationship that undoubtedly affected our working practices.[2] Initially, I think, the project members were surprised at our rather unlikely rapport – we had seemingly very little in common except that we were both Asian women, and this became the assumed basis for our interaction. Perhaps ironically, what Yasmin and I actually had in common was that neither of us were what anyone generally expected an Asian woman to be. Our friendship was, nevertheless, an important factor in structuring the young men's interactions with me. At a general level, then, the presence of another woman in the project made my position at once more comfortable and less a subject for comment, while Yasmin's position of trust and authority with the members acted partly as a protective shield and an emblem of my own trustworthiness.

More specifically, however, being variously described as Yasmin's 'sidekick', her 'best friend' or, during one of our frequent comic wranglings as 'like those two women out of Birds of a Feather', I became almost inseparable from Yasmin in the minds of the young men – half of a double act: 'Yazz' and Claire. Within this, I was undoubtedly cast as the straight (wo)man – a 'decent', 'respectable' and conventional Asian woman who Yasmin was, at various times, accused of 'corrupting'. Although this image has been gradually dismembered over the past two years, particularly amongst the junior members, it is still one that structures my relationship with the senior group and the project's more occasional visitors. The complexities of gendered categorizations of this kind will be considered in greater detail in a later chapter.

The senior group actually exists as a far more fractured category than its label suggests, encompassing at least three distinct subsets, broadly defined. My interaction with each subset varied, over time and in kind, and also in relation to the individuals within these groups.

The first of these subsets formed part of the original group I had intended to focus the study on – and who mainly disappeared from the scene after the summer project of 1995. Aged between twenty and twenty-three years, this was the oldest grouping, although age was not a sole defining factor. Several had been with the project since its earliest days and had been an active part of its turbulent history. Most had moved on from the project during my fieldwork although several were occasional visitors. Partly because of this infrequency, my interaction with this group was minimal and, with two exceptions, often rather tense. Seeing themselves as the 'elders' of the project and the local youth community, they adopted a generally hyper-masculinized and authoritarian approach to the project and its workers. Towards me, in particular, as a woman and an outsider, both spatially and culturally, the attitude was one of suspicion and sometimes of muted hostility. One or two refused to interact with me at all; others thought it amusing to address me only in Bengali; with others there was minimal and largely superficial contact; while one attempted vaguely to flirt with me and then gave up. The exceptions were Omar, a twenty-two year old who worked in a bank, and Hashim, who had once been part of this group, but was now employed as a youth worker in the project. My contact with Omar was too infrequent for us to establish any significant relationship, although we had a number of long and interesting conversations, which form part of the backdrop to the study. Hashim and I have, however, become good friends during the course of our work together, and he was able to give me unique insights into the history of the project and the area, and the dynamics of the older group.

The second group was without doubt the most dominant presence in the project in the early days of my fieldwork and remains a defining authority. Generally referred to by the younger project members and workers as 'the older lot' (a relative term), their ages range, at the time of writing, from eighteen to twenty-one years old. As mentioned earlier, my relationship with this group was marked by greater distance and formality than with the younger members, a function partly of a combination of age and gender factors. As the senior members of the project, and as adult male members of the community, their relationship to me as a single woman was automatically more carefully circumscribed and limited, although this was partly mediated by the difference in our respective ages. These distances were enhanced initially by a dislike of outsiders and newcomers arising from the history of the project; they were likewise decreased and muted as our interaction grew, particularly with those who had younger brothers in the junior group, where it was easier to place me in more of a familial care role.

Certainly in the earliest days of my fieldwork, my relationship to this group was marked by feelings of intimidation on my part and a barely concealed suspicion on theirs. As I moved into a new and more defined role as a volunteer worker some of this suspicion decreased and my presence as researcher seems to have been largely forgotten, arising occasionally in conversations or sudden questions. However, as a youth worker, my presence raised new issues around notions of authority and control, which were often problematic. Although partially expressed as gendered antagonisms, these were mainly to do with the legacy of tensions between project members and staff, which Hashim and Sher Khan avoided largely because they were older members of the Abbey Street neighbourhood. The confrontations were few, and generally enacted by only one or two members of the group, mainly involving small, engineered conflicts over the payment of subscription money or the theft of five pence lollies from the canteen. My general response was to smile and abdicate responsibility to Yasmin with whom, with the exception of the incident at Christmas, they had a far more equable relationship.

On only one occasion did a confrontation between myself and a member of this group become more serious. The situation again involved Liaquot, who had apparently made threats to slap me because someone had told him I had called him a 'stupid bastard' several weeks before. Yasmin closed the session and Liaquot and I discussed the situation, reaching an uneasy truce. The incident distressed me greatly because by this stage, over sixteen months since the project reopened, I had established very good relationships with the majority of the project members, some of whom now stood by to make sure Liaquot did not carry out his threat. They later reassured me that Liaquot was known for picking fights with workers over minor or imagined issues, had done the same thing several times before and that his actions had nothing to do with me personally nor with the feelings of anyone else in the project. Nevertheless, the episode did rattle my sense of 'belonging' and acceptance within the project and placed me on my guard as to the complexity and vulnerability of my position there in relation to its members.

On the whole, my relationship with most of the senior group remained instrumental – I worked in the club, helped them fill out application forms for jobs and for college and made up foursomes for Coalbridge.[3] During more recent months, leading up to the interviews and subsequently, many of these formalities have become translated into more personal and individuated friendships – I have cheered on the senior football team in their matches (most of which they lost), fed them chocolate biscuits and oranges at half time, celebrated family weddings, waited anxiously for the outcome of court cases, fretted in vain over fights, gossiped about girlfriends, laughed over photographs, discussed religion and politics and sociology and – on one occasion – the methods and ethics of ethnography. I finally asked only four of the young men to take part in the interviews, partly because they were the more authoritative presences in the group, and, in two cases, had younger brothers in the junior group, but largely on the totally unobjective basis that these were the people I liked most and felt most comfortable with. Those I interviewed were Shahin, whose two younger brothers, Khalid and Hanif, also attended the project; Humzah, Ifti's older brother; Zohar and S. Ahmed. Interestingly, with this group, the process of interviewing itself helped to establish stronger bonds of understanding and trust, and closed some of the distances between us. Although I did not know them as well as I had come to know the junior members, their openness about their personal lives and thoughts and experiences touched me greatly.

The last subset of the senior group is its smallest and in some ways its most ill-defined. Consisting of only four regular project members, aged sixteen to seventeen, they constituted initially a breakaway faction of the older group, the dynamics of which division will be considered in later chapters. This grouping was, as a general rule, the quietest and most self-contained, attending the project regularly but making few demands on its facilities or resources. Its character is one of gentle and unassuming self-effacement, and this was evident in the nature of our relationship. On one level, then, I had little interaction with them, except during the day-to-day running of the project sessions, and while this necessarily distanced our interaction, it also freed it from the issues of conflict and control, which sometimes marked other relationships. In particular, as a younger group within the context of the project, the anxieties of gender-specific formalities did not seem to apply as it did for the older members. This allowed the growth of an affectionate and good-humoured set of relations in which, although personal knowledge was often slighter on both sides than with the other groups, trust grew without issue and without trial. This was partly because the members of this subset seemed not to find themselves in as many problems as both the older and the younger groups; our relationship was accordingly less intense and more relaxed. Although during the course of the fieldwork I sat with them in police stations and youth courts, and on occasion commiserated over fight injuries, our interaction was mainly incident free – we talked about college and career ambitions, played the Grapevine[4] game, planned celebratory meals at MacDonalds that never happened, and sat glued to Eastenders, occasionally ducking table tennis balls fired by Shakiel.

I interviewed only two of this group; Khalid, Shahin's younger brother, and Shakiel. Of the other two regulars Ashraf, Faruk's older brother, was unwilling to be interviewed mainly, I think, due to shyness, and Mehraj and I arranged two interviews, one of which he forgot and the other of which I was too tired to undertake – the moment simply passed.

It is the junior group, generally referred to as 'the little ones', with whom I had the greatest and closest contact, and who form the heart of the present study. Aged fourteen to sixteen years at the time of writing, these young men form a relatively stable and cohesive core group of friends who, with the exception of one member, Ismat, attend the same local school, the Thomas More school, and constitute the active centre of the SAYO project. The junior group has ten regular members – Hanif, Ifti, Jamal, Mohammed, Faruk, Shafiq, Ismat, Sayeed, Enam and Adil – with whom most of my fieldwork time has been spent, certainly in the last eighteen months. Although the junior session also has a large number of occasional users who also feature in the study, and with some of whom I have developed close and affectionate contacts, these remain peripheral to the main focus. This is largely to do with a split in the ranks of the junior group in the summer of 1996, between the core group and a smaller cluster of friends from the neighbouring Amersham estate. This division resulted in some of the young men I had come to know disappearing from the project for some time, and resurfacing only periodically – and with new companions – for sports competitions, football training and residential trips. There are also a number of young men from the Stoneleigh Estate who only use the project on Saturday mornings for football training, partly because of the negative reputation the project has attracted in the local area.

As I mentioned earlier, my relationship with this group grew naturally and almost without conscious effort from either side. As they began to use the project more throughout 1996, I was an already established feature of club sessions; none of them recall my arrival and I was therefore never a 'stranger' – I simply moved from the background to the foreground. In addition, because these young men had never really taken part in the more turbulent period of the club – indeed, only those with older brothers in the project were aware of its history – they did not share the same immediate suspicions and hostilities evidenced by some older members.

It is interesting to contrast the role that the structures of age, gender and ethnicity played in this interaction, particularly in comparison with the senior members. Within the project's structures, and more generally, this group was regarded by the senior members as almost a generation apart. Although separated in age by only two or three years in some cases, distinctions of age, family position and authority functioned to designate the group's members as being, if no longer children, at least not yet fully adult members of the community – they were in name and in practice 'the little ones'. The intricacies of these group interactions will be explored later; what it did mean in terms of their relationships with me, however, was that it freed them from some of the constraints around gender and sexuality that marked my relationships with the senior members. Where, as a single adult woman, I was regarded by the latter as within the same generational, and potentially sexual matrix, I was perceived by the junior members as a generation above, with a position of authority and respectability to match. This position was both facilitated and mediated by my gender and ethnicity, which located me with relative ease within existing cultural frameworks, and which, ironically, allowed for greater familiarity than with the older groups.

As a woman, the young men were thus able to relate to me without some of the defensiveness or sometimes ebullient humour with which they often tested male 'outsiders'; as our relationship developed they also felt able to discuss and display vulnerabilities, fears and tensions that they did not approach as openly with male workers or the senior members. The flip side to this was a tendency to regard me, at least initially, as being rather delicate, vague and unworldly. This was consolidated through additional ethnicity and class categorizations, which placed me as a 'nice' and 'decent' educated (and therefore impractical and naive) Asian woman, who could be easily shocked and upset. Several years on this image has been only partially dismantled – the young men are no longer surprised by my swearing or my temper tantrums (my tendency to road rage is a source of constant delight to them), even if they blame these 'changes' on Yasmin – but their relationship to me is marked by a gentle protectiveness, teasing and concern for my well being. An integral part of this position is its implacable denial of my sexuality; as a 'decent' and unmarried Asian woman I am not regarded nor imagined as an autonomous sexual being. Although the young men delight in matchmaking me with every 'eligible' (and unlikely) single man of our acquaintance, from youth workers on exchange visits to our Duke of Edinburgh worker and, most of all, to Hashim, my co-worker with whom I have a long standing fantasy engagement, these were always performed in the strict understanding that there was absolutely no possibility of their becoming reality. Inherent in this is the silent policing of gender relations, which was also present, though in a different way, with the senior members.

Ultimately, however, it is impossible to separate out such structuring factors from myself as a person, a thirty-something Asian woman, or from them as individuals, who are only so partially captioned as fifteen-year-old Bengali young men. Our interaction was at once more personal, more haphazard, more time- and place- specific, and more holistic than such a description allows. Undoubtedly, the combination of my being an Asian woman, just about old enough to be their mother (and on more than one occasion actually mistaken by outsiders as such), led to the creation of very close and affectionate bonds, which had strong pseudo-familial undertones on both sides. More than this, however, I became a peculiar mixture of mother-substitute, older sister, youth worker, teacher, taxi-driver, confidante and ally, which they articulated simply as being 'a friend'.

It is almost impossible for me to unpack the complex weaving of the strands of my relationship with these young men without losing its energy, humour and fun. Over the past two years, we have travelled to Nottingham, Manchester and Bradford, visited Sega World, screamed on rides at the American Adventure and Alton Towers, slept through Toy Story, danced (or perhaps I mean 'raved'), gone dry-slope ski-ing and bowling, cele-brated birthdays and weddings and Eids, cooked pizza and lasagne and jam tarts, completed a music project, trekked ten miles in the rain and mud and cold and got lost, slept in tents and in dormitories, put together a cultural display and triumphed in a fashion show. I have stuck more plasters on their knees and hands than I care to count, taken them to hospital, held their hands in police stations, sat with them in court, given character references, helped arrange work placements, dropped them home from club, taken them for ice cream, taught them to cook, played hide and seek and Murder in the Dark until 5a.m., cheered them on in football (I am undoubtedly SAYO's most loyal – and possibly only – fan), discussed *Macbeth* and *Animal Farm*, taken countless photos, admired the latest trends in coloured contact lenses, helped them apply to Further Education college and watched them receive their Duke of Edinburgh's Bronze award, an achievement award for the fashion show and, most recently, celebrated their NRA (National Record of Achieve-ment) day and saw them leave school.

They, for their part, have cheated me at cards, and taught me to cheat, given me concerned advice on my personal safety, carried my shopping, looked for my book in shops, stayed at my house, met my friends and asked them outrageously personal questions, tested out their flirting techniques on me, kept me purposely awake all night on residentials just to see me lose my temper (now famously known as 'Claire doing a Bradford' after one particularly long sleepless night), decorated my car with balloons and flowers (in case I never get married), 'protected' me from unwanted admirers, leapt out in front of my car on more occasions than I dare remember, mobbed me so often while driving down Abbey Street that the police have certainly marked my car, and taken me home to meet their families.

Driving through the school one lunchtime my car was again mobbed by a group of 'the little ones', who stopped me to exchange news and catch up on the gossip. A teacher walking past looked with some curiosity at the sight of a dozen young men, infamous in the school for their reputation as gang members and troublemakers, clustered round my Micra, sticking their heads in the windows and arranging themselves in dramatic poses across the bonnet. One of the young men, Hanif, noticed the teacher and called to him: 'Sir, sir, Do you fancy her? She's our youth worker. She's too clever for you though, sir, she's got a doctorate. She went to Oxford.' Adding to the teacher's mounting confusion and embarrassment, Sayeed added, more prosaically: 'Yeah, Oxford Street. She bought it at Selfridges.'

What this scene evokes for me is the conflation of structures, emotions, perceptions and humour that marks out my research and personal relationships with this group, and more generally. It displays at once a recognition of gender and 'class' factors, age and sexuality, reflects a sense of ownership of me by the group and captures the transformation of these categories and emotions into a more localized and personal set of understandings mediated by mixture of humour, pride and affection. What has evolved over the past two years is a set of relationships that cannot easily be dissected, compartmentalized and evaluated, that are not simply about hierarchy and inequality and that are definitely not about objectivity, while at the same time encapsulate a depth of understanding and knowledge which go beyond anthropological narcissism. For both myself and the young men there exists a mutuality of trust, respect and affection, a sense of sharing in each other's experiences and participation in each other's lives.

I interviewed all but three of this core group; both Shafiq and Enam were too shy to be involved in the interviewing process, while Adil failed to turn up on three occasions, after which I gave up. Theirs were the most detailed interviews and perhaps the most open, related on the whole to incidents and events we had shared over the past months. As in all cases, I asked the young men to select their own names for the book, primarily because I wanted them to feel a sense of ownership of their voices and their part in the research, partly to convey a sense of their self-creation in the work, but also to acknowledge the interactive process of the research and its transformation into 'fiction' (Clifford, 1988). The others who feature in the study were given names by me, and are crucial in providing both breadth and texture to the work.

On Terror and Love . . .

The preceding account of my fieldwork and the relationships it has generated is not intended as an authoritative or exhaustive statement. Nor is it an emblem of personal authenticity, designed to quietly reassert a publicly denied position of privileged knowledge through the covert accumulation of pseudo-experiential credentials – as an Asian, as a woman, as working class, as 'being there', as a 'native'. It is simply one version of events built on my memories and thoughts and emotions, and through which I have tried to make sense of my experience of fieldwork.

That said, there is an acutely personal dimension to this study, which has indelibly marked these relationships and the ways in which I want to write about them. It has been, and remains, a very personal journey – an exploration of my own identifications which began with *The Art of Being Black*, and which exploded in this study in ways I could not begin to imagine when I first arrived at the SAYO project. The present study is unthinkable without this dimension, which is woven into every encounter and understanding, at least on my part. It is an element of which most of the young men are, at best, only dimly aware, yet one which has been so important to me, on a very private level, that to deny it would be to lose a crucial facet of the portrait presented here. This section, then, is my attempt to explain it, most of all to these young men who have come to mean so much to me.

To begin, then, with a potted autobiography: I was born in 1965 and fostered from birth, and later adopted, by a white English family. My father is a haulage contractor, now retired; my mother worked as a secretary. I grew up with my two brothers and a sister (another sister followed later) in various small villages in Oxfordshire and went to school in a local market town. I was the only 'black' child in my primary and secondary school, but – some racist name calling aside – survived without major conflict. I always knew I was adopted, mainly because my family are white and blonde and blue eyed, and I am brown and black haired and brown eyed and it was kind of hard to overlook; and while I was a child I assumed it was because my mother had too many children and could not afford to keep me – a product of watching too many Blue Peter appeals, probably. When I was fourteen, my mother told me that my birth mother had actually been a history student at Oxford, who had been forced to leave me in England and return to India, where she had married and undoubtedly had other children.

My desire to 'be Asian' and discover my 'roots' grew through my teenage years, but was impossible to satisfy. There was no visible Asian community where I lived and, in fact, I met my first Asian person when I was nineteen and went to Oxford to study English Literature. When I was sixteen, I persuaded my parents (who have always been, I think, remarkably tolerant of my many self inventions), to buy me a *saree* for my birthday. I remember being devastated at discovering that I did not know how to put it on, feeling that if I were a 'real' Indian I would somehow have naturally known and it would have fallen into place, pleats and all, with no safety pins. Although these feelings seem a little ridiculous now, they still exercise a hold over me and display the intensity of my desire for an 'Asian' identity within my imagination. When I arrived in Oxford, and made my first Indian and Pakistani friends (interestingly, mainly from Britain), I took the opportunity to explore this new identity – joined the Asian society, wore *salwar kameez* and *sarees*, started to learn to cook Indian food (I once started to learn Urdu, but could not get beyond 'this is a table' before a sense of futility took over), visited and was welcomed by my friends' families, who initially claimed me as a 'lost' daughter.

To say this experiment backfired on me is perhaps something of an overstatement, but even until today it does not feel like it. After one terrible weekend at a friend's brother's wedding, when I was sat on and pushed around and asked very personal questions about why my mother had abandoned me and been climbed over by countless children and given a sack of onions to peel and talked at in Punjabi and, finally, laughed at publicly for not understanding 'my' language – my desire to be Indian largely evaporated. It was replaced instead with a terror of Asian families and a defensive assertion of an identity which, if it was not exactly English, was definitely 'not Asian'.

It was with the same defensive 'not Asian' identity, partially mediated by my experiences of *The Art of Being Black*, that I approached the SAYO project. It would be true to say that a large measure of the terror I felt at beginning the fieldwork arose from this more personal source – I was less terrified of the young men I had been told about than what their reaction might be to me personally. It was, I suppose, this fear of an altogether more personal rejection that prevented much of my early interaction. It also constructed barriers in my own imagination about the fieldwork – my sense of alienness and distance was at least as much self created as tangible, and it took me some time before I dared dismantle these walls.

As the fieldwork progressed, my more private journey of discovery kept pace; as I came to know the young men, and to accept that they were not the guardians of some imagined but nonetheless much envied cultural authenticity, many of my fears also dissipated. A major player in this process was again Yasmin, who in the past two years has hurtled me through the complexities of a belated 'cultural education' with good humour, tolerance and a healthy disregard for over-essentialized cultural representations and my own manifold paranoias. From shopping for *lehngas* in Green Street, through Brick Lane and the Asian club scene to gold shops in Wembley and Bollywood extravaganzas, the past twenty-four months have been something of a personal revelation – as well as great fun.

More than this 'education', however, the acceptance by Yasmin and the young men of me as a person, without judgement, or assessment or constraint has been perhaps the most surprising – and without doubt the most rewarding – aspect of our encounter. Although most of the young men know of my background, it has never become an issue or a barrier – I am simply Claire, their youth worker, their friend or, as Hanif once told me with exaggerated affection, 'the light in our lives'. Although I think the young men have always thought of me as 'Asian', or perhaps more accurately as 'Indian' rather than 'English', this has never been a category that has carried conditions with it. It has been rather an accepted and unscrutinized facet of my personality, along with my temper and bizarre sense of humour. For example, on discovering I was mixed-race – of an Indian mother and an Irish father – the only comment was a solemn 'Ah well, that explains why she's mad then.'

For me, their acceptance has meant more than any of these young men could imagine. It has, put simply, taken much of the terror out of my relationship to 'the Asian community', both real and imagined, and replaced it with a sense of 'belonging'. Which is not to lay claim to an essentialized and authentic 'Asianness', but rather to recognise the heterogeneity and inclusiveness of that term, the identities and experiences it encompasses, and the space within it for understanding and friendship and love between very different people.

This understanding has marked the scope, substance and direction of this work in significant ways. To distinguish between the intellectual project and its more private, emotional dimension has become impossible for me, as well as undesirable. The study is about people I care about deeply and with whom I have developed bonds that explode any simple discrete notion of the research relationship. Through the research I have been able to explore for the first time in my life my sense of being part of a 'community' – of workers, of friends, of families – which once seemed so unreachable and mysterious. Although my position is still marginal, and not always comfortable, it at least no longer feels as isolated and as isolating as it once did. My 'Asianness' now fits me better, and if it still startles me when the young men treat me as a 'conventional' Indian woman, it at least no longer feels like an ill-fitting pretence.

The correlation – or perhaps I mean confusion – of life and work, the private and the public, subjectivity and objectivity, the search for personal identities and collective identifications runs throughout this study. The focus on family relationships, for example, springs from my own very personal curiosity about Asian family life, which I had never experienced and, at times, so longed for. I remember vividly sitting in Heathrow airport several years ago waiting for a friend to arrive from America and watching an Asian family next to me. A little girl was running around, closely monitored by her slightly older and very protective brother. The scene fascinated me – and I wondered what it would be like to be part of a family that looked like me and that seemed to share a closeness that I did not feel with my own family, much as I love them. One of the areas that has absorbed me most over the past two years has been the ties between families, and particularly between siblings, real and 'fictive' – primarily, I suppose, because it was something I had simply never known before. What I discovered, of course, was a very complex, shifting and indiv-iduated set of relationships and hierarchies; but what I also found was a sense of support and caring which drew me in. I have 'collected' several new families through this research, who have become an integral part of my life. With a number of 'the little ones', particularly, I have found the younger brothers I never had and with whom, as several of my friends have observed, I am reliving aspects of my childhood. Or perhaps that is just an excuse for screaming at funfairs and playing hide and seek.

In the summer of 1996, I finally made contact with my birth mother in India and we met in London at the end of July. She was, I confess, not at all how I had envisaged her – very forthright, down-to-earth and completely terrifying, a consultant with the United Nations on child labour in India. I look very much like her, which surprised us both; and we share a fiery temper and a passion for our respective areas of work. We met for only three days at this time, and I introduced her to my friends in London, and met hers, and we went shopping together and ate polite meals out. What was most important to me at that time was that she met the young men I had been working with – my 'other' Asian family, who suddenly seemed much more real to me than the family I was suddenly confronted with.

We went to the project on a Saturday morning shortly before she was due to leave and I introduced her to several of the junior members I was closest to. They seemed a little confused as to what our relationship was, and I felt too overcome by the newness and strangeness of it to explain at the time. Only Ifti, who is one of the young men I am closest to, knew who she was and he was, I think, at least as nervous as me. It was an extraordinary encounter, to introduce the mother I had never known, a Bengali Hindu woman whose family were originally from Sylhet, to these young men whose families, though Muslim, are also mainly from Sylhet, and who are now such a central part of my life. Yet it also provided a sense of continuity for me, and of resolution between my past, my present life and a newly imagined future. Had I not known Yasmin and these young men, I could never have faced this meeting without terror, while meeting my birth mother gave me the answers I needed to finally move on. It seemed only natural, then, that when I travelled to India that summer to meet my brother and grandmother, that Yasmin should travel with me, to complete this cycle.

Conclusion

Several weeks ago,[5] during my usual round of lifts home after the evening club session, Hanif turned to me with a knowing smile and asked: 'So, Claire, the new Asian folk devil, what do you think?' After the initial shock wore off, I realized, to my confusion, that Hanif was referring to my introductory chapter. I had given a copy to Shahin, his older brother, who is currently doing A-level sociology, to read and comment on, after he had agreed to act as my 'gentle reader'. He had not only read it, but had passed it on to both of his younger brothers; something I had not realized, nor ever really contemplated, until Hanif's rather pointed allusion. Yasmin told me later that Hanif had told her that he had read the chapter, and that it was really exciting and 'full of gangs and stuff' – which sort of missed the point, but was at least a positive response.

What Hanif's question to me most clearly illustrates is the processual and unfinished nature of this study, even as I write it. For me, largely because of the close personal ties which are woven through the research, there is no sense of completion, no moving away from the fieldwork site, no autonomous reflection. I still attend every club session, and the project office has become my second home; most of my free time is spent either with Yasmin or my 'other' families. For the young men, similarly, there is no definable separation or closure; there has been no leave taking. With many, the progression of the book has become a subject of concern and interest, as well as a favourite way of winding me up. 'So, Claire, have you finished writing the book yet?' is a frequent, once genuine and now increasingly ironic question which confronts me. To which my usual response is 'Ask me if I've started it.' What I am writing about, how I am writing it, or why I am not writing it, have become topics of discussion both with me and amongst the project members, as have the many variations on the sardonic comment 'I bet that's going in the book', or 'Put that in the book, Claire.'

The dialogic foundation on which this book is built is perhaps not as apparent in the final product as I would like. Although I am attempting to write more accessibly, to replace an emphasis on overt theorisation with a less intimidating and exclusory emphasis on 'ethnographic', though not 'thick' description (Geertz, 1983) and to involve the young men at every stage of its production, inevitably the present text reduces and silences the multi-vocality of the lived experience. It loses, by default, the immediacy, the energy and sheer exuberance of these young men. It also loses the frustrations and joys and laughter we have shared throughout the study, and still share. The present chapter has tried to make clear some of these processes. In acknowledging the interplay of subjectivities, the aim is not to disavow the work's wider responsibilities, nor to undermine its claims to a broader significance. If the experiences and voices contained here are selected and mediated by its author, refracted through me rather than simply reflected by me, they also go beyond my own position to a more collective project. During one of the discussions that informed this chapter, when I was explaining 'innocence' to Humzah and moaning about how difficult it was to untangle all the thoughts and feelings which make up my work, he asked me: 'But who are you writing it for?' After some thought, I told him that, ultimately, I felt my responsibility was to the young men, so I supposed I was writing for them. Smiling, he said, reassuringly: 'Well, that's okay then, because we trust you.' It is a position this study takes seriously – although its success as yet remains to be seen.

Notes

1 Amitabh was so-named by the young men due to his resemblance to Bollywood icon, Amitabh Bachchan.
2 It is this personal friendship that underpinned my decision not to interview Yasmin. Yasmin and I have spent so much time together during the past four years, in work and outside, and I have learned so

much from her that, to a large extent, our views and aims in relation to the project have become one and the same. I decided that to interview Yasmin would be rather like talking to myself; her knowledge and experience, along with those of the young men, runs through this text, which is formed in dialogue – almost sentence by sentence – with her.

3 A card game.
4 A sex education game.
5 The first draft of this chapter was written in early 1998.

–3–

The Setting

In April 1996, the junior members of the SAYO project travelled to Bradford on a three-day residential visit to a Muslim youth project in the City. After a sports day, several hours in the local casualty department, shopping and cooking, a visit to the National Film Museum, a concert of Bengali music and two – what seemed like very long – nights of Hide and Seek, Murder in the Dark and midnight walks, we visited Bradford City Centre on the final morning, ending up in Pizza Hut for lunch before the journey home. As we watched Faruk, our youngest member, devour his pizza and the rest of several others, Sher Khan, one of our co-workers, commented that he hoped Faruk would get fat.[1] Faruk, who is our tallest – and probably our skinniest – member, laughed and retorted smugly, 'No, I don't put on weight, you know – I just get taller.' Laughing, I asked, 'How tall are you now Faruk?' Faruk looked at me and answered with unblinking candour, 'Well, the last time I was arrested and taken to the police station, they said I was 5'10".'

While Faruk's remark made us all laugh, however unintentionally, it also held a certain poignancy – at least for me. That a fourteen-year-old could, or should, view his physical development through his encounters with the local police was bizarre enough: beyond this, that these encounters should be endowed by the same fourteen year-old with the aura of normalcy – as constituting almost an expected and inevitable part of life – seemed to border on tragedy. Yet over the past two-and-a-half years that I have spent with the SAYO project, such events have been a common, if not yet quite commonplace, occurrence. Such encounters between the young men and the institutions which so often frame their experiences – the project, the Youth Service, the police, the school – form an integral and inescapable part of the historical, local, and contemporary development of individual and collective identifications, the impact of which can be neither underestimated nor ignored. As will become clearer in the following chapters, the identifications of this group of young men are structured through, though not determined by, a set of institutional representations, which in turn draw upon and reinforce a set of commonplace understandings about Asian, and especially Muslim, young men. This was most clearly apparent in the police and school responses to the clashes between the local Bengali and African-Caribbean young men in the summer of 1996, which was referred to earlier and which will be considered in greater detail later on. However, more generally, it can be argued that these understandings – particularly focused on representations of socio-economic and cultural deprivation and 'special needs' – are a formative influence on the way in which the Bengali community on the Stoneleigh Estate, and the SAYO project itself, has developed and been perceived. More than this, these representations, which have broadly functioned to construct the local Bengali young men as 'problem', have a tangible impact on the experiences of these young men. Although the present work has sought to place these structures within a wider context of individual and collective agency, and local, historical process, their significance must be acknowledged. Reflecting back on *The Art of Being Black* (Alexander, 1996), I cannot escape a sneaking feeling that in seeking to counteract dominant, negative and essentializing images of black youth, I perhaps under-emphasized the explicit structural constraints that informed the lives and experiences of those young men and women. While I still strongly affirm the complex primacy of agency over structural over-determination – which is why the present chapter comes *after* my more personal introduction to the research project and its participants – the often 'in-your-face' encounters, conflicts and confrontations with the institutions of 'authority' are something that it has been impossible to escape. Perhaps this is because of the younger age range of my informants this time around, who are more obviously still enmeshed with various institutions; perhaps it is the more clearly defined, local base of the research project or, indeed, the institutional framework of the research base itself in the SAYO project; or perhaps, five years on, I am less naive, or simply less optimistic.

Writing this, I am thinking of one visit to the local police station with Shafiq, one of our junior members, then aged fourteen, who had been arrested for apparently shouting threats at the Deputy Head of Thomas More school during a minor disturbance on the school grounds between the police and some of the school pupils.[2] Although both Shafiq and the Deputy Head himself denied the accusation, one zealous young policeman insisted on the arrest and took Shafiq, handcuffed, in the back of a police van, to the local station. I had witnessed the events and promised Shafiq that I would meet him at the police station. When I arrived and was allowed in, some time later, Shafiq was in a cell, crying and shaking. He was cautioned and told to empty his pockets, the contents of which consisted, almost in true *Boys' Own* style, of a biro, a broken pencil and several grubby tissues. Although Shafiq is hardly an angel, the gap between the image of a dangerous assailant and this slight figure of a scared fourteen year-old schoolboy seemed at once absurd and intensely revealing.

Under the protests of myself and the supposed 'victim', the Deputy Head, the Charge Office admitted that he felt the policeman concerned had, in his inexperience, perhaps overreacted in arresting Shafiq. Nevertheless, it took several hours before Shafiq was released, on bail to return five weeks later, at which time he was formally cautioned. The rationale seemed to be along the lines of a 'short, sharp shock' tactic – that if Shafiq had not actually done anything this time, it was nevertheless a good opportunity to give him a fright in advance of any future misdemeanours. The assumption, both at the time of the arrest and subsequently, was that Shafiq was bound to be guilty of *something* – a representation that drew on and reinforced a wider set of common-sense understandings about Asian youth, and a more localized articulation of these images centred on and about the Stoneleigh Estate.

The present chapter is concerned with this latter articulation, and has a dual motivation. Firstly, the chapter aims to paint in the background to the study – its physical, historical and statistical setting, against which the project, its subjects and their identifications are to be understood. Secondly, implicit within this description, and inescapable from it, is an exploration of the ways in which institutional and societal representations of Asian/Muslim young men play an active role in shaping this backdrop and its subsequent performances. The aim here, however, is not to posit a deterministic, top down and uni-dimensional script, but to examine the negotiations and dialogues, conflicts and commonalities, which mark out the history of the locale in relation to the SAYO project and its members.

Setting the Scene I: the National Picture

The guilty-by-representation approach enacted in Shafiq's treatment partly reflects the refocused public and media spotlight on Asian youth – and more specifically on Muslim young men – in recent years. The emergence of 'the Asian Gang', traced in Chapter 1, mixes common-sense notions of culture conflict and culture of poverty, to evoke a vision of a reactionary inner-city/urban subculture, which has been taken up, fleshed out, reiterated and expounded in media, political and academic discourse, as the new 'British Muslim underclass'. Receiving its most notorious performance in the 1993 *Panorama* documentary *Purdah in the Underclass*, concerns about an emergent Muslim ghetto culture have come to form a primary and largely unexamined motif in contemporary racial politics and ethnicity theory. More precisely, Britain's largest Muslim communities, from Pakistan and Bangladesh,[3] have moved centre-stage in debates around 'race', ethnicity and identity – particularly, and crucially, in rethinking the parameters of discrimination and disadvantage.

An unforeseen, but perhaps inescapable, consequence of the emphasis on multiculturalism and 'difference' amongst Britain's hitherto largely undifferentiated black communities has, then, been the apparent growth of a divide between those groups achieving material success and a degree of social acceptability, and those increasingly viewed as outcasts – economic, social and cultural pariahs. The major axis of this division has been articulated though religion, with Britain's south Asian Muslim communities constructed in opposition to their more successful non-Muslim counterparts, and increasingly in overwhelmingly problem-oriented terms – an opposition encapsulated in Modood's distinction between the 'achievers' and the disadvantaged 'believers' (Modood, 1992: 43). As I have argued elsewhere (Alexander, 1998), rather than shattering racialized images through the assertion and celebration of difference, the unintended side effect of this reconceptualization has been to polarize debates around a new dualism – a movement from a black/white divide to a Muslim/non-Muslim dichotomy, in which Muslim groups are, ironically, positioned in relation to the same series of negative labels and images that earlier sought to define 'black'/African-Caribbean groups and from which the champions of 'diversity' such as Modood so struggled to free themselves. Paradoxically then, seeking to explore the differential positioning and experiences of South Asian groups has at the same time served to reify and enmesh Pakistani and Bangladeshi communities in a morass of deprivations. As the latest PSI Survey *Ethnic Minorities in Britain: Diversity and Disadvantage* comments in its introduction, 'Many of the following chapters show that the experience of Pakistanis and Bangladeshis has been *different* from that of Indians and African Asians – *usually worse*' (Modood et al., 1997: 17, my emphasis).

Certainly, the figures paint a depressing, if persuasive, picture of these communities – under-represented in Higher and Further Education, forming the sector with the largest proportion of young people (aged sixteen to twenty-four years old) without qualifications; disproportionately over-represented in the unemployment statistics (generally double that of whites and Indians, and reaching up to forty seven per cent amongst men in the London region in 1994); with employed Bangladeshi men earning a third less than their white counterparts, and with apparent downward mobility in the professional and managerial occupations (from ten per cent to seven per cent between 1982 and 1994); concentrated in social housing in inner-city and metropolitan areas with high levels of harassment and poor amenities. Commenting on household income, Richard Berthoud notes, 'The author of this chapter has been analysing household incomes for more than twenty years. Pakistanis and Bangladeshis are *easily the poorest group* he has ever encountered' (Modood et al., 1997: 161, my emphasis). Modood concludes in his chapter on employment:

> the prediction that Pakistanis and Bangladeshis will develop a similar class profile to other South Asians grossly understates the current scale of the disadvantage of Pakistanis and Bangladeshis, and takes no account either of the *cultural differences* between South Asians . . . or of a political alienation . . . which is itself a product of and further stimulates anti-Muslim prejudice (Modood, 1990), or *of anxiety about a possible trend of criminalization among young Pakistanis and Bangladeshis, which in some ways parallels the experience of Caribbean male youth* (Modood et al., 1997: 147, my emphasis).

While not wishing to dispute the findings of the PSI Survey, a number of questions can be raised about their broader interpretation and, more significantly, about their role in creating a series of images about Britain's Muslims, which casts them in almost exclusively negative terms – or to quote Modood 'different [and] . . . *usually worse*' (Modood et al., 1997: 17). Firstly, there is an almost uniform conflation of Pakistani and Bangladeshi communities throughout into an undifferentiated category of 'Muslims' – Berthoud, for example writes of Pakistanis and Bangladeshis as '*the* poorest group' (Modood et al., 1997: 161) – which in turn is placed in opposition to other South Asian groups and defined in terms of immutable 'cultural differences' (Modood et al., 1997: 147). Secondly, this new category is constructed through the lense of multiple and cumulative 'severe disadvantage' and alienation which, it seems knows no bounds nor offers much room for optimism.[4] Thirdly, this 'severe disadvantage' is most pronounced in relation to young people, who are represented as alienated from society, with the seemingly inevitable move towards criminality and criminalization (seen by Modood as apparently indistinguishable processes). It is revealing that Modood draws a direct comparison between these unquestioned possibilities and the experience of African-Caribbean young men, reflecting both the implicit gendering of youth concerns and the repositioning of Muslim young men within an already racialized framework of social marginalization and threat.

The centrality of this broader portrait to the invention of 'the Asian Gang' is obvious and draws on the same commonsense linkages between cultural difference, economic deprivation and social breakdown – evoking a series of negative images and labels through which Britain's Muslim communities are defined and understood. With regard to Muslim groups, it seems, the emphasis is less on diversity than disadvantage.

Setting the Scene II: a Local Portrait

The Stoneleigh Estate forms the central residential area in More Ward of a south-east London borough. A sprawling development of red brick inter-war local authority housing, rimmed by newer grey concrete blocks of flats and maisonettes, the estate lies in the triangular segment between three major roads feeding access across the river to the City and the West End, although it is barely visible from any of these thoroughfares. Divided by Abbey Street, the estate has two small parks, a mosque, an adventure playground and playscheme, a community centre, a doctor's surgery and a nursery. Abbey Street itself curves from the County Court building and local police station at one end along the outskirts of the red brick blocks to the Philip Sidney primary school and the Thomas More secondary school, which the majority of the local school children attend. The street boasts a newsagents, a launderette, a chemist, a barber's shop, a cafe, a small grocery store and off-licence, a halal meat store, an advice centre and three pubs.

More Ward has a population of over 9,000 people, thirty-one per cent of whom live on the Stoneleigh Estate. Described as having the most severe problems in relation to household indicators in the borough (itself ranked second overall in London for its levels of deprivation),[5] the ward has, as the tellingly titled *Poverty Profile* of 1996 states, 'always had a reputation for serious deprivation' (*Poverty Profile*, April 1996). Now ranking as the fifth most deprived ward in the borough, More Ward has twenty- five per cent unemployment, a figure that rises to thirty-two per cent for men on the Stoneleigh Estate itself. In 1980, an Urban Aid application described the estate and its surrounds as 'a prime example of inner city urban decay, and suffers from some of the worst social stress and deprivation in [the borough]'.[6] A 1997 application for Single Regeneration Budget (SRB) funding for the ward estimates that eighty per cent of the households live in purpose-built accommodation, two-thirds of which is local authority housing , with nearly sixty per cent of households dependent on housing benefit, less than a third owning a car (falling to twenty-nine per cent on the Stoneleigh Estate), and eighty-two per cent of schoolchildren at the local school eligible for free school meals. The application states that 'the Ward has particular problems in relation to unemployment, education performance, crime and racist behaviour' (Community Regeneration Report, 1997).

Such a portrait of More Ward, and of the Stoneleigh Estate, inevitably combines the statistical data with an element of utilitarian vested interest and special pleading. What is of particular relevance to the present work, however, is the representation of the area that emerges and that functions as a crucial agent in the creation of meanings for the actions of its inhabitants. Note, for example, the seamless association of the 'inner-city/urban' with 'decay', 'social stress' and 'deprivation', and with the notion of 'particular problems'. In the SRB bid, in addition, there is the implicit and explicit linkage between the 'particular problems' of the estate and youth – education, youth unemployment (thirty-four per cent and twenty-seven per cent for young men and young women, aged sixteen to twenty-four, respectively), youth crime (vandalism, drugs offences, crime and 'community problems' are the identified areas of concern, all directed at young offenders), and the effects of racial harassment on young people.[7]

As this final element suggests, there is also a powerful association between the 'problems' of More Ward and its black and ethnic minority population. Thirty-one per cent of More Ward's inhabitants are Black or Asian (compared with twenty-five per cent across the borough); with ten per cent of African descent (and including a large number of recently arrived Somali families), and eight per cent of Bangladeshi origin. Eighteen per cent of the residents on the Stoneleigh Estate are of Bangladeshi origin (approximately 1,200 people), and are described in the SRB report as experiencing 'particular disadvantage'.[8] This resonates revealingly with the conclusions of the PSI Survey on the national picture. Noting the ward's 'reputation for serious deprivation', the 1996 Poverty Profile continues:

> it comes out fifth worst in the borough. It shares similar characteristics, of very high proportions of lone parents, ethnic minority groups, and people with disabilities, with the four preceding wards on the scale. These are the groups who mostly lack access to basic amenities in the community which has *contributed to their state of acute deprivation*. (*Poverty Profile* 1996, my emphasis)

The mere presence of an ethnic minority population, it would seem, provides a causal framework for inner-city deprivation, which is self-explanatory – a pre-defined and self-evident 'problem' group who, along with similarly disadvantaged categories, are implicitly scapegoated as lacking the social and cultural capital required to access resources and thereby '[contribute] to their state of acute deprivation'. Significantly, this same equation of ethnic minority communities with deprivation was employed by the local Thomas More school to deflect its imminent failure by Ofsted inspectors in 1995, by claiming the presence of large proportions of ethnic minority pupils demanded special dispensation.[9] The SRB Report notes that over a third of students were recently assessed as having 'special educational needs'; a category that, in the period of my fieldwork, included a number of the young men who attended the SAYO project.[10]

The Bengali community on the Stoneleigh Estate in particular has been cast as a 'problem' community, defined by the twin axes of 'need' and 'threat' – a reputation that seems to have grown alongside its expansion into the only significant Asian community in the borough, providing a focal point of identification for Bengalis in surrounding areas. This representation is most clearly reflected in, and has perhaps the greatest impact on, the Bengali young men of the area, who are its most visible and active element. At an official level, the young men exemplify the dual pathologization of youth and of 'race'/ethnicity; while within the locale, the transformation of the community and the landscape by the activities of these young men in recent years has earned them something of a reputation as troublemakers, both within the Bengali community itself, and outside. This labelling process can be traced in part to the pathologization of the Bengali community at a national and local level; in part to the changing nature of community activism on the Stoneleigh Estate in recent years, and in part to the history of this group of young men over the previous five years.

Certainly there are clear continuities between the profile of the Stoneleigh Bengali community and the assumptions of 'need' and 'disadvantage' that permeate the portrait of the Muslim 'underclass' at a national level: there is additionally the same slippage between 'disadvantaged' and 'problem' communities, and the same focus on 'youth' as the crucible for these moral panics. This is not to argue for a simplistic translation of images from the national to the local, but to suggest that a set of images and codes have emerged that provide a framework within which local events can be placed and deciphered; and which too easily silence more local-historical or alternative readings.

The positioning of the young men from the Stoneleigh Estate against the broader local and national backdrop of the Muslim 'underclass', then, predetermines their representation within a limited range of understandings and as constituting a 'problem' group. The representation of the junior members of the SAYO project as a 'gang' in the newspaper report at the opening of Chapter 1 should be read against this broader conceptual canvas, as should the police targeting of Bengali youth on the estate.

Two significant representational by-products of this intersection of ethnicity, generation and locale are worth mentioning here, and should be born in mind during the rest of this chapter. Firstly, that although a number of the first generation of young men from the estate have grown up, married, and moved away, the reputation has remained intact, transferring to their younger brothers and friends without significant alteration. This has particular consequences for peer-group relations, especially amongst the younger members, which will be explored in later chapters. Secondly, that as the Stoneleigh Estate has developed as a focal point for the wider Bengali population in the borough, it has also become a primary site of identification for young men from outside its immediate confines. These young men are thus identified, and identify themselves, as Stoneleigh youth, and thus become subject to – or, indeed, partake of – the reputation of the local community. Significant numbers of the SAYO project members have either moved from the estate in recent years or, indeed, have never lived in More Ward, yet this local identity remains strong despite – or perhaps because of – its negative connotations.

One of the most evocative images of the Stoneleigh Estate, for me, is of the Bengali young men sitting and talking on a small stretch of wall on the corner of Abbey Street, next to the grocers and the 'Nigerian phone box'.[11] In a recent video about life on the estate, Ismat, one of the junior members, described this spot as 'the heart of the Stoneleigh'. For Ismat, his friends, and the other young men of the SAYO project, this curiously undefined corner is not only a place to meet, but a space that they claim as their own – an articulation of their own deeply gendered and generational identity, part of a more broadly imagined territorial and ethnic identification – a community within a community. Significantly, a place which is perceived by the young men as a space of solidarity, and celebrated as such, has also become a symbol of exactly those problems associated with the Bengali young men of the estate – labelled, targeted and subject to surveillance by the police and the wider community.[12] The young men who inhabit this corner (and who incidentally are the core group of the SAYO project) have become synonymous with, and to a large extent held responsible for, the problems of their community – both 'ethnic' and territorial.

Such a definition is, however, by no means uncontested; and this contestation – of images, meanings, reputations, identities – forms a crucial struggle for these young men: for physical, institutional, cultural and ideological space.

Contested Histories, Contesting Images: the Rise and Fall and Rise of the SAYO Project

In the course of writing this chapter, an anonymous letter arrived on the desks of a local newspaper and the borough's Director of Education. Ostensibly from 'a group of worried and anxious mothers . . . from a number of different nationality and culture' (sic, February 4th 1998), the letter complained of the apparently preferential treatment being meted out to Asian young people at the Thomas More youth club, at the expense of other local youth. In a curious and angry mish-mash of misinformation, accusation and barely veiled racial hostility, the authors of the letter assert that 'there seems to be favouritism by the service for *certain races* getting more than the rest' (my emphasis). Noting that 'the tabloids see youth clubs as places where *gang members* meet up' (my emphasis), the letter continues by blaming the Asian young men for 'intimidating the other young people as they have this idea that the club belongs to them so any other kids that go there are not made to feel welcome.' Accusing the youth service of heightening 'racial tension' by 'segregating' youth provision, of rewarding 'numerous attacks on the other kids by the Asian kids' with 'weekend trips, nights out to discos, holidays' and of promoting drug and alcohol abuse through staff and members smoking cigarettes together outside the club building, the authors conclude dramatically,

> If the service don't do their work properly . . . may heaven's forbid when someone's childs gets killed in Thomas More because the staff in the school and club are not doing their jobs properly. [sic]

While this is not the place to set this particular record of complaint straight, nor to argue the case for special provisions for minority groups – ethnic or otherwise – the letter is significant for a number of reasons. Firstly, it points to the increasing profile of the SAYO project in the local area, and to its recent successes in fundraising for residential exchanges within Britain, training opportunities for its members and its most current achievement – a trip by nine junior members to Tunisia that same month. Secondly, it relates these successes not to the activities or efforts of the project members themselves, or their workers, but to the 'favouritism' of the youth service in response to an imagined special pleading for resources. Thirdly, it paints a picture of the Bengali young men on the estate, and who attend the project, as troublemakers, gang members and social deviants, who intimidate and attack other local youth and prevent them from attending even generic youth provisions. Implicit in the latter two points is a dual representation of the SAYO project and its members, which can be mapped against wider representations of the Bengali community locally and the 'Muslim underclass' nationally – that of Muslim young men as victim and as threat. Set in opposition to these more dominant themes is the first point – the assertion of potential and its fulfilment. It is worth noting that this assertion of agency is always riven with its denial: in this case, for example, success is recast rather as the compensation for acknowledged inadequacy and deprivation – of 'special need'[13] – the inescapable fusion and confusion of subject and image. However subordinated or silenced, this voice of contestation remains an important one, and it is this process of representation, objectification and contestation that marks out the complex history of the SAYO project.

It is against this wider conceptual backdrop – of representations of inner city decay and cultural deprivation – that the development of the SAYO project must be understood. In particular, the designation of the Bengali young men of the Stoneleigh Estate as a 'problem' group has been structured into the fabric of the project, and has functioned to interpret and translate much of its activities, its internal conflicts and its external interactions.

The project itself started as part of a wider initiative to develop youth provision for the Asian community in the ward about ten years ago. It is significant that at this point, the provision developed very much from a perception of 'special need' – a recognition that Asian young people were either not using, or were being excluded from, existing youth provision on the estate. One of the estate's first Bengali residents – and the first generation of Bengali youth – Silver, now twenty-three and a playworker in the area, told me that as he grew up the small community was subject to constant attacks:

> Living on the [Stoneleigh] Estate as a seven, eight, nine, ten year old, I remember playing football outside the house and white kids coming, and then you would automatically go home. No-one says anything to each other, it was just automatically understood, you would just pack up your bags and go home. (interview, 3 September 1996)

Julia, the Neighbourhood Development Worker who first established separate provision, similarly noted:

The Squires youth club at that time – Asian young people couldn't even dream to set foot in there . . . at the time, which is something that has changed now, I think, there was a lot of harassment for Asian young people by other young people . . . and it was very intimidating for them to walk in there. (interview, 18 October 1996)

The Asian project began in the local community centre, Coronation Hall, one evening a week in 1988. Two initial definitions of 'need' were built into this small beginning, which provide a revealing contrast with its later developments. Firstly, there is the construction of 'need' through the ascription of 'victim' status; and secondly, there is the cross-cutting definition of 'cultural need'. Thus, initial provision was aimed specifically at Asian young women, who were perceived to be, as it were, 'doubly disadvantaged' through both racist exclusion and gendered cultural expectations. The project was established and staffed by women, including Silver's elder sister. Asian young men, interestingly, did not form part of the equation – at this stage at least they were effectively invisible.[14] Under pressure from the young men, however, first a joint provision and then two separate groups were established: *Salam Bhano* for young women and *Salam Bhayo* for young men.

The provision expanded to two sessions for each group under the control of the Stoneleigh Estate Play Association (SEPA), and in 1990, the local council established a full-time post for Asian youth work. The first full-time worker, Shopna, had previously been employed as a part-time worker with the young women's group, and now assumed overall responsibility for both provisions. A short time later, a male worker, Helal, was employed part-time to run the young men's sessions. During this period, from 1990–2, the joint Asian provision became one of the most successful projects in the borough, initiating youth work training for both male and female members, and facilitating placements in the After Schools Service, with the support particularly of Majid, then Youth Officer. Shopna told me:

At the end it got very difficult, but in the beginning it was very, very good. The Asian project thrived because it was the biggest asset of the Youth Service at that time . . . before that they didn't know Asian young people existed. And so suddenly there's all these active Asian young people going around, including young women – doing Induction courses, becoming part of the Youth Service. (interview, 10 December 1996)

Within the young men's group at this time, however, a number of tensions emerged, which were to fracture the joint provision, and fundamentally alter the development of the SAYO project. Understandings of this period are, however, widely discrepant, and point to an ongoing contestation of images, aims and expectations that were structured into the project itself. At one level, then, as Julia informed me (interview, 18 October 1996), the Youth Service had set up the Asian project with an overarching definition of (young women's) need, but with little perception of what this actually entailed on the ground, and no acknowledgement of the specific needs of young men. Majid similarly told me that when he assumed responsibility for Asian youth work in the borough in 1990, the project was viewed at once as a high profile publicity exercise, and as a compensatory gesture:

> It was the only project working with Asian young people in the youth service in the Borough, in any shape or form . . . there was no monitored Asian youth people in any of the generic youth provision, so it was seen as 'oh, yes, this is a good project'. (interview, 7 November 1996)

The young men's provision within this was seen very much as an afterthought; badly resourced and – at least until Helal arrived – erratically co-ordinated. Majid, for example, told me that the boys group was supported initially as a way of making contact with the young women through their families, and later to defuse the disruption caused to the young women's session by the bored young men. This instrumental, and perhaps rather cynical, definition of an almost secondhand 'need' left a legacy of inequality – part-real, part-perceived – in the SAYO provision, which became a tangible source of resentment as the two projects developed. At the same time, then, as the young men's group developed under Helal, establishing a management committee, undertaking training residentials and establishing an informal mentoring programme (Majid, 7 November 1996), tensions increased with the young women's group, and particularly with Shopna, the full-time worker. Finally tensions erupted into confrontations between staff and members, with the young men accusing Shopna of misuse of funds and club equipment. Complaints were directed to the Council, while Shopna filed counter-claims of sexual harassment. These accusations and counter-accusations ultimately exploded into open conflict, with one of the members attacking Shopna physically, and an ongoing campaign of abusive phone calls. Shopna was moved to work solely with young women, and the young men's project was moved to a new site in the Thomas More School. These 'facts' are subject to a number of competing interpretations, which cast varying degrees of light and shade on the representation of the SAYO project and its members at this time.

The problems of the SAYO project at this time functioned at two levels: firstly, the organizational/structural response of the Youth Service which, as mentioned previously, sought to combine unspecified perceptions of 'cultural need' with a strong emphasis on visibility and institutional self-promotion. Ideologies of specialist provision, underpinned with unexamined notions of cultural difference, meant that overall scrutiny of the *quality* of the work being undertaken was abandoned in favour of multicultural rhetoric and utilitarian wish fulfillment. The successes of the Asian projects at this time could then be traced rather to the personal support of individuals, such as Majid, rather than to a more structural support base, while the combination of institutional disinterest and benign neglect perpetuated the illusion of strength which belied the reality of mismanagement, miscommunication and 'corruption' on the ground. Majid told me:

> Because of my commitment to the Project . . . I was actually playing quite a role, which was more akin to a full-time youth worker than an officer, and I was blinding myself to the amount I was actually doing as opposed to the youth workers . . . So our main worker was actually not a good youth worker, but the success of the project was seeming as if she was. (interview, 7 November 1996)

This structural blindspot then provided a framework for the second level of conflicts which marked the SAYO project, which were more personal, and centred on the relationship between Shopna herself and the project members. This focused around two distinct, but effectively inseparable, issues: firstly, there were accusations of corruption in the running of the project, and secondly, there were objections to the personal conduct of Shopna, both as a youth worker and as a woman. It is worth noting here that this second, gendered element only became significant within the context of the more general dissatisfaction with the running of the young men's session, but has generally been understood as the primary motivating factor in the dispute. The accusations of corruption partially have their root in the resentment of the unequal, hand-me-down provision reaching the young men's group, which was mentioned earlier. It is interesting, if not surprising, that Shopna herself blames much of the conflict on these structural inadequacies:

> At the end it did get very difficult, but it wasn't difficult because of the young people or the workers. I think it was difficult because of the funding situation and lack of understanding of the Youth Service . . . the workers were left with

the backlash; so where the young people got angry, they took it out on the workers. They felt it was the workers who were not providing. (interview, 10 December1996)

Certainly, it was felt that *Salam Bhano*, the young women's group, was being resourced at the expense of the young men's organisation,[15] a feeling fuelled by Shopna's admitted reluctance to assume responsibility for the young men – as she told me 'I wasn't really their worker'. (interview, 10 December 1996) More than this, however, the young men claimed that equipment bought for the SAYO project, including a hi-fi system TV and video and a washing machine, had disappeared from the club building: the hi-fi system was, apparently, later seen in Shopna's house, where she claimed she was keeping it for insurance purposes (S. Ahmed, interview, 6 November 1996; Hashim, interview, 24 October 1996).

In addition, Shopna bought in first her brother, then her cousin to staff the project – a series of moves that was seen as especially insulting to the young men – including Hashim and S. Ahmed – who had completed their basic youth work training and who had expectations of paid work with the project. Hashim, who was one of the first generation of young men to use the club, and at the time of my fieldwork was employed as a youth worker with the project,[16] summed up this period:

When Shopna came into the organization we felt that we were shut out for some reason; we never had a say in the club and we never knew what was going on in the backroom – we just come into club, we played club-based activities and went home . . . When she come into the club, she brought in some youth workers, her brother, then her cousin, and we thought 'What's going on – I mean, this is becoming like a family tree here.' And then we just took it – fair enough if they perform then that's fine. But it never happened . . . It got really bad, really; we tried to communicate . . . but she ignored us totally . . . So I mean it come to a stage where no one really come into the club anymore. (interview, 24 October1996)

Majid's portrait of this period bears striking similarity to this account. He told me:

Her [Shopna's] relationship with the young men was being severely undermined, not simply because of their attitude to her as a young woman, but because there was a lot of corruption issues, from their perspective – the club wasn't being opened, there were members of her family being brought in . . . Yes, I think a lot of [their views] were justified. (interview, 7 November 1996)

The present study is obviously unable to comment on the 'facts' or justifications of this period of the project's history. A number of observations can be made, however, on the perspectives that were articulated around these events, and that are of significance to the project's more recent development. Firstly, the articulation of gender relations in this period becomes a contested arena, and one that has enduring repercussions in the representation of the SAYO project and its members. On the one hand, then, there is the assumption of the centrality of gender bias in these encounters; as Julia insisted to me on a number of occasions that 'the young men have got a terrible attitude to women' (interview, 18 October 1996). This is given the additional weight of an ethnicized 'authenticity' through the evocation of religio-cultural attitudes;[17] thus Shopna told me:

> It was very naive of me to think I can leave my work at work and just go, because at the end of the day this is a very close knit community . . . when problems arise, it's like 'Well, what is a woman doing in a man's job?' (interview, 10 October 1996)

On the other hand, however, the young men's perspective was less overtly concerned with gender than with the more tangible, material consequences of what they perceived to be organizational incompetence, or worse. All the young men I interviewed denied the significance of gender in these events; S. Ahmed told me with some emphasis:

> Well, to me we had Julia as a woman, Sober's sister as a woman, Jahid's sister as a woman, Malkit as a woman, Zubaida as a woman, and now we've got Yazz as a woman. So when Shahin and them done the interview,[18] we had a choice between a woman and a man, but we didn't take that choice – why do you think we chose a woman? (interview, 6 November 1996)

It is probably true that although the cause of their conflict with Shopna did not originate in gender concerns, their response was nevertheless explicitly gendered – or as Julia put it 'Once they were on the attack, they used the fact that she was a woman' (interview, 18 October 1996). Similarly, Silver, who was employed part-time on the young men's project towards the end of this period, told me, 'I don't think it's because she was a woman, but if she was a man, I don't think it would have been like that' (interview, 3 September 1996). It is also true that gendered concerns became explicitly bound up with the other issues, particularly due to Shopna's apparent romantic involvement with a co-worker, and this in turn was understood and articulated through a cultural lense. Majid, who had responsibility for the Asian projects at this time, noted:

> that's why I'm saying the moral issues did it. It's just that initially it was very difficult to accept what the attitude was, because I was unaware about what they [the members] knew of Shopna and her relationships, and the corruptions that were going on . . . So when you've actually got young men being quite verbally insulting to women, there is that immediate assumption that you make . . . but if you look at it now and you look at Yasmin, you can see, well, that isn't actually the connection. I think . . . without a doubt their view of how they were being served by youth workers was completely justified. (interview, 7 November 1996)

Some of the complexities of these attitudes towards gender will be considered in a later chapter. What is of significance to the present discussion, however, is the way in which this debate served to shift the emphasis away from the young men's complaints and delegitimate them, portraying them as perpetrators rather than victims of misconduct: it is significant that in the wake of Shopna's accusations of sexual harassment the then Principal Youth Officer insisted that the young men undergo a series of anti-sexist training workshops before the project could reopen – a pattern of blame attribution repeated later in the project's history.

Of equal significance, however, was the challenge to the dominant institutional credo of 'special provision' undertaken by the young men in these encounters. This was enacted as a rearticulation of ownership by the members, marked by a shift in language from questions of 'need' to assertions of 'right'. Hashim made this point to me strongly:

> it came to a stage where on-one really come into the club anymore – everyone preferred to stay out there in the street, you know, than come in here, because it was like the same old thing over and over again. And then . . . we decided to say 'hold on a second this is *our* club, why should people from outside just come in and throw us out and do their own thing'. So we decided to come back in the club and then, definitely, there was a change of attitude towards the youth club at that time. (interview, 24 October 1996)

Although, under Majid's guidance, the young men of the project initially attempted to make their complaints through official channels, counter-claims of sexual harassment thwarted these attempts and, by their own admission, the encounters became more personal and more bitter – 'there was problems, there was fighting, there was swearing' (Hashim, 24 October 1996). S. Ahmed similarly told me:

people were really angry . . . I was angry as well, like you lose your temper and we used to – like when we had meetings we always used to say something but they would always be on the right side . . . they said this and that, but it just didn't go, so they moved her on and we got a new worker. (interview, 6 November 1996)

This feeling of disempowerment when confronted with the workings of the Youth Service was to leave an enduring sense of mistrust which underlay the next years of the project's growth. As Majid admitted to me, the Youth Service itself avoided the issues at hand, rather than confronting them directly:

without a doubt their [the members] view of how they were being served by youth workers was completely justified. That's why she was moved; although in the context of a local authority, when there's allegations of sexual harassment by young men, you take sideways steps rather than getting into the nitty gritty of it. (interview, 7 November 1996)

The Youth Service response to these conflicts was then to split the Asian provision; with *Salam Bhano* remaining under the control of Shopna and gradually disintegrating to the present situation, where there is a full-time Asian young women's worker in post, but no work actually being undertaken.[19] The young men's group, meanwhile, drifted into an institutional wilderness – or as Majid put it: 'The project just didn't happen, it just became a void' (interview, 7 November 1996).

This dual process of delegitimation and avoidance in the face of the increased assertiveness of the Stoneleigh Bengali young men signalled a broader reconceptualization of the SAYO project. From a perspective defined through a significantly feminized doctrine of 'special need' and victimhood, the SAYO project now came to occupy a more problematic status – the young men themselves *became* the problem. Ironically, it was this recategorization of the project's members as 'problem' that was to provide a renewed impetus for its development. This was partially due to the conflicts between members and staff within the project itself, but was largely tied to a wider perception of the Stoneleigh Estate – and particularly its Bengali young men – as constituting a community 'problem'. Majid thus told me:

[There was] a significant shift because as those young men got older, they also got to be seen to be more troublesome, both in terms of school and generally on the estate. (interview, 7 November 1996)

The summer of 1993, in particular, saw a number of attacks on Bengali youth on the Stoneleigh Estate by white youth from neighbouring estates. A report by an area monitoring project states:

> In the summer of 1993 there were a number of attacks against Bengali youth on the Estate by white youths from the neighbouring Amersham development, an estate targeted by the BNP for regular leafleting and recruitment drives. On each occasion, the police were called out. None of the perpetrators were apprehended but a number of Asian youth, including a youth worker,[20] were arrested. The lack of police assistance forced the Asian youth to defend themselves and it is only since they have adopted such a stance that the attacks have ceased.

The report continues, revealingly, 'The militancy and hostility harboured by the Bengali youth in the area has been highlighted by a number of people.' The tension was heightened at this time by a firebomb attack on the mosque on Abbey Street, which precipitated a 'mini riot' amongst the young men. The history of these developments will be traced in greater detail in the next chapter; however, what is of significance here is two things: firstly, the changing perception of Stoneleigh Bengali youth, both amongst themselves and their immediate community, and with the institutions that encountered them; and secondly, the response of these institutions to these redefinitions, in particular the interaction between the police and the youth service.

As the monitoring report clearly shows, the summer of 1993 marked a turning point in the perceptions of Bengali youth on the Stoneleigh Estate. Most notably, the young men were attributed a 'problem' status, marked by 'militancy and hostility'. As Hashim, who was one of the main combatants in this period, told me:

> It just shows, the police always have the wrong people; I mean, these perpetrators just come to cause a lot of trouble and then run and they [the police] don't do anything, it was the Asians [who were arrested] most of the time. So we felt a bit bewildered basically, you know, not receiving any help from the police or the community in any way – it seemed as if we were labelled as the troublemakers. (interview, 24 October 1996)

Silver, who witnessed these developments from the sidelines, similarly commented on the transformation amongst younger members of the community:

> Me and my friends took a lot of shit, we never really rebelled that much. And then, when we had enough sense we would just steer clear of it . . . but what

these kids were doing, they would walk alongside them to see what would happen and if they started, they would give back as good as they got. Which was their right and I respect them for it. And sometimes I don't think they thought it through properly, but they were saying 'we're not going to take any shit anymore'. (interview, 3 September 1996)

Amitabh, who worked for the Area Monitoring Project around this period, and later as a race equality officer on the estate, noted this change in attitude amongst the young people and told me, 'it was like fighting fire with fire' (interview, 8 November 1996). When I asked him if he saw this as a positive development, he responded:

I think it's because they have no option, absolutely no option: whether it's positive or not . . . the outcome is positive, but I also think it creates a lot of resentment and hostility in the young people themselves. They realize that the only way they're going to deal with the situation is through violence. Which is quite sad, but that's how they've had to deal with it. (interview, 8 November 1996)

This sense of inevitability, of last resort, has not, however, prevented these young men from being stigmatized – a fact of which they are fully aware. Hashim told me:

the label's stuck with us for a long time, I think it still is stuck to us . . . the white community here, they used to see us as a minor problem, but now it's like a big thing. Everyone on the street is thinking, oh God, this is escalating with the Asian guys here and there is a lot of problems . . . We seem to be the ones that are labelled as troublemakers. (interview, 24 October 1996)

This label is of equal – or perhaps even greater – significance within the local Bengali community. S. Ahmed told me:

Most of the Asian people here think that all the boys are corrupted – like they take drugs, they don't go to the Mosque, they're bad . . . but the problem is, if we wasn't there, the old men wouldn't be allowed to go to the Mosque, because people would bully them, but they don't see it that way. (interview, 6 November 1996)

This image has repercussions for the SAYO project itself, which has gained something of a reputation for attracting troublemakers, the origins of which can be traced particularly to this period. Amitabh commented:

I think there's a stigma attached to the youth club and the youths who actually use the youth club. And I think certain kids are kept away from it delib-erately . . . They think that group is trouble. (interview, 8 November 1996)

As Silver put it to me:

The parents are thinking, if my son associates with these kids, he's going to have that funny haircut, he's going to have that cigarette behind his ear or he's going to be wearing those sorts of clothes, and I don't want that. (interview, 3 September 1996)

What is of primary importance to the present chapter, however, is the ways in which these images fed an institutional response. Julia commented:

Because the boys also became more dangerous and like there were a couple of mini-riots, and people thought that . . . you know, the police are still waiting for this big riot that is going to happen on the Stoneleigh. (interview, 18 October 1996)

Majid informed me that it was the response to these incidents that restarted the SAYO project:

The project just didn't happen, it just became a void . . . Then there was a big police incident prior to the summer and the police were saying 'there's going to be a riot on the estate', and I was asked to get involved. And so we organized a summer scheme. (interview, 7 November 1996)

Julia, who was area worker at the time, was rather more cynical about the underlying rationale for this renewed interest on the part of the youth service:

Julia: they realised that not only were those boys in need of some sorts of service, they also realised they were becoming dangerous.
Claire: Which was more important?
Julia: The danger, because the police really pressed on the youth service. After that mini-riot to do with the Mosque, I seem to remember, within a week they organised a six-week holiday project, which no young person in Southwark had. They recruited people from the street with no induction, and I think the instruction of the workers was 'keep them off the street.' As it was, maybe they did some interesting things as well, but the aim of that holiday project – where a lot of money went into it, because there was a high level of staffing, but they did no preparation – but it was *just* to keep them off the street. (interview, 18 October 1996)

This policy of containment partly had its roots in earlier perceptions of the young men as disrupting the 'real' goal of Asian provision – i.e. for young women – but now assumed a new urgency, significantly under pressure from the police. There was, however, an acknowledged tension between this institutional imaging and the motivations of workers involved in the project at this time. As Majid told me:

> For the service, it was about let's keep them off the streets, there's going to be a riot, the police are telling us that, so let's put some resources in . . . and yeah, I spent a lot of money on them, for two reasons – one, because I think they deserved it and because in the past their money has been squandered, and [secondly] I think to get them back into that relationship [with the youth service]: it was about saying 'yeah, you are justified' (interview, 7 November 1996)

Julia similarly told me:

> From the point of view of the workers, there's always been a different attitude. It wasn't about keeping kids off the street, it was about providing for a group of young people who weren't getting a fair deal in a mainstream situation . . . It was also about trying to channel that energy that had become apparent and had become uncontrollable in some situations. (interview, 18 October 1996)

There is a conflation of images of 'need', 'threat' and 'rights' in these responses that both partially coalesces with, and contests, the dominant representation of perceived danger. The summer project was, by all accounts, a successful one, yet one which can be characterized more as a reactive, reflex action than as laying a stable foundation for future development. As Silver, who worked on the summer project said: 'They said, oh, there's shit happening on the Stoneleigh Estate, quick let's get someone in' (interview, 3 September 1996). After the project ended, this knee-jerk response was succeeded by a part-time provision, headed by Hassan,[21] an unqualified and inexperienced worker from east London. Hassan had worked on the summer project and had established an apparently strong relationship with the young men through this period, and through his involvement with the local mosque. Majid told me:

> their relationship with the worker was quite good to start with. He was very, very religious, but they bought into that; they saw him as quite a champion of them at that time. (interview, 7 November 1996)

Julia was rather more sceptical of the recruitment process – or lack of it – claiming that the Youth Service opted for easy 'tokenism', that they 'would employ anyone who looks Asian enough' (interview, 18 October 1996). She continued:

> They took [Hassan] because he was around, because he looked smart enough in his appearance, *modern* enough, but at the same time he could understand the Asian kids because he was religious. (my emphasis)

The construction of the SAYO project firmly in terms of religio-cultural 'difference' – or perhaps in terms of religio-cultural anachronism[22] – is clear in this approach, and is combined with an opportunistic essentialism, which sought to place Hassan in a role as mediator, gatekeeper and cultural buffer. Silver, who was the only strand of continuity between these transformations, informed me that the project was allocated only ten hours for part-time staff provision, and had no budget. Hassan himself was employed on only fifteen hours per week and was otherwise committed to his law degree – a division of labour that was to lead to conflicting priorities as time went on. Silver commented to me 'they were setting us up to fail' (interview, 3 September 1996). Julia similarly noted that the decision to employ Hassan – because he was Bengali and a Muslim (and perhaps also because he was a man) – substituted theories of unexamined cultural specificity for a more subtle analysis of the actual problems confronting the SAYO project:

> I don't think anyone took much time in analysing their situation, because if they had they would have come up with the decision that he was not the right person. (interview, 18 October 1996)

Unaware of the project's recent history (and given the misconstruction of the recent past as a gendered issue, such an account would probably have hindered rather than assisted the work), Hassan ironically repeated crucial patterns within it, bringing in his own staff from east London and administering the project in increasingly erratic fashion. Majid commented:

> the same sort of problems then started emerging – like he wasn't opening, he had commitments in his other job that stopped him opening; and then I think they said, 'oh, this is just the same as we've gone though, a waste of time', and the relationship with the youth worker broke down again. (interview, 7 November 1996)

A further salient factor in this reaction was the role of religion. Although at first, as both Majid and Julia make clear, Hassan's strong religious identification was seen as a source of contact and solidarity with, and by, the young men, this later proved a significant point of contention. Hashim explained to me:

> Hassan was bringing a lot of religious people into the club and it seemed as if they were from a different planet – they never understood the background we were coming from, you see. (interview, 24 October 1996)

Although the young men did not object to Hassan's attempts at religious guidance per se – and, in fact, were initially very attracted to this element – the tone of patriarchal authority and condemnation that accompanied it seems to have worn thin, especially when combined with the absence of adequate service provision. A major turning point was a residential weekend in Birmingham the Christmas before I arrived at the project. S. Ahmed described it to me:

> Well, he used to take us to these Islamic things. But we didn't mind going to the Islamic things: once we went to some Christmas thing in Birmingham and – he's so clever, yeah – he took us there during Christmas, so we don't get to do anything, everything's closed. When we got there we didn't have nothing except to go to the lectures every day, and the food wasn't all that. And everyone started arguing about that. And like he goes 'we saved the money and we can buy something for the club', but when we come back, he goes 'we've got no more money left, its gone'. (interview, 6 November 1996)

The suspicion of ongoing corruption and a more general dissatisfaction became inseparable from a distrust of Hassan's religious affiliation. This was in turn bound up with a growing resentment of Hassan's projection of a personal superiority, which was part of his religious identification and its proselytizing mission: what S. Ahmed referred to as his 'cleverness'. Hashim explained:

> they said they didn't like him, he was a bit too religious for them, he was coming at them really hard . . . That was his personality, that's how he kept going on and on over the time he's been here. He used to see himself as superior than any others in this place. (interview, 24 October 1996)

Along with other members of the staff he recruited, Hassan was a committed member of the Young Muslim Organization in east London. His stance towards the SAYO project, even in the short time that I knew him, seemed to be one of a disinterested, distant, and more than slightly disdainful, patriarchal mission of conversion. Integral to this was a view of the project's members of being in need of redemption – of being without religion, culture or respect, as he told me repeatedly. His interaction with the young men was structured though, and attempted to enforce, a notion of cultural respect – as their *bhaya* (older brother) and religious mentor – that was, however, strictly unilateral. This became focused in daily, mainly minor, conflicts around issues of perceived disrespect – around choice or volume of music, and particularly around smoking. The young men were increasingly alienated during these confrontations, which embodied institutional, religious and cultural hierarchies, yet which were simultaneously regarded and experienced as illegitimate. Hashim told me:

> So that's when it really started off, you know. That's when we realized he doesn't understand anything that we've gone through over the last couple of years – and then he comes in from a different place and he lectures us about different things – you know, it just didn't link in together. (interview, 24 October 1996)

These tensions finally erupted, a few weeks into my fieldwork, with the open confrontation between Hassan and the project's senior members referred to in the previous chapter. The incident built up over the course of the evening with a series of minor clashes over the music and smoking in the club building, which culminated in one of the panes of glass in the front door being smashed – though, I think, more by mistake than intent. Hassan emerged from the club office, where he spent most of his time, and the ensuing argument became more accusatory and more personal. As I watched the tension escalate and I saw the young men's mood shift from a rather shamefaced defiance to undisguised fury, I decided it was time to leave. S. Ahmed told me what happened afterwards:

> Like someone broke the window over there, and it was Mustafa that broke the window, but Hassan knows because Aklak told him . . . So we didn't know that Aklak had told Hassan that it was Mustafa, we thought he didn't know. So like he called up a meeting, so we're sitting around the meeting and he goes, he was saying 'who broke it?' So no-one admitted and so he's doing all these indirect cusses – like he's saying 'whoever broke it, their mum and dad don't use condoms'. He was saying all these things, and Mustafa was sitting there getting vexed . . . So Mustafa went 'whoever said that I'll fuck them off.' And like when we were going out, Hassan goes 'did you say something, Mustafa?' and then Musafa goes 'wait there'. So like Hassan came out and it's like Hassan wants to fight him because he took his coat off . . . and like,

he come towards Mustafa . . . and Mustafa just punched him and he dropped on the floor. And he got up and said 'you'll regret it', and that was it, and then he took Mustafa to court. (interview, 6 November 1996)

As Silver commented to me wryly, 'he [Hassan] tried to use psychology to sort of get the person to come out of the group and it worked – the person that smashed the window smashed him as well' (interview, 3 September 1996).

After this incident, a number of meetings took place between the Youth Service, staff and project members, but the issues remained unresolved. The SAYO project closed down indefinitely, and Hassan's contract was not renewed by the Youth Service. After several months and more training – this time in conflict management – the interviews were undertaken, this time with the full participation of the project members. In July – and significantly, in time for the summer (the period perceived as the time with most potential for conflict on the estate) – the SAYO project re-opened under a new full-time worker, Yasmin.

The development of the SAYO project under Yasmin's guidance over the past three years is hard to encapsulate in a few paragraphs, in part because many of its encounters, complexities and transformations form the substance of the rest of this account. More than this, however, the rebirth and growth of the project, which coincided largely with the period of my involvement with it, has become so much a part of my work and my own personal history that the grain and texture of this time are so intensely interwoven into my memory and affections as to be effectively inseparable from them. For me, as for other workers during this time,[23] the maturation of the project has been a process of growing together with its members, of sharing their ambitions, and ideals and hopes. It is marked as much by personal milestones as institutional ones, and it is impossible to distinguish the latter from the former. Several weeks ago, Farhan and I were watching 'the little ones' playing football, and reflecting that not only were they no longer so little, but that they were barely recognizable as the withdrawn and often rather sullen group we had met in the summer of 1995. In that year, Hanif had commented to Yasmin and myself that 'the thing is, no-one really likes us'; it seems ironic that, three years on, the project's members have been recognized throughout the borough as so amiable and co-operative that there are voices that doubt the need for separate youth provision at all.

Acknowledging my implication in the history that follows, a number of developments can be discerned over the past three years that reflect processes of both continuity and change. Some of these were touched on in the previous chapter – the expansion of the provision to full-time status, the change of days, the division of sessions between junior and senior members,[24] the level and forms of activity that were instituted. Thinking back to those early days, I recall an atmosphere of profound cynicism on the part of members and those staff, like Julia, who had been part of the project's recent history. From an institutional point of view, the project's expansion was underpinned and legitimated by a notion of the Asian young men as an ongoing and growing problem. This representation proved remarkably resilient, even as the project was transformed, and it remains a significant one. In particular, the activities of the young men in challenging the dominant problem-oriented definition of the provision has been to some extent rendered illegitimate through this lense – translated into a reinscription of, rather than opposition to, the dominant ideology of need and threat. When I conducted my interview with Julia in the autumn of 1996, this attitude remained stubbornly predominant. She told me, 'I see the older group being set in their own ways and very little change', and while admitting that 'the younger ones have been much more responsive', their activities were neverthless similarly viewed as manipulative and potentially explosive. Ironically, 'empowerment' for these young people – part of the Youth Service credo – is then recast as the actions of incipient fifth columnists: Julia thus asserted 'when they became aware of their rights, they were using them, whether they were in the right or not' (interview, 18 October 1996).

The attitude of the young men was similarly intransigent – riven with the expectation of repeated history and repeated failure. The incident at Christmas 1995, involving S. Ahmed and Liaquot, mentioned in the last chapter, is to be understood as the expression of frustration at prophecies fulfilled – or perhaps more accurately, prophecies self-fulfilled. S. Ahmed told me, with striking honesty, in our interview a year later:

> The Club's running good now. Like before, when Yazz first come I did have a bit of a problem . . . because I didn't know her at that time really well, she just come and I underestimated her. I didn't know how she's going to be like, but it's like from the past; for me, I thought the same thing's going to happen again, because of what's happened in the past . . . and I know I was wrong, and what Yazz is doing, she's doing right now. (interview, 6 November 1996)

It is impossible to separate out the development of the SAYO project from the personality and vision of Yasmin herself, whose single-minded energy and belief in the potential of the project and its members was often, and certainly in its early stages, its only driving force. Yasmin was recruited from Camden where she had been active in various youth organizations and had worked in close association with Majid several years earlier. She was the unanimous choice of the young men and although many people – myself included – were surprised at the appointment of a young woman, and expected the worst, she established an open, if not totally unproblematic, relationship with the project's members astonishingly quickly. Majid told me:

> I've known Yasmin for a long time, we have done work together in Camden and she's brilliant . . . her commitment and her approach is always her young people centred, she's never concerned about herself, she doesn't put those sorts of things before her job and she has high standards. (interview, 7 November 1996)

With the extension of the project, Yasmin has been able to maintain a consistent and varied provision, and has developed a frank and non-hierarchical style of organization and management, based on mutual respect and trust:

> Yasmin talks to them more openly than most youth worker would, but then I think she trusts them and they know that level of authority she's sharing with them. (Majid, 7 November 1996)

This more open style of management constrast sharply with the more rigidly hierarchical structures favoured by both Hassan and Shopna, which attempted to exploit culturally based notions of 'family' and respect to enforce control and compliance. In addition, Yasmin displayed a blatant disregard for the 'reputation' of the project and its members, substituting her own more exacting set of expectations. As Majid told me:

> She's not patronising, which is the other thing. She has very high standards herself and she knows their potential. She knows they know it so she won't let them cross those barriers, which they appreciate and have come to know quickly, which is also good. (interview, 7 November 1996)

Only one member of Hassan's staff, Aziz, remained at the project when it reopened. Yasmin recruited Farhan from east London, and then Hashim, who had grown up on the Stoneleigh Estate, trained as a youth worker during Helal's time at the club, and had been an active (sometimes proactive) member of the project in recent years. Although Hashim's position was a complex one, due to his role as community 'elder'/older brother in relation to the younger members, his presence as a worker was an important stabilizing influence and his appointment was regarded by the other young men as very much an emblem of faith, helping to defuse the few minor conflicts that arose during the first eighteen months. As Hashim told me:

> Like outside they know what I've been through and they know I've been hanging around with their older brothers and they know what we've been through . . . that's why the respect is there. (interview, 24 October 1996)

At the end of 1995, Sher Khan joined the project, initially as a volunteer but later as a paid worker, and he now stands as one of the cornerstones of the project's activities. The closeness, support and informality of the relationships between staff, and between staff and members, has become a defining feature of the project and has provided a stable foundation for its emergent links with the wider community. Hashim commented:

> I mean, I sit down in the club and think . . . like about the younger ones doing like this fashion show and everything, and I'm thinking a couple of years ago that would have been really difficult . . . so it's definitely improved, there's no doubt about it, it's changed . . . so it's all credit to Yazz.

The first fashion show in October 1996 proved to be a watershed for the SAYO project, and something of a test case. Part of the junior member's Duke of Edinburgh's Award Scheme, it was also very much a focal point of conflicting expectations and a trial of faith that enveloped the whole project. The senior members refused to take part, and attended the show reluctantly in an almost tangible dread of its failure and their implied disgrace; the junior members co-operated with a mixture of terror, feelings of inevitable doom and a blind trust that Yasmin and the rest of us would not let them down. With hindsight, I think before the show only Yasmin, Sher Khan and myself had any confidence in what was about to happen, and even Sher Khan and I were keeping our fingers crossed. In the audience were Julia, representatives from the Youth Service and the police; significantly absent were the school administration, and the media, while Shopna refused to attend. In his opening speech, Majid made the significance of the event clear:

> this show demonstrates the fact that within [the borough] young people are creative imaginative and extremely talented . . . Speaking to the members of SAYO, I was struck by the fact that they said that many of us perceived them as gangleaders, non-achievers and troublesome . . . This show illustrates one important lesson for us all: the important thing is not that we should attempt

to teach young people but that all young people should be given the opportunity to learn.

The fashion show *was* a triumph, on a number of levels: firstly, it brought staff and members together for the first time working on a significant event and for a common goal; secondly, it affirmed the junior member's trust in Yasmin and re-established bridges with the seniors, after the conflicts of the year before; thirdly, it allowed the members to view themselves and their project through a lense undistorted by the trials of the previous years (and after the tribulations of the spring and summer of that year), and from this, lastly, to turn this vision outwards and challenge the external gaze. S. Ahmed told me, 'it's the best thing I've seen for the club . . . it surprised me, no joke, that's the best thing I've seen this club do' (interview, 6 November1996).

The contestation of images and expectations that *Style and Culture '96* enacted can be understood crucially as the distinction between external definition and internal subversion – what Majid captures as the difference between the desire to *teach* and the provision of the opportunity to *learn*. What is at stake, then, is the understanding of the notion of empowerment itself, as something to be given, or chances to be taken. It is also the difference between definitions of 'need' and of 'right' which so characterizes the history of the SAYO project. Where 'need' is characterised as a lack, and becomes too easily synonymous with 'problem', the discourse of 'rights' opens up the possibility of equality, mutuality and transformation. Silver thus commented to me, 'These kids have been given the space, they've been given the opportunity to express themselves, to be free, and they've taken that, to a certain extent' (interview, 3 September 1996).

The success of *Style and Culture '96* has been followed by a series of chances taken and fulfilled. October 1997 saw a second fashion show, entitled *Independence Day,*[25] which brought together staff, senior and junior members in an impressive – if not entirely flawless – show of unity and purpose. Significantly, the show's opening speech this time around was delivered by one of the project's senior members, Shahin. In April 1997, the project's members held a youth forum with local youth service officials, councillors and SRB representatives, a forerunner to the borough's plans for a Youth Parliament. In the summer of 1997, we began training for a senior member's management committee with a residential in Leicester, followed by another session in Oxford in April 1998. The committee, consisting of ten junior and senior members, is now up and running, raising funds, producing a quarterly newsletter and hosting events on a community-wide basis. In association with the new *Kickstart*[26] initiative, several of the project's members have begun volunteer training, including S. Ahmed, who is hoping to start a Diploma in Youth and Community work qualification at Greenwich University this Autumn (1998).

In a recent video about the estate made by the junior members with funding from the local SRB, some of the senior members, including Shahin and S. Ahmed, reflected on the transformation of the project:

Shahin: Especially with the Bengali community, when the young people say to their parents that they want to go to the youth club, their parents think it's a bad thing, they're going to go over there and do whatever. But I think the workers have been really helpful in showing to the parents that it's not just going to a club and there is more . . . and I think the parents have realised, and the whole community has realised, because the youth provision has been supportive and has had a great impact.

Zohar: Personally, I think that most of us have got a lot of support from the youth club – like jobwise, education, training, application forms – like that's the first place we'd go to.

Many of the new initiative launched by the SAYO project are in their early stages and their future success or failure still remains very much to be seen. It would be naive to assume that the reinvention of the SAYO project will ever be complete, or that it will escape from its history and location – the anonymous letter mentioned earlier is a clear indication of the way in which perceptions of the project's development are fissured with ambiguities and accusations, labels, unrelenting cynicism and unforgiving memories.

It is true, moreover, that the success of the SAYO project has within it the seeds of its own destruction. While there are those who view the project's existence as inherently illegitimate, there are also those who view its new found energy as proof that the provision no longer has a role. The project then runs the risk of being damned for representing a problem and for *not* representing a problem – or, at least, not *enough* of a problem, anymore. The inherent fallacy of both perspectives is the shared assumption that the primary impetus for youth provision in areas like the Stoneleigh Estate, is the articulation of the need–problem axes. To redefine these originaries is then to remove the rationale for the provision. While it can be argued that the SAYO project's genesis in the exclusion of Asian young people from generic provision no longer holds great validity, it is also true that the defining ethos of the project has been contested and radically translated in recent years. External ideologies of 'need' and 'threat' have then been replaced by internal assertions of 'community', however variously imagined; what Silver described as 'a sense of identity and a sense of common purpose' (interview, 3 September 1996).

This is not to reinvent the SAYO project and its members as a troop of boy scouts. Nor is it to underestimate the resilience of previous or alternative narratives. Moreover, although it is true that most of its internal battles have been fought and laid to rest, the larger campaign has only just begun – and its outcome seems less certain.

Conclusion

The history of the SAYO project recounted above is not intended as a blueprint for youth provision – Asian or otherwise – nor should it be read as an attack on the institutions and individuals involved. As Silver pointed out to me:

> When problems happen, it's not necessarily a bad thing. Sometimes problems need to happen for you to know what's going on . . . And when they do, it's how you deal with them.

What is interesting for me, in terms of the present study, is three things: firstly, the complex set of local-historical circumstances that produced the project and the interventions that transformed it; secondly, the interplay of institutional definitions of 'special need', problem and threat that characterize the project and the contestation of these definitions by its members; and thirdly, the interaction between these mediating institutions and the wider set of representations concerning black young people (especially young men) and ethnic minority communities (especially Muslims). The ways in which these representations frame and inform localized images of 'the inner city', 'deprivation' and 'decay', and translate them into moral panics about 'crime', 'drugs' and 'youth', mediated by assumptions of 'need' and 'threat', are crucial to an understanding of the background and setting of the present study, and the ethnographic material that follows. It also points to the relationship between the highly localized, historically specific and personal account and its wider ramifications. Emphasizing the particularities of the present study does not deny its relevance to other groups of young men, other spaces and other projects. It is within these wider processes of representation, objectification, legislation and contestation that the SAYO project's history takes on both shape and significance.

Notes

1 The actual content of his remark loses something in this narration!

2 Shafiq was not involved in these initial events and had, in fact, gone to the school office to get help.

3 The 1991 Census recorded numbers of 477,000 Pakistani and 163,000 Bangladeshi people (Modood et al., 1997: 13).

4 This disadvantage, it should be noted, is linked explicitly by Modood to the existence of 'anti-Muslim prejudice', which serves to reinforce the notion of a homogeneous and monodimensional 'Muslim' identity which is the object of discrimination; to place these communities apart from other racialized minority groups in a newly constituted 'hierarchy of oppression'; and to further define this identity solely in terms of deprivation, victimhood and a potentially dangerous alienation.

5 Centec Key Statistics, January 1996.

6 Extract from *Community Profile* by 'Julia' (Neighbourhood Youth Development Worker) 1992.

7 A recent report by a Detached Youth Work team shows that thirty per cent of black/ethnic minority young people had experienced racial harassment and that in almost half the incidents a weapon had been used.

8 Rates of adult unemployment amongst Bengalis on the estate are estimated at sixty per cent for men and eighty per cent for women (SRB Report).

9 The SRB Report estimates that fifty-nine per cent of pupils speak English as a second language, with twenty per cent speaking Bengali as a first language. How these figures explain high levels of truancy, unauthorized absence and school exclusions remains unclear.

10 The rationale for this categorization remains unclear, but it included pupils with 'behavioural/discipline problems' which illustrates revealingly the slippage between the attribution of 'need' and the ascription of 'problem' status.

11 The 'Nigerian phone box' was so labelled by the Bengali young men because of its popularity amongst the local African community. It forms a significant marker in the perceptual landscape of the estate for the SAYO members, as a meeting point and general place of gathering – so much so that it was rumoured that several of the young men gave out its number to young women as a point of contact!

12 This section of Abbey Street is heavily policed and is unfailingly a first port of call if there is any trouble in the area.

13 The relationship of this image to wider representations of Asian youth was clearly demonstrated during the recent trip to Tunisia. Reflecting the accusations and attitudes of the anonymous letter writers, other British holiday makers assumed the group had travelled under the auspices of the Probation Service!

14 I have written elsewhere about the construction of invisibility in Asian masculinities (in Hesse 2000).

15 The equipment cupboard at the youth club still contains battered, now mainly empty, boxes of games, labelled *Salam Bhano*, which were designated solely for use with the young women's group and which, as some of the young men still rather bitterly recall, they were not allowed to use.

16 Hashim left the project in November 1997 to open a takeaway in Portsmouth.

17 It could be argued that in accusing the young men of sexual harassment, Shopna herself was playing the 'ethnicity card' around the institutional assumption of patriarchal gender bias.

18 Shahin and Zohar were on the interview panel at the time that Yasmin was appointed.

19 A recent appraisal of youth service provision in the area identified a clear absence of youth work with Asian young women.

20 The youth worker arrested was Silver, whom the police suspected of being a drug dealer – apparently because he drove a car and carried a mobile phone.

21 I was unable to locate Hassan to interview him about his involvement with the SAYO project.

22 The perception of the project members as patriarchal and repressive after the incidents with Shopna outlined earlier helped reinforce this image.

23 This period of the SAYO project has been marked by a remarkable stability in staffing – Yasmin and myself for three years, Farhan and Sher Khan for two-and-a-half years, Hashim for two years (up to his departure last November), Amitabh has been an intermittent presence for over three years, while Silver has recently rejoined the Project.

24 A division that has now ceased to be of relevance, so that most sessions are now mixed in ages.

25 The title has an intentionally multi-layered meaning, which encapsulates the historical commemoration of fifty years of Indian and Pakistani Independence and twenty-five years of Bangladeshi Independence; the assertion of alternative images and a recognition of the iconoclastic potential of the show.

26 An initiative funded by Crime Concern and Legal and General aimed at working with local young people to develop activities to enhance personal development and divert them from crime.

–4–

'The Gang'

In April 1996, a letter was sent from Yasmin and Amitabh to the Board of Governors of Thomas More School. Instigated by the apparently unprocedural expulsion by the school administration of a year-ten Bengali pupil, Malik, the letter went on to detail a number of incidents and wider concerns around the treatment of a group of Bengali young men in years nine and ten, the majority of whom attended the SAYO project. Malik's expulsion was the culmination of a series of clashes between these young men and the school, which had occasioned flurries of – mainly undocumented – short- term exclusions and unofficial threats of expulsion. The letter identified an 'atmosphere of distrust' between the Bengali students and the school, in which the former were consistently portrayed as a 'gang', accused of drug dealing and extortion[1] within school and targeted accordingly as troublemakers and deviants.[2] At its lowest point, the young men were identified in school assembly as the primary reason for the school's recent Ofsted failure and threatened with wearing luminous green jumpers to mark their pariah – or perhaps more accurately, their scapegoat – status. The letter goes on to highlight the growing tension between the school and the Youth Service – and particularly the SAYO project itself – in which previous attempts to facilitate and mediate between the young men, the community and the school had met with overt hostility, non-cooperation, suspicion and 'mockery' from the latter. The letter concludes with a number of suggestions for improving communication between the local community and the school, for representing the interests of young people and for helping to resolve the conflicts, in partnership with the school administration, between groups of young people both in school and in the immediate environs of the Stoneleigh Estate.

The incidents preceding the letter, and detailed within it, are closely tied to the then- ongoing confrontations between these Bengali young men and a group of black (African and African-Caribbean) young men in the school, which scarred the spring and summer of 1996. The details of these confrontations are explored below, but what is of immediate interest here is the set of institutional representations at play in the run up to the events, in the interpretation of the conflicts and in the determination of the school's rather belated and ill-directed response. The letter argues that the school's failure to deal with the conflict decisively in its early stages had a threefold effect: firstly, it enabled the escalation of the conflict in school; secondly, this escalation precipitated the knee-jerk rash of exclusions as a last-ditch attempt to reinstate control in a situation of institutional incoherence and playground disorder; and thirdly, these exclusions then helped to shift the conflict to the area outside the school, where the absence of any institutional framework led to increased levels of violence and the eventual intervention of local police and the SPG.

This initial failure can however be traced, at least in part, to a misinterpretation of the dynamics of the conflict – most notably as 'racial' in origin – which in turn rested on the portrayal of the groups involved, and particularly the Bengali young men, as a 'gang'. There is a specific local history to this representation which will be traced below, but it can also be argued that the school's response, along with that of the police, the local media and the Youth Service administration, was in large measure informed and guided by a set of assumptions drawn from wider representations of youth 'gang' subculture, complete with its peculiar 'ethnicized' reinvention. As I have argued in Chapter 1 and elsewhere, the naturalization of racialized/ethnicized groups in both media and academic portrayals of 'gangs' and 'gang warfare' legitimates a New Racist hands-off (or perhaps more accurately hands-up) account of seemingly intractable conflict between bounded and opposed homogeneous absolutes, which renders mediation futile and resolution impossible.[3]

The response of the school, then, was to attempt to remove rather than resolve the conflict, an abdication of responsibility additionally legitimated through the appeal to the already well-established position of the Bengali young men as local folk devils. This is not to suggest conscious discrimination on the part of the school administration – though it often seemed like that – but that a dominant perception of both the nature of the conflict and of the groups involved, compounded undoubtedly by the pressures of the Ofsted inspection, resulted in a process of labelling, institutional denial and attempted eleventh-hour containment, which went far beyond the bounds of the current conflict to a more fundamental set of questions concerning the relationship between the school and the local community, its role and obligations to its students and a more general ideological crisis concerning the racialisation of youth violence in education in the wake of the murder of Headmaster Philip Lawrence in December 1995.

At a more immediate level, the actions of the school administration generated a crisis of confidence within the local Bengali community, and particularly amongst the young men of the SAYO project who were most directly involved, which has left an enduring legacy of distrust on all sides. As Majid commented to me:

> If you look in the school . . . it's been demonstrated through some of the outcomes, that they are treating them [the Bengali young men] appallingly. They're not all angels, but you know, some of the young people have been excluded from school without just cause, some have been excluded without due process and that system of unfairness and unjustness . . . reverberates around everyone, so even when the school's being just in the way they're treating someone and they are doing it fairly, it becomes known to everyone else that this must be unfair because they treated everyone else unfair. (interview, 7 November 1996)

Most notably perhaps, after the young men involved completed their GCSEs and left school, there has been a continued gulf between the Youth Service and the school,[4] a situation made all the more unfortunate by the youth club's location within school grounds.

The letter itself precipitated a furore beyond all expectations, with the school administration accusing Yasmin and Amitabh of 'racism',[5] of provoking the conflict between the Bengali and black youths for their own (unspecified) ends, and threatening them with libel action in the courts. Staff in the school were instructed to cut all lines of communication with the youth centre and the Head insisted that the Council take out grievances against both Amitabh and Yasmin for overstepping the bounds of their job remit and for misrepresenting their position in relation to the community and the young men. To this end, several of the young men were pressured by the school into recanting their initial complaints, and Yasmin and Amitabh were instructed by the Youth Service and Equalities Unit respectively to cease mediating for the young people, and even to refrain from informing them of their rights! In a rerun of the earlier Shopna debacle, while Julia flapped and accused the young men of 'manipulating' the goodwill of Yasmin and other project workers, the Youth Service undertook a 'damage limitation'[6] exercise with the school, which effectively evaded dealing with the substantive issues in favour of a largely ineffective gesture towards institutional co-operation and solidarity. Partially as a result of this, and as a token of faith (whether good or bad remains a matter of perspective) to the school, first Amitabh and then Julia were removed from the Stoneleigh Estate, with Amitabh transferring to the council administration building several miles away, and Julia[7] assuming responsibility for youth work in another part of the borough. A new Area Youth Development Worker, Steve, arrived in More Ward in

November 1996, and has since waged an ongoing battle with the school administration over jurisdiction, role and liability, most notably in relation to the SAYO project. In his first meeting with the school administration, the Head told Steve that she wished the youth club were 'located on Mars'. Although the young men's final year in school was largely incident-free, this institutional tension has remained undiminished and the school's perception of the group has remained stubbornly resilient. It is revealing, I think, that the school was conspicuously absent from both fashion shows and has remained hostile to any school's work initiatives from the youth club – most especially those aimed at working with Bengali students.

This confrontation is recounted here partly by way of background to the account presented in the remainder of this chapter, but also because it illuminates some of the linkages and some of the spaces between increasingly hegemonic popular and institutional representations of so-called ethnic conflict and gang subculture in Britain, and its street-level performance. This is not to posit an outdated and over-simplistic representation-versus-reality dichotomy, but to recognize the interplay between representation, performance, subversion and constraint. What the school's actions also clearly illustrate is the intransigence of dominant discourses, whether concerning 'race', or youth, or gangs, or masculinity, in the face of its more complex and ambivalent manifestations, and their consequent inability to (re)act in any meaningful way.

The following chapters will attempt to trace out some of these manifestations, to reveal the shifting and often contradictory matrices within which experience is formulated, read and misread. The focus is explicitly on the interaction of 'race', ethnicity and masculinity – firstly, through peer group formulation and secondly, through the articulation of discourses of community, kinship and authority. The present chapter focuses on the articulation of these elements through the conflicts that ran throughout the period of my fieldwork, and will explore the discrepant interpretation of these events, their local-historical context and their broader significance for the re-imagination of 'the Gang'.

Spring/Summer 1996: Anatomy of a Racial Conflict?

Despite the reactions of the school, the police and the media – and indeed the way it sometimes felt to all of us at the SAYO project – the events that took place in the first half of 1996 were largely unconnected, sporadic and small-scale clashes with disparate groups and individuals. What bound these events together into an apparently more sinister whole was the overarching discourse of 'race' – in all these cases black versus Asian –

and of 'gangs'. These coalesced and served to focus concern on the comparatively small number of fights involving the Bengali young men of the SAYO project to the exclusion of the broader spectrum of scuffles and confrontations that took place during this time, involving all groups (including young women) for a variety of reasons and sometimes for no reason at all.

The series of encounters that dominated the spring and summer of 1996 involved the Bengali young men in year ten of Thomas More school, who constituted the core of the SAYO project at this time and who were the focus of the letter mentioned above (as well as the primary targets of the school's disciplinary endeavours).[8] The impetus for the conflict was barely discernible, even at the time, and in the months that followed became lost in a haze of half-remembered slights and minor playground standoffs.[9]

Ifti told me that their first hostile encounter with their main antagonist, Hansel started with a joke originating, ironically enough, in the perception of the Bengali young men as a 'gang':

> You know, like when we walk around the school, yeah, like playing something and we're running – that's when people think we're fighting and everyone will start running. And one day Hanif comes out 'let's run for a joke', because like we're bored in school, nothing to do at lunchtime and breaktime, so Hanif says, 'let's have a little joke, let's have a little run and everyone will start following'. And we start running, yeah and we come next to the [school hall] and there's two long black boys, fifth years, and they just sticked their leg out and Malik buckled up, Malik flew, yeah, and then I flew. And I went 'Oh my God, what are you doing, what are you sticking your leg out for when we're running?' . . . And the boy grabbed me and the boy start punching. And then we both got angry and hit them back . . . And he had another tall friend, and he come and pushed me and grabbed me and hooked me on the wall and his friend punched me on my face and then they went off. (interview, 28 September 1996)

The 'tall friend' who attacked Ifti was Hansel. The following day, Ifti's older brother Humzah came into the school looking for Hansel and a fight broke out in the library, during which the police were called. As a result of this, Ifti was suspended from school for three days, of which he commented to me 'And that was an alright reason'. This was followed by one-on-one fights with first Jamal and then Sayeed, all of which occurred during school time and on school premises. On several occasions, the Bengali young men approached the school for assistance but no action was taken. Sayeed told me that after his fight with Hansel:

We went to Miss King [Head of year ten] and we said 'Miss, there's going to be a fight and we're just warning everyone', yeah, and after that the teacher thought that *we* started it, but we don't start it. (interview, 5 November 1996)

For several days after this last fight, the majority of these Bengali young men stayed away from school to avoid repercussions. On the first day that Hanif returned to school, alone, he was attacked by Hansel and his friends in the school canteen during lunchbreak, suffering head injuries and a black eye. That afternoon, as news of the incident spread, large numbers of the older group gathered outside the school and again the police intervened, arresting Ashraf, Faruk's older brother, for possessing an offensive weapon.[10] The following afternoon, a number of the junior group, supported by some friends from East London, saw Hansel in the street, chased him into a garden and beat him with belts and sticks. Although it was rumoured that Hansel had suffered a broken shoulder and fractured skull,[11] he escaped with a fractured arm and bruises to his legs. A number of the young men were picked up by the police from their homes and questioned about the incident, but none were charged. The next day, and despite his exclusion from school after the attack on Hanif, Hansel and some friends from nearby Clifton walked back into Thomas More School, this time attacking Sayeed and Faruk, beating Sayeed with a belt and opening a gash on his forehead. The attack was witnessed by a number of teachers, and even by the Head herself, although it was several hours before the police were called.

Shortly after the attack on Sayeed, a large number of black youths from Clifton arrived at the Thomas More School, looking for the Bengali group. Ifti told me that he and his friends decided to go off the school premises to fight because of the presence of Ofsted inspectors on site at that time. The fight never took place, but it was this non-incident which prompted the across-the-board exclusion-that-wasn't[12] of the Bengali young men and which in turn initiated the protest from Yasmin and Amitabh. Jamal explained – or rather, did not:

We wasn't excluded, they threatened us and they showed us that we was excluded, but it wasn't written down, that exclusion, they really just gave us a two-day, three-day holiday. (interview, 17 October 1996)

The attack on Sayeed was the final serious encounter between these groups, although there were a number of ongoing minor scuffles, for example, when Hansel attacked Musleh,[13] hitting him and robbing him of his jacket. Rumours spread that the same group were due to return in large numbers to the estate, precipitating the flurry of activity in preparation reported in the local press. The confrontation never took place and Hansel himself returned to Nigeria, after which there was a long period of relative calm. A year later, Hansel returned and a number of the young men were picked up again by the police and requestioned about the attack, but the case was finally dropped. Having said that, since leaving school, Ifti has experienced a number of run-ins with some of these young men, which can be traced directly to these earlier troubles.

These relatively few encounters were transformed by a dual discourse, closely intertwined, of 'gangs' and of 'race', which served to obscure the more mundane – perhaps even banal – explanations in favour of dramatic caricatures. As Chapter 1 argued, the imagery of inner-city gang subculture is woven throughout the press article covering these events, and suffused with ethnicized meanings. These meanings are then read into encounters, providing a framework of greater organization and premeditated hostility than the events themselves – however serious – actually warranted. It is worth noting again here that as Ifti's earlier account shows the conception of the Bengali young men as a 'gang' was already in place and was threaded throughout the actions of the protagonists and the reactions of outsiders, such as the school, the police and the press. This latter stance can be distinguished by its assumption of guilt and the attribution of blame that, as Sayeed's comment above clearly demonstrates, precluded the school from taking any measures, even when requested. The Bengali young men I spoke to were, without exception, aware both of the label and of its implications for their own position. As Hanif put it:

Last year, year ten, it was like anything that happened in the school he [the Deputy Head] was coming and blaming it on us . . . He used to think of us as a gang. (interview, 26 September 1996)

Sayeed similarly told me:

The [Deputy] Headmaster told us that he thinks we are a gang, yeah. We said we are just a group of boys hanging around together, that's not a gang. (interview, 5 November 1996)

What seems to have defined the boundaries of this 'gang' was its ethnic formation – that the young men assumed to be involved were all Asian and, with one exception, Adil, exclusively Bengali. It is worth noting that despite this rather tidy label, the designated group did not include all Bengali young men in the school (being primarily limited to year ten pupils), nor even all Bengali young men in this year (though it did include some Chinese year mates). In addition, the boundaries of this collective were, as the following chapter shows, loosely and often ambiguously defined. At its broadest application, the label served to target the Bengali young men who would gather on the mound, a sheltered grassy knoll behind the main school building, to smoke, talk to girls and occasionally bunk lessons. When I asked Ifti if the young men were indeed a gang, he retorted, somewhat indignantly:

> *Ifti*:   Of course not. Like they [the school] see the black youths hanging around together – we're like all together hanging around the mound, smoking and everything; we do everything there – so what's the wrong about that? Just say we're over there kotching,[14] there's black youths over there, why don't you go and call them a gang?
> *Claire*: Why do they think you are a gang?
> *Ifti*:   I don't know, I haven't got a clue. (interview, 28 September 1996)

Hanif similarly told me:

> We used to say, all the black youths hand about together as well, so we'd say, why don't you call them a gang? And he [the Deputy Head] goes some of the activities and that we do, he calls us a gang. (interview, 26 September 1996)

When I asked what activities, Hanif replied, 'I think it's just that some of us got caught stealing some books from the stock cupboard . . . fighting, using some kind of gun, smoking illegal substances.' As mentioned earlier, the incident with the gun concerned Malik's alleged use of a Magnum-style water pistol to extort money from other pupils. One interesting consequence of the 'gang' label in this scenario is the attribution – and often acceptance – of collective responsibility (and guilt) for individual misconduct, an assumption and misattribution of 'community' identification I want to return to in the following chapters. Sayeed's explanation for the label was, characteristically, more straightforward, 'Because we fight in a group, that's it; like if there was a fight there would be a circle or something like that' (interview, 5 November 1996).

The association of 'gangs' with criminality and violence is a primary – and often circularly – defining characteristic of this label, attributed by the school administration and resisted by the young men with equal vigour. In addition, the labelling process provides a degree of internal structure and coherence to the group that did not in reality exist:

Claire: So there's not like any organization?
Sayeed: No, no organization.
Claire: No leaders or anything like that?
Sayeed: No we're all the same.

The Deputy Head, who was a pivotal figure in this series of claims and counterclaims even went so far as to identify specific roles; casting Ifti as the 'gang leader', Hanif as 'the mouth' and Sayeed as 'the hitman'. As Ifti told me, his role as leader enabled the school administration to target him in its search for control:

> they pick on us, especially me . . . because like every little thing that goes on, yeah, like a small fight's gone on over there, they'll come to me straight – 'oh, you're the leader, you're the ringleader, you'll have to find out who's started it or you ain't getting off the hook'. I ain't done nothing, I don't know nothing, how am I going to find out? (interview 28 September 1996)

In the few weeks of most intense activity, Ifti seemed to spend more time in the Deputy Head's office than in classes, or he simply stayed away from school. Ironically, given his ascribed status as 'leader', Ifti's position was particularly vulnerable due to the Deputy Head's relationship with his father, a prominent member of the local Mosque, who tended, like many local Bengali parents, to assume the infallibility of the school institution and the automatic culpability of their offspring. In the worst of the crisis, and during yet another session of questioning, the Deputy Head attempted to make Ifti take an oath on the Qu'ran. After the letter arrived, he persuaded Ifti's father that the letter contained specific complaints made in his name, soliciting a denial that was later used as the foundation of the school's attack on Yasmin and Amitabh.

More generally, the 'gang' formation facilitated a process of identification and control in which the Deputy Head told the young men that he intended to remove them all from the school permanently. Ifti told me that after Malik's exclusion the Deputy Head announced:

> 'One of your leaders is out' – and he's not our leader at all, no-one's our leader. So he goes, 'your next leader' – me – I'm going to go. 'And the mouthy one', Hanif, 'and the hitman', Sayeed. 'All three are going by next April, you're going out.'

On one occasion, after a clash between Sayeed and Hansel, the Deputy Head told Sayeed to choose a new school in readiness for his imminent exclusion; Sayeed told me:

I was sitting down in the [main hall] with all my other friends, we were writing a statement [about the fights] and he comes up to me, he goes 'take this book, choose a school', yeah. I goes 'why?' He goes 'you have to go to a new school, because you're going to be permanently excluded.' I goes 'alright'. I was looking through the book, yeah, then I goes up to him and goes 'here you are, your book, I got a school' yeah, and he goes, 'No, I was only joking.' (interview, 5 November 1996)

In the same 'joking' vein, and around the same time, was the incident referred to earlier, after the Ofsted inspection debacle, in which the school administration identified the Bengali young men in assembly as the main reason for the school's poor performance and threatened them with luminous green sweaters. Ifti recalled:

It was only the Asian youth, yeah, and you know what they were saying? In assembly, they was going, 'If you see anybody wearing green jumpers, avoid them, they're the bullies, they're the thieves, they're this and that.' And we're only the ones that got in the fight, not for robbing anyone or anything like that. (interview, 28 September 1996).

To add insult to injury, he added, 'and they were school made, you know, all the fluffy things – embarrassing jumpers.'

Interwoven throughout this evocation of 'the gang' is a less explicit assertion of the racialized basis of collective identity. It is this raced identity that becomes paramount, obscuring alternative formulations around gender, age, territory, friendship or indeed their more fluid divisions or solidarities. It is significant that the young men themselves used 'race' to articulate these divisions – as Hanif explained to me, 'It's just that all the black youths stay together, all the Bengalis like stay together, there's a few Chinese with us' (interview, 26 September 1996). Similarly, when I asked Jamal if there were any gangs in the school, he replied, 'Not gangs, we're just like separated – blacks, Bengalis' (interview, 10 October 1996) It is worth noting, however, that Thomas More School has an eighty per cent black African and African-Caribbean school body, and that these separated groups actually refer to considerably smaller divisions centred on gender, year group, peer group alliances and friendship rather than racial classifications, and encompassed only a fraction of the school's overall population. It is also interesting that the young men seem to accept these classifications, often unthinkingly, as natural and inevitable whilst also clearly recognizing their more contextual and situational performances. As a brief example, around the same period as the conflict with Hansel, the Bengali young men got into a fight with

a newly arrived Somalian pupil. Several weeks later, returning home from
school, Ifti saw the same young man being attacked by some black boys
from the neighbouring Amersham estate and intervened to assist him.
He told me afterwards that he had felt sorry for him and also that (on this
occasion at least) he wanted to help a fellow Muslim. Most significantly,
the young men were unanimous in rejecting 'race' as a valid rationale
for conflict:

Claire: Is it a race thing?
Ifti: No, it's not that, *them* black people try to prove that they're badder
than *us*. We ain't proving them that we're bad, they're just showing
themselves up.
Claire: So you're not fighting them because they're black?
Ifti: No, they want to fight, they're the one's that like cause it . . . Little
things and then it turns into a big thing. (interview, 28 September
1996)

The same tension between 'race' and racialized hostility surfaced in my
interview with Hanif:

Claire: Do you fight them because they're black?
Hanif: No, it's because some of them have an attitude problem . . . not all of
them are bad, some of them are alright. (interview, 26 September 1996)

The issue of control, 'race' and gender has a specific historical
provenance to which I want to return below – one that has left a legacy
which frames the events of early 1996. However, with these past events,
as with the events presently under discussion, 'race' becomes a category
so suffused with alternative local and shifting meanings as to become
less an explanation than a cipher – or indeed, a convenient red herring.
Nevertheless, there was a clear recognition amongst the young men of
the power of a raced interpretation of the conflict with Hansel, an
interpretation they vigorously refused:

all they [the school] could see was we were a gang out to get the black boy,
that's all they could see, but they couldn't see what he done wrong. (Jamal,
interview, 10 October 1996)

The conflation, and confusion, of 'race' and identity – the collective
and the personal – privileges the timeless and universal and obscures the
crucial significance of the latter; the local, the immediate, the personalities
and the passions. It is this more personal history, in which 'race' serves
as an ambiguous marker rather than a simple motivation, which can be

traced clearly in these events. Ifti thus told me that their first encounters
with Hansel were relatively amiable:

> *Ifti:* Like this what happened, yeah, he [Hansel] came in school, he come
> in new and we got along safe with him and everything, he was talking
> to us . . . [And then] one day, you know Kenny and the other black
> boys? He used to hang around with them and then he thought he was
> a bad boy, bigged himself up, and that time Jamal beated him up – he
> beated him up three times . . .
>
> *Claire:* For what reason?
>
> *Ifti:* He'd done something wrong, I don't remember . . . a few days later,
> Hansel went tougher and badder and bad . . . he thought he was a bad
> boy. (interview, 28 September 1996)

The question of individual action and responsibility highlighted in these
accounts constitutes a crucial dimension within the conflicts that should
not be underplayed, and that problematizes any simplistic racialized
interpretation. This realization was brought home to me very clearly one
afternoon, during the last throes of the conflict, on the day that Hansel
had waylaid Musleh on his way into the youth club, and robbed him of
his jacket. Myself, Femi (our Duke of Edinburgh's Award worker) and
the junior members of the SAYO project were leaving the school grounds
on our way to Riley's, a local snooker hall, where they were working on
the skills section of their bronze award, when we met Musleh, looking
shaken and with a bloodied lip. As he told us of this latest encounter with
Hansel, the young men grew increasingly angry and agitated. Femi and I
made attempts to calm the situation, and failed, and as we entered the
estate, the young men surrounded a lone black young man known to be a
friend of Hansel's. Several times they asked Musleh, 'Was he there? Was
he one of them?' Musleh seemed uncertain but finally said no, the young
man was not there. The group apologized to him and after conciliatory
comments from both sides – and sighs of relief from Femi and myself –
we carried on to Riley's without further incident. After the session, the
young men went in search of Hansel, but this time without success.

What this non-incident made clear to me was the issue of personal
motivation, responsibility and retribution that imploded the anonymity
of 'race' as a rationale. Although the young man was black, was known
to be a friend of Hansel's and had, moreover, been implicated in some of
the earlier incidents, this was not considered a sufficient reason to attack
him – he was not responsible and could not, it seemed, therefore be held
accountable – at least not in this instance. By contrast, of the attack on
Hansel, Jamal, who had been ill at home that day, told me:

I think it's good; like I ain't a violent person, but *I think it's good they didn't let him get away with what he done* . . . Because I didn't really want my friend to get punched in the eye and get a black eye and let him like get away with it – no, *I'd get him back for what he did.* (interview, 10 October 1996, my emphasis)

It is interesting to contrast these more up-close-and-personal inter-pretations with accounts of an unrelated incident around the same time, and which finally led to Malik's exclusion from school. On this occasion, Malik attacked a white boy, Daryl Andrews, for no apparent reason except that, as Malik told me afterwards, he 'didn't like his hairstyle'. Hanif, who witnessed the attack, described it:

Malik just went behind him and grabbed his hair and goes 'White boy, I don't like your hair' and just kneed him in the head, so that boy started crying and running off. (interview, 26 September 1996)

Ifti similarly told me:

He's (Malik) just walking yeah, Daryl Andrews didn't do nothing to him, he's just going to his lesson. Malik just grabbed his hair, kneed him in the face and said 'You white cunt.' The boy was crying and everything. (interview, 28 September 1996)

In the wake of the attack, Daryl Andrews' mother called the police and Malik was arrested. He appeared in Court several months later and was given six months conditional discharge. He was also, of course, excluded from school and after this time effectively disappeared from the project. One of the reasons for this, which I want to return to in the following chapters, was the general disapprobation felt and expressed by his peer group, partly as a result of his attack on Daryl Andrews. As both Ifti and Hanif made clear, Malik's actions were unwarranted because 'Daryl Andrews didn't do nothing to him'; racialized antagonism was simply not a good enough reason. As Hanif told me, 'he shouldn't have done what he did to that white boy, that white boy didn't do nothing . . . Malik's a bully' (interview, 26 September 1996). Or as Ifti put it, 'Malik's an idiot. He shouldn't have done that. I told him he shouldn't have done that. He sold it, big time' (interview, 28 September 1996).

The spectre of 'race' must then be viewed and understood through a more local and personal lense, which fragments any more universal perception of difference reified and naturalized in notions of 'the Gang'. Central to the conflict was a more specific, time-bound and localized notion of personal and collective positionality, articulated in a discourse of antagonists and allies, guilt and responsibility and most notably, of 'control'. This locked these few specific events into a longer history of conflict in and around the school and the Stoneleigh Estate. Where for the school, police and media, this reinforced the belief in a more general gendered/raced hostility, symbolized in the image of 'the Gang', for the young men, the conflict was read against a very particular collective local history which at least partially dictated their understanding and subsequent response. Ironically, this local history was also used to (mis)inform institutional mythmaking about 'gangs' on the estate, which in turn fed the institutional reaction.

Making Myths: from the 'Notorious BIG' to the Triads

The events of 1996 were, for the junior members of the SAYO project clearly and crucially connected to the history of not only their peer group but that of their 'community', in a variety of imaginings. Most specifically, the conflict with Hansel formed part of a continuum of battles waged by the Bengali young men of the Stoneleigh Estate, within and outside the Thomas More school, over the past years and that formed the core of a sense of collective identity – and of 'reputation', hard won and jealously guarded. Of the recent struggle, Jamal commented:

> *Jamal*: That's started since the blacks try and overcome . . . they think they can dominate the school, but we're not giving them the chance to do that. Because the rest of the Bengali boys just let them push them around and we don't want to take that from them; we stand up for ourselves.
>
> *Claire*: And has that been the case before your time? Was that the case with the older boys as well?
>
> *Jamal*: Yeah, that was the case with them as well, but they had trouble with the year younger than them, not the black boys in their year, because they got along with them . . .
>
> *Claire*: So why has it started up again with your year?
>
> *Jamal*: Because of them, the blacks are now trying to be like the ones two years above them, they're trying to be like them ones, but we're standing up for ourselves, not giving them the chance.
>
> *Claire*: Is it all of the black boys?
>
> *Jamal*: Not all of them – it's only the ones that think they're big and hard, them ones. (interview, 10 October 1996)

Jamal's explanation conveys the sense of continuity with earlier conflicts, read as part of a history of black versus Bengali struggle.

However, as argued earlier, the use of 'race' as a signifier is located against more local and time bound circumstances – the earlier confrontations, as with the more recent ones, are with a specific faction of individuals and personalities. The struggles of the older group were, as described in more detail below, with a group of black young men in a different year group 'not the black boys in their year, because they got along with them'. Similarly the conflicts of 1996 were with a small group of black young men 'the ones that think they're big and hard, them ones'.

The gendered nature of these conflicts are crucial to an understanding of this history, in its present and past performances.[15] These are confrontations between young men and are centred crucially on the issue of control, of 'standing up for ourselves'. Jamal's account reveals a significant tension between a recognition of vulnerability – 'because the rest of the Bengali boys let them push them around' – and a determination to challenge this position – 'we're standing up for ourselves, not giving them the chance' – a determination which proves particularly ironic given the group's more usually perceived role as perpetrators and aggressors. Implicit in this tension is the playing out of a wider ideological construction of Asian masculinities as weak and feminized, and their more recent reinvention, particularly through the invocation of 'the Gang', of a racialized (hyper)masculinity. It is interesting that Jamal choses to distinguish himself and his friends from a wider Bengali peer group, and to cast the latter in a more traditional 'typical' role, creating a perceptual divide that, if not always lived through, did both generate and draw upon ambivalent reactions within the local (particularly older) Bengali community. The gendered perceptions of 'community', authority, responsibility, friendship and family implicit in the issue of 'control' will be explored in the following chapters. What is also at stake in Jamal's interpretation is a longer and broader history of the Bengali community on the Stoneleigh Estate; one in which 'race' assumes at once a more abstract and more immediately uni-dimensional significance.

The recent history of the Stoneleigh Estate was touched on briefly in the last chapter, while examining the emergence of the Bengali young men as a 'problem'. As was argued then, the SAYO project itself had its roots in a dual perception of the Bengali community – and particularly its young people – as vulnerable and later as constituting a potential threat. Silver told me:

One of the fundamental problems [growing up] was racism.[16] I mean, I remember as a child running away and being beaten up and things like that . . . The racism was a big problem. I have memories of when we used to live on the Taylor[17] when we first come . . . and we used to live next door to skinheads and they used to piss on our door and shit on our door and put matches through the letterbox and throw bottles at my dad and stuff like that. (interview, 3 October 1996)

As the Stoneleigh Bengali community grew in strength and became established, and more particularly, as its young people grew up, the situation was transformed:

Things are different now because they're quite established in terms of people knowing now generally not to mess around with the kids from the Stoneleigh Estate, the Bengali kids. That's not to say there are no problems, but they know that they're not going to be able to beat kids up and get away with it, they know there's going to be retaliation . . . They know that the Bengali kids are as crazy as the black kids and the white kids, in terms of they don't give a shit; if they get trouble, they give it back.

This transformation was effected by the young men on the estate and hard fought in the face of opposition from their attackers, the police and their own community. The borough's monitoring project notes: 'The Stoneleigh represents a pocket of dense ethnic minority inhabitants surrounded by predominantly white areas'.[18] The early years of the 1990s saw a high incidence of racial attacks on and around the estate, most particularly by white youths on the Bengali inhabitants; it was indeed these attacks that served as the impetus for the establishment of a monitoring project on the estate. The Report highlights four major incidents between 1993 and 1995 which were explicitly racially motiv-ated: firstly, in 1993 a series of attacks from the neighbouring Amersham development, in which retaliating Asian youth were arrested and which led to the summer project discussed in Chapter 3; secondly, in November 1994, when between thirty and forty football supporters 'including individuals wearing fascist regalia' abused and attacked a number of black people on the estate; thirdly a firebomb attack on a local Bengali family in March 1995;[19] and, fourthly, in May 1995, an attack by between thirty and forty white males, armed with baseball bats and knives, on local Bengali youth. The Report also draws attention to a series of black/Asian confrontations in the summer of 1994, to which I want to return below. It is significant that the Report contrasts these incidents with the four outlined above, 'Detailed investigation clearly identified that these incidents were not racially motivated. Rather they arose out of a personal dispute between two youths which had escalated.' Ironically, it is these later encounters that provide the foundation for the making of the myth of 'the Asian Gang' in the area. It is also ironic – but revealing – that, as the Report notes, it is these last incidents rather than the other events, which sparked a huge public outcry and a flurry of meetings between the police, the community and community workers, leading to the establishment of the Stoneleigh Anti-Racist Group and a report by the Police Community Consultative Group on *racial* attacks in the area.[20]

These earlier battles were fought by an older group of Bengali youth, the first generation to have grown up, gone to school and on to work in the area. Many of these had, by the time of my fieldwork, married and moved away, but had left a legacy of resistance to their younger brothers, which they in turn re-enacted, if sometimes with less justification. Hashim, who formed part of this older group, along with S. Ahmed and Mustafa, told me:

> Well at first, because there was a few families there and it was like a small community, we had no support from our parents, or the police, or anyone, so we really just used to take it – get done and everything and start a new day again . . . Slowly we had other people coming onto the Estate as well, there was other families there . . . and it came to a stage where we thought to ourselves, well, there's more than enough here to defend ourselves. So we fought back defending ourselves, and when these boys used to come down we never used to run or anything, just stand up for ourselves and have fights and everything . . . slowly people across the way [on the Amersham Estate], they got this message, that we are not actually going to take crap from anyone; if they've got a problem we will stand up for ourselves as well . . . It got to a stage where we just couldn't take it – even calling names, we used to get into fights and everything. (interview, 24 October 1996)

S. Ahmed similarly recalled:

> Like before this area used to be really bad. Asian people had a hard time, well, I had a hard time when I used to be young – our older lot, they didn't help us. Like when the boys come down to fight us, we used to run away. Now we all grew up, me and Mustafa and that, we all started fighting back; we didn't want to take no more so we fighted back. (interview, 6 November 1996)

Remembering the fights with the neighbouring estate, S. Ahmed told me:

> In the summers it used to be worse,[21] everyday – not even one day that I missed you had to fight. The other side of the road hated us . . . [it's] changed enough, they don't come down no more. It's like our own area now; it's like the Asian boys here, they rule this place, like Stoneleigh, they have their rights.

The notion of 'control' originates in this assurance of personal and collective safety, of 'ownership' of the area; what Hashim described as, 'being able to walk down the street without having any fear or anything' (interview, 24 October 1996). This certainty was achieved through the assertion of a collective identity, structured around area, ethnicity and gender, although interestingly, in the light of later developments, not of age. Hashim told me, 'we formed a kind of group, we all used to hang around in a group, so that if anything did happen, there was enough of us to handle the situation' (interview 24 October 1996). This group, as in its later incarnations, had no formal structure but shared a unity of purpose, 'with one aim and that was being able to live a normal life on the estate.'

Hashim was also at the forefront of the confrontations between black and Asian youths in the summer of 1994. He told me:

> This happened . . . two years ago. I was just about to go to work . . . and I was walking past and like about three or four black guys, they came up to me and they wanted some money from me. But me, I'm not one of those kinds of person – I don't know, I mean, over the years I've been fighting and everything, it's come to a stage where I think, no, no-one's going to mess around with me in my own area . . . one threw a punch and I got involved in a fight.

The fight escalated when a number of other Bengali young men came to Hashim's aid, and the police arrived, arresting the Asian group. While Hashim was still in jail, the incident grew still further:

> After a couple of days these black boys came back with their friends . . . and I heard there was a big fight and they were looking for me and they were looking for the boys that were involved in that fight and it escalated into a big, big thing. I mean, we had riots and we were actually going around in cars with petrol bombs.

This series of clashes culminated in a now almost legendary attack on the local Abbey Street Mosque one Friday afternoon during prayer time. Hashim recalled:

> Everyone was in the Friday prayer and then everyone got out and we could see those boys coming over to us and they had long machetes and then they were actually chasing me and Haroon in the Mosque . . . and every Asian man, every Asian boy just stood there and they just saw us getting chased; no-one did anything.

When Hashim's father came out of the Mosque, he and a number of the other older men picked up sticks and bricks and started chasing after the boys. A group of between twenty and twenty-five men finally drove the attackers off the estate, before the police blocked off the area and arrested seven of the Asian young men.

During the same period as these events on the estate, a series of conflicts were also taking place in Thomas More School, involving the then year eleven young men, including Shahin, Humzah and Liaquot. While there is no direct connection between the events in school and those faced by Hashim and his cohorts, the accounts mirror the same concerns over control and autonomy, the same sense of inhabiting the 'frontline' and the same determination to effect meaningful change. It is these struggles in particular that Jamal earlier related to their conflicts with Hansel. Interestingly, Shahin's carefully self-edited account of his time in school bears a striking resemblance to the later narratives of his youngest brother, Hanif and his friends:

> *Shahin*: Humzah and them lot, they had a fight when we was in school with some of the black boys that were younger than us, they had a fight with them.
> *Claire*: Over what sort of thing?
> *Shahin*: I'm not too sure, just over the usual things ain't it? Like when they beat up one person then you go and beat someone up, yeah?
> *Claire*: Were there gangs in school when you were at school?
> *Shahin*: I don't know – there used to be other schools coming down and other groups – they used to come for certain people.
> *Claire*: But not within the school?
> *Shahin*: It wasn't really gangs, just like groups. I wouldn't call it gangs, just a group of friends that stick together . . . It's always been like that at Thomas More. You've got the Bengalis that will always be on the mound, and that pattern's been happening for the last six, seven years, they're always on the mound . . . Everyone was alright with me. I used to stay with Chinese people, white people, black people, everyone,[22] you know what I mean. But like with the Bengalis and the blacks in my year, no-one had no trouble, everyone was alright – it's just other years. (interview, 26 September 1996)

Shahin's account shares the same stress on individual interaction and motivation, the same common-sense assertion of naturalized group boundaries, whether ethnic (Bengalis, Chinese, blacks), or territorial, and the same counterveiling denial of the salience of racialized or ethnicized identities. There is also, of course, the same resistance to the idea of 'gang' identification – a resistance which in Shahin's case encompasses a resounding silence. Humzah told me:

Ours was the first group to be seen as a gang – it was like the first thing that started everything . . . see, when we left they're still talking about us. (interview, 5 October 1996)

Like Hashim, Humzah's narrative is one of resistance and transformation:

It's just the way the school was in the first place. It was like we were ashamed to be Bengali or something – people are running you down, pushing you, cussing you, that's how it was.

Returning from an extended stay in Bangladesh to year nine, Humzah told me:

When we were third years, that time we had no control over the school – anything happen, the boys used to get the fifth years. And our fifth years were like dopey idiots, they didn't even get into it. We had no-one to back us up.

On his first day back, Humzah got into a fight in defence of Mehraj and found himself at the forefront of a series of conflicts that was to eventually mould the Bengali young men (or at least some of them) into an apparently united fighting force:

I can tell you hundreds, but forget it – there were fights and fights and fights. All these boys [the Bengalis] were wimps, you know that? Every single one of them were wimps, and then suddenly everyone started to get guts.

In year ten, Humzah became friends with Shahin, who until this point had mainly socialized with the African-Caribbean youth from his own area. Humzah told me, 'Suddenly at the end, we all used to sit down on the mound and talk and have a laugh . . . everyone was together.' This coming together created an image of collective strength and confidence that belied the rather more prosaic reality:

The thing is, you get a group of fifteen boys and only two of them fight, the rest are just there. The thing is, one person can't do it, you need fifteen people there, because at least the other people don't know that they're not going to fight.

Together with Shahin, Humzah fought and won a number of minor battles, both within school and against other schools attracting, like his brother Ifti after him, a reputation as a leader and a troublemaker, 'At the time there was not many people that would fight . . . When you start winning fights, then you get known.' After one particularly fierce encounter, when Liaquot was attacked by some African-Caribbean boys in school, the Bengali group became the focus of outside attention, and some fledgling mythmaking. Humzah told me:

> *Humzah*: We started giving names, just as a joke – it was just as a joke, just on our own . . . it was BBB, one was – that was the older ones gave that and we carried it through.
> *Claire*: What did it mean?
> *Humzah*: (laughing) Bengali Bad Boys! . . . Taz came up with this one, this was the maddest one – he come up with B.I.G. Have you heard of it? . . . I wrote it everywhere. You know what it meant? Bengali International Gangsters!

What started life as a private joke soon took on a life of its own:

> I remember boys used to come and they're asking about the BBB and we're like, 'how do you know about the BBB, we were just talking about it ourselves'. . . That's when the Triads came.

The role of the Triads in London schools throughout this period has been a focus of huge media controversy, notably in the wake of the murder of Philip Lawrence by so-called Triad gangleader, Learco Chindamo in 1995. The links between school-based gangs and the Triad organization are much debated and remain unclear, and the present study does not pretend to shed any light on this issue. I myself remain rather gratefully hazy on this point, except to note that the police and community organizations were greatly concerned about Triad activity on the Stoneleigh Estate throughout this period. It is interesting to note in passing, given the concerns with racial tension and its supposed links with gang violence during this time, that these acknowledged gangs were not racially exclusive in their recruitment and internal organization. According to Humzah,[23] he and Shahin were initially recruited through Shahin's neighbours, who were Chinese. He confided:

> I'm going to tell you the roots now . . . So we were known as this Bengali group and we had all these fights . . . We were fighting, always fighting, every day I used to have two fights, three fights.

Faced with a big confrontation with a group from a nearby area in the wake of the Liaquot fight, however, the reputation proved unsustainable and a number of the Bengali young men fled the fight: 'So we were shamed up . . . we were thinking we were so shamed we're saying we're not going to go back in school no more.' The Stoneleigh young men turned first to contacts in north London for support and then to the Triads. Humzah explained that this search for support, and for control, was the primary motivation for their involvement; 'We didn't know all this Triads stuff and all they said was that they just wanted them boys to know we had numbers.' Shahin's neighbours lent the required support and another confrontation was arranged. On this occasion, the Bengali young men were joined by over sixty Chinese youths, armed with knives and choppers, who assembled in the Stoneleigh Adventure Playground. A number of black young men were spotted but, significantly, as Humzah told me, 'See, the thing was, we didn't really know if these black boys were involved, they might just be normal boys sitting there.' As on many occasions throughout my fieldwork, the expected confrontation never took place, and the situation was resolved – after a fashion: 'After that we never saw them boys ever again, they never bothered to come back again.'

After this incident, a number of the Bengali young men, including Shahin and Humzah, joined the 14K gang. According to Humzah, the intention was primarily to offer mutual support and assistance when necessary: 'What it is, it's like, whenever they need help they will call you. I mean, anyone in the gang needs help you help them.' The new members were given money on recruitment, but Humzah and others who joined denied that there was anything more sinister involved:

> Friends . . . that's how they were. So we had no problems because we didn't have orders or things like that. If we wanted to do it we'd do it, if we didn't want to, we didn't do it.

Involvement with the 14K group centred around fighting with other groups and both Humzah and Shahin proved so adept as to progress to the position of *Dai-lo's*, which allowed them to recruit other members. Humzah continued:

> And then we had so many fights and there was a time when we didn't have to fight. It's like there were no fights anymore, no-one wanted to fight . . . That's when it was the fun days in the school.

For Humzah and the others, membership of the 14K ended with their school career, 'We left the Triads when we left school.' However, others of the young men, including Malik, who had joined a rival gang, the

SWs,[24] found membership rather more taxing and harder to leave behind. Humzah commented: 'If you were to join SWs and you wanted to get out then it's hard; you'll find it very hard because they won't let go of you.' Although initially the two groups were joined together in the school, eventually a split took place, causing schisms within and without the Bengali young men in the area. Tensions also developed within the gangs; in one incident, one Bengali young man from the nearby Buckingham estate, Kemal, joined the SWs and when he wanted to leave was told he would have to find £301 to buy himself out. Ismat told me, 'he did get into a bit of trouble with all this Triad business . . . he had to pay some money, which he couldn't, so he got beaten up' (interview, 11 October 1996). One of the key figures in the attack was Malik, who had also joined the SWs. Ismat continued:

> Kemal was joined to the SWs, so was Malik and Kemal had to pay some money and he couldn't pay. So one day, after school, Kemal was on his bike, Malik called him over: 'Give me a go on your bike.' So he was on his foot, [Malik] rode off with the bike, called for the older people in SW, some five or six of them – they grabbed Kemal and beat him up.

Malik's betrayal in the light of the mythology of Asian gangs in the area, then and now, is at once revealing and ironic, a fact not lost on Ismat:

> The trouble is that Malik helped them beat Kemal, even though Kemal and Malik live in the same area and all that and knew each other; so he's like two-faced with Kemal . . . Everyone didn't really trust him or anything.

Kemal remained living in the area, but was moved to a school in east London, where he made new friends, maintaining only sporadic links with the Stoneleigh Estate. He does, however, make a re-appearance in the following chapter.

Humzah told me that Shahin also had problems with the SWs and finally left the 14K group because of their unwillingness to back him up.[25] After another Bengali young man from the SWs attacked Shahin, the Stoneleigh Bengali young men left the 14Ks and joined with the older group on the estate to deal with the SWs. Triad activity on the estate and in the school seems to have since ceased, except as part of a collective memory – and indeed, a selective amnesia.

It is significant that none of the junior members of the SAYO project were actively involved with the Triad activities and that, of the core group, only Ismat was recruited.[26] He was dismissive of his involvement:

They came round my school . . . [and] this Chinese boy asked me if I wanted to follow him. I said 'what do you mean follow?' and he's like, 'do you want to join my gang?' I said, 'well, I don't know, do you want me to?' and he said 'yeah'. So I said 'yeah' and like after that day, still the same – nothing really happened, even if I was in or not in, still the same.

Other members of the junior group were prevented from joining the Triads by the older lot, particularly their older brothers. Humzah insisted:

I told them to stay out of it. I told them, look, you don't need to join them, we're here, you get it? They understood that . . . None of these lot joined because they know it's not worth it. (interview, 5 October 1996)

For Humzah, the question of collective security was the primary rationale for his involvement and this in turn negated the same rationale for the younger group, who could rely on his protection – a protection he and his friends had not been able to rely on:

If they [their older group] was to come one day in school, walk around the whole school and go out, that's it, that would have been much easier; everything would have been much easier. No-one would have joined the Triads – we didn't need to join the Triads. We didn't have no back up, no nothing, so we *had* to.

The role of familial and community responsibilities will be considered in later chapters. What is salient, however, is the ambivalent legacy bequeathed by this recent history for the Bengali young men of the SAYO project. The junior members have, then, inherited a reputation for aggression based on a history of community vulnerability; for territorial exclusivity based on a complex web of shifting alliances and local transgressions; and for ethnic chauvinism – or worse – based on a playground joke and a reactive affiliation to an organization that though profoundly raced in its popular imaginings, was markedly inclusive in its formulation. Rather paradoxically, they themselves have developed an ingrained suspicion of gang identification – whether actual, assumed or attributed. Hanif thus commented to me about the early conflict with Hansel, 'he joined *some stupid gang* and thought he was a hard nut' (interview, 26 September 1996, my emphasis)

Hansel was rumoured to have joined a 'gang' in a nearby area, called the SBDs (Silent but Deadly) (Ifti, interview, 28 September 1996). Ifti remarked dismissively:

They're all idiots, though . . . Some of the gang, yeah, like they try to give their gang like they're bad, but at the end we found out they're idiots, 'cause when we fighted them, all of them run off.

This is, however, counterbalanced by an equally ingrained sense of reputations once lost and staunchly defended – a mixture of confidence, of sometimes empty bravado and of a strongly defined, if rarely expressed, fear/intolerance of failure. This has in turn led to an undoubted element of sometimes reckless 'proving oneself' in and through conflicts, mixed with the certainty of back up in the event of possible defeat. This mixture was potently demonstrated in the last significant confrontation involving the members of the SAYO project – junior and senior – which took place during a general club session one Tuesday night in March 1998. The incident was sparked by an argument between Faruk and an African-Caribbean young man, again from Clifton, who were attending a popular music project in the Thomas More club building. Buoyed by the presence of the older SAYO members, Faruk initiated a minor scuffle, then turned to Humzah, Shahin and the others for support. Mindful of their seniority and weary of intervening in the younger group's sometimes self-generated problems, the older members proposed a one-on-one fight between Faruk and the young man, and a large group of the SAYO project members, other young people from the estate and the young man's friends, gathered. Clearly not expecting to have to follow up his actions alone, Faruk hesitated and then backed down, to the collective shame of the Bengali young men present. His opponent left, returning shortly after with a larger group of friends, and after an exchange of insults and counter-insults, a fight broke out. The older group chased a number of the outsiders through the estate, finally catching up with one on the main road and beating him severely. There were ongoing repercussions to this event, to which I want to return in the next chapter, but it is recounted here for several reasons. Firstly, Faruk's initial actions were determined by a combination of self promotion and an apparently unfounded over-confidence in his support base, leading to a position of unexpected individual responsibility he was unprepared to fulfil. Secondly, the senior members response demonstrated at once a recognition of the importance of individual action – of being able to stand up for oneself – and a reluctance to get involved in such a conflict (particularly in light of the age of the protagonists) without just cause. This was, however, ultimately tempered by a sense of collective implication in Faruk's actions – of collective shame – which was consolidated by a perceived need to defend their reputation, both as a group and as an area. It was this reputation that was placed in question by the returning outsiders and that determined their final response. It is interesting to note two elements in particular – firstly, that the young men were not primarily concerned to defend Faruk himself, who was generally felt to have let the group down; and secondly, the response and the subsequent events were framed not by ethnicity but by an identity based primarily on territory. There is a significant tension between the assertion of individual action and the acceptance of collective responsibility in this encounter that undermines any straightforward notion of group ident- ification, or indeed of collective will; similarly the privileging of a territorial, ethnically/racially inclusive identification on this and other occasions problematizes the ascription of apparently simple racialized divisions. These ambivalences will be revisited in the following discussion of peer group formation.

The older group's perception of some of these later stuggles reflect these ambiguities. Hashim told me:

> I'm a bit worried about the younger group because they seem to be – to get caught. I mean a couple of years ago, we used to get into fights only if it was necessary, in terms of defending ourselves; but with the younger group I'm not too sure. I have heard a lot of rumours . . . that they're actually going over to other areas trying to cause problems. I don't really want to comment on it, but I don't think that's right. (interview, 24 October 1996)

For Hashim, the struggles of his peer group are the foundation of this new confidence and of its sometimes negative effects; thus he continued:

> they're probably doing it because they've not been in a time when we were actually having problems, they don't know how it feels like to be picked on by people from a different area . . . they're young and, you know, they've got a big group and society has changed.

Humzah similarly commented:

> See these younger lot, they were influenced by knowing about us, by our year . . . and now they thought, yeah, no-one would really fight them and that's when they really changed. Afterwards they like took advantage and they used to go around fighting people . . . and then the olders said, 'No, we're not going to help you no more' . . . So we stopped them, but when we left I don't know what they're doing now. (interview, 5 October 1996)[27]

There is a kind of poetic irony to this mythmaking – a story of victims- briefly-turned-heroes-turned-villains, which has consistently haunted the

Bengali young men of the Stoneleigh Estate. It is, in many ways, a tale that has nowhere to go, that perhaps needs and has sometimes invented new enemies and that at the same time has developed something of a life of its own, outgrowing and enveloping its more mundane foundations to assume extravagant, and profoundly ambivalent, proportions. While this myth has proved markedly intractable, this ambivalence can be seen in the splintered perspectives of the young men themselves, with the older group remembering a past of vulnerability, lauding a golden age of unity, strength and purpose and critiquing the uses and misuses of their legacy; while the younger group in their turn view this history with a mixture of second-hand pride, sometimes distanced scepticism and a sense both of regret at having missed the action and the assurance of its continuity in their time. Quite what the new generation,[28] now coming through Thomas More School will do with this legacy remains to be seen.

Conclusion

A number of isolated incidents and occasional no-shows aside, the intervening two years on the Stoneleigh Estate have been relatively trouble-free. The junior members' final year at school was concentrated more on individual GCSE performance than their previous collective endeavours, and most have since moved on to college outside of the local area. The atmosphere within the Thomas More School also seems to have calmed, though mild hostilities with the Youth Centre and the security guard on the gate remain intact. As the following chapters illustrate, these life-changes have also precipitated a loosening of the group's internal structures, leading to divisions that have clearly manifested a number of latent tensions. Although these divisions are by no means absolute or permanent, the sense of collective identity and mutual struggle now seems muted, except in the now fortunately rare incidents of conflict that have arisen, mainly outside the area.

Two-and-a-half years on, and with the benefit of hindsight, the events of 1996 no longer seem as dramatic nor as earth shattering as they did at the time – at least to me. Certainly those few fraught months did mark a watershed in the SAYO project, in the establishment of strong and enduring bonds between staff and members which have laid a solid foundation for the project's development. However, the time that has followed has distanced – if not entirely removed – the feelings of dread, occasional horror and frequent personal distress that those often intense and sometimes apparently meaningless episodes of violence provoked in me. I have sat at too many hospital bedsides, examined too many scars, witnessed too much pain and frustration and anger, and breathed sighs of relief at too many lucky escapes, in the aftermath of these events to take this history and these stories lightly or objectively – or indeed simply as history or stories. That being said, the mundanity – even the sheer banality – of many of these conflicts should not be lost in the appeal to sensationalism and outrage; indeed, it is their very ordinariness that begs to be understood.

In focusing on the sequence of events outlined above, the aim has not been to sensationalize, but to examine firstly, the discourses which frame and determine the interpretation of such conflicts; and secondly, to explore the more complex matrices of personal, local, historical, gendered and generational factors that at once challenge, inform, and are informed by these discourses. The following chapters will explore in greater detail the complex mechanisms of group identification, hierarchy and control that were manifest not only in such incidents of violence but in the everyday lives and experiences of this group of young men. Certainly, these identifications find their most dramatic performance in instances of conflict but are perhaps more salient – and undoubtedly more pervasive – in less extreme, day-to-day interactions. While conflict remains a present, if less dominant, theme in what follows, the aim is not to dissect or explain the violence in itself but rather to explore what these – and other – events reveal about the nature of these more complex identifications; in particular about the creation and performance of racialized masculinities. The following chapter will focus on peer group formation and change, and will return again to the myth of 'the Asian Gang'.

Notes

1 On one occasion, the Deputy Head claimed that the young men were seen in school with a Magnum gun – the 'gun', it later transpired, was actually a water pistol.
2 It is also worth noting here that it is this group of young men targeted by the school as having 'special needs' (see Chapter 3). This labelling is ironically offset by the school's expressed inability to guarantee the safety of the young men in their care, which led to the Deputy Head instructing one recent victim of an attack on the school premises not to return to school 'for his own safety'.

3 Some of the implications of the misnaming of 'ethnic/racial' conflict are explored in 'Re-imagining the Muslim community', *Innovations* Journal, Vol. 11, No. 4.

4 My own association with Yasmin and the SAYO project at this time has meant that I have been unable to approach the school for interviews.

5 An interesting twist on the racialization of the conflict in the school itself, with the school administration representing itself as 'black' and pitted against the Youth Service, embodied in the SAYO project, as unproblematically 'Asian'.

6 The term 'damage limitation' was used by the Youth Service administrator at the time to Yasmin.

7 Julia was attributed the blame for the conflict for her supposed failure to 'manage' Yasmin appropriately, and was given a 'transfer-or-be disciplined' ultimatum.

8 Their antagonist was a Nigerian young man, Hansel, and a loose-knit group of unidentified friends, from both within and outside the school.

9 The account that follows is the conglomeration of my notes at the time, interviews with the Bengali young men concerned, and a collective memory of incidents and understandings.

10 Ashraf was carrying a wooden chair leg.

11 This was information from the police and the Deputy Head.

12 The young men were informed by the Deputy Head that they were excluded for three days (preceding half term); however, a letter sent to the parents informed them that the young men were able to come back into school immediately once an appropriate adult had visited the school administration; this apparently explained the absence of any formal procedures taken by the school.

13 Musleh is a friend from the neighbouring Amersham Estate who was a regular member of the project at this time.

14 'Hanging out'.

15 See my article 'Dis-Entangling the Asian Gang' in B. Hesse (ed.) *Un/Settled Multiculturalisms*, Zed Press (forthcoming).

16 One of the consequences of deconstructing 'race' as a category is that this ignores its more immediate material, physical and psychological effects. Racism is no longer a fashionable object of enquiry, but remains a salient and powerful presence nevertheless.

17 A neighbouring estate.

18 Report by Ethnic Monitoring Project, 1997.

19 This incident involved Zohar's family. Their front door was wired

shut and a petrol bomb was put through the letterbox. The family only escaped by climbing through the bathroom window.

20 Both the SARG and the monitoring project based on the estate are now defunct.

21 Summers are still generally held to be the worst time for fighting; indeed, the increased frequency of fights is held to be a harbinger of the season.

22 It is significant that Shahin did not live on the Stoneleigh Estate and came from a more predominantly white area. He only became close to the Bengali group in the fourth year of school.

23 It is significant that Shahin and others involved with the Triads during this period chose not to tell me about this episode in their lives, though we have discussed it afterwards, usually with some awkwardness.

24 Based on the WSWs – Wo-Sing-Wo faction.

25 Some links were maintained with old friends, however, which were activated in some later encounters.

26 Malik lived on a different estate and maintained only tenuous links with the older Bengali group on the Stoneleigh Estate. Interestingly, Ismat who attended a different school, has no sibling in the older group and has a rather more distant relationship with this group that his more locally based peers.

27 Humzah's comments are interesting in light of the discussion about Faruk's actions above.

28 At the time of writing, this group, affectionately dubbed 'the teenies' by Yasmin and myself, are aged thirteen to fourteen years old and are surprisingly trouble free.

–5–

Friends

In May 1997, six of the senior members of the SAYO project (including S. Ahmed, Shahin, Humzah and Zohar) travelled with Yasmin, Sher Khan and myself to Leicester for a residential training weekend – the first steps in the setting up of the project's senior member's committee. Early on Sunday morning, as we all slept, we had unexpected visitors – around 6 a.m., four of the other senior members, including Liaquot, arrived to see their friends, announcing their presence with squealing tyres and blaring horn. First I and then S. Ahmed told them to leave, and after some angry exchanges, they did so – although not before letting the air out of one of the tyres on the minibus. Returning later that evening to the Stoneleigh Estate, we found my car, which had been parked on the estate for the weekend, with its rear window smashed. Nothing had been taken, and it was assumed by all of us that the motive had been some form of revenge by our earlier visitors, although this has always been denied. Liaquot and the others were waiting on the corner, next to the Nigerian 'phone box, laughing, and were joined by a rather shamefaced Humzah and S. Ahmed. Shahin, Zohar and the others comforted me, muttering quiet curses towards their friends before drifting off with them, while Shafiq and several of the other 'little ones' gathered round, visibly distressed, apologizing for their failure to look after my car. Over the next few days a number of the young men, completely disconnected from the incident, approached me individually and apologized to me. Their assumption of some form of culpability confused me, while their private demonstrations of concern touched me greatly – although it is significant that no public disapproval over the vandalism was ever voiced.

One day, twelve months later, the co-ordinator of the Stoneleigh Estate Play Association (SEPA), had money taken from his wallet. The wallet had been in his jacket, hung on his office door in the SEPA building, which had been closed to users that day. The money, £230, was the biggest portion of my rent, which I had asked Mark, the co-ordinator, to pass on to Silver, from whom I was then renting a room. The only people other than SEPA staff who had been in the building that day were Saira,

Yasmin's younger sister, on a work placement, and two of the SAYO
junior members, Shafiq and Faruk, who had conveniently vanished. When
Silver arrived, and the theft was discovered, Silver disappeared onto the
estate to find the young men, recruiting a number of the other little ones
and S. Ahmed in his search.

Rumours about the theft spread like wildfire, and it was soon confirmed
by Ismat that he had seen Shafiq and Faruk with the money. Silver and S.
Ahmed finally found the young men and an angry confrontation ensued,
with protests of outraged innocence giving way to personal insults and
threats. Silver finally demanded that the young men meet him with the
money half an hour later on the corner of Abbey Street. When we went
over, a number of the junior members had assembled, along with several
of the older group. Shafiq and Faruk arrived several minutes later, still
denying their involvement. After a tense fifteen-minute stand off, Mohammed (who had been with them earlier and seen the money) stood up and
accused his friends to their face. The others then joined Mohammed in a
chorus of condemnation, accusing them of betraying Silver, Mark and
myself. Faced with this ostracism, Shafiq and Faruk agreed to return the
money – minus £30 they had already spent – and the money was returned
to S. Ahmed shortly afterwards. Faruk and Shafiq were banned from SEPA
and the SAYO project for the summer, and until today Shafiq has never
returned to the project; nor, it seems, has he ever quite forgiven Silver or
myself for initiating the rift with his friends, however temporary.

Apart from the occasional ripples in my relationship with the SAYO
project, these two incidents are also significant – both in their similarities
and differences – in demonstrating the complex dynamics of group
identification, fragmentation and imagination. In both cases the primary
identification was structured around peer group – around friends – with
its powerful evocation of group loyalty, shared history and collective
solidarity. On both occasions, the boundaries between individual and
collective action – and individual and collective responsibility – became
blurred, with members of the peer group assuming the burden of group
loyalty, and also of group culpability and shame. With the first incident,
this collective identification at once presented a stance of public solidarity
and cohesion, masking the 'backstage', largely private dissent and
frustration, and effectively muting any explicit expression of division.
To articulate any anger or attribute blame, either publicly or privately,
would then be read as a sign of disloyalty; of siding with me – an outsider,
a woman and someone who had already clashed with individuals in the
group – and thus inevitably against them. It was this basis, rather than
the initial incident, which established the moral parameters for interpreting

and reacting to the events, and on which appropriate action was demanded. Thus, even though both Zohar and Shahin fractured this unity by helping me clean the glass from my car before joining their friends, it was nonetheless inevitable that this temporary rift would be obscured, if not entirely healed, by their collective departure. Interestingly, in the days that followed, very few of the SAYO members, younger or older, would attribute direct blame on the individuals concerned, and I learned to accept that this reluctance was no reflection on their relationship with me. Indeed, the bonds established with the senior members in Leicester served to mediate tensions within the project through the demonstration of support which was more expansive than divisive: thus, when Liaquot and friends first returned to the project – and were, I think, surprised to see me still there – S. Ahmed made a gentle, but determined, point of sitting with me and talking over the residential, despite his friend's obvious hostility. This quiet gesture of concern and conciliation was at once pointed and non-confrontational, and helped prevent any escalation of tension or attempts to intimidate me, which then largely subsided, and have now reached a point of polite avoidance.

In the second incident, these peer group ties were also clearly evident; firstly, in the reliance by Shafiq and Faruk on their friends' unquestioned support for them, if not their actions; secondly, in the immediate assumption of culpability by the rest of the group for their friends' actions; and thirdly, in their belief – later partially justified – that other people, and particularly those in authority, would label, blame and punish them collectively. Hearing of the theft, Jamal and Hanif came at once to apologize to me and seemed taken aback when I told them that as far as I was concerned they had nothing to do with the event and would certainly neither hold them responsible nor alter my affection for them as individuals (nor, in fact as a group, since I had been some years in learning not to take some actions/events personally). Ironically, but I think revealingly, others on the estate were less circumspect and in the weeks that followed I heard several people who knew the young men or had worked with them, express sweeping opinions that 'the Asian kids' had messed up, betrayed them and could no longer be trusted *as a group*. As I will argue later, this collective labelling, the history of which has been discussed in earlier chapters, has been a crucial factor in the formulation and maintenance of peer group boundaries and loyalties. As with the first incident, the moral parameters were established on the basis of group loyalty rather than the theft itself. Where this has been maintained by collective silence during similar past incidents (it later transpired that both Mark and myself had been the victims of small thefts in the past that went largely unnoticed; indeed, Shafiq and Faruk had been unwittingly 'lucky' in finding so much money in Mark's wallet that day), on this occasion these ties were fractured by crosscutting relationships articulated around family roles and responsibilities, and notions of 'community' – most particularly around 'brothers' – which mediated peer group loyalties and opened space for dissent and distancing not possible during the earlier event. It was this fracturing that Shafiq, in particular, found so hard to forgive and that placed his friends, Silver and myself, in the 'wrong': for several days afterwards, then, Shafiq and Faruk would not talk to their friends and tensions still remain, while as I mentioned earlier, Shafiq has not returned to the project after the summer ban and still avoids me in the street whenever possible.

The role of Silver and S. Ahmed in this encounter is particularly revealing. Both had grown up on the estate and their relationship as 'elders' in the community of young men, commanding considerable authority and respect as *bhayas* (older brothers) was a crucial factor in transgressing and fragmenting peer group solidarity. This stance was further strengthened through their connection with the families of the young men, which was appealed to as a source of legitimation and of potential retribution, should the money not be returned. It was this combination – of respect and potential shame – that proved so compelling on the whole peer group and resulted in the public isolation of the culprits; something I had never witnessed before, nor since. The bonds of respect for 'brothers', then, here contested peer group loyalties – an encounter between competing notions of 'community' that proved at once dramatic and deeply distressing for all those caught in the crossfire. For Silver, particularly, Shafiq and Faruk's actions assumed the proportions of almost filial betrayal, especially in his confrontation with Shafiq, when the younger boy threatened to take off his shoe to the older man – an action laden with culturally targeted and purposive insult. The intensity of the fallout from the incident over the following days and weeks took me by surprise – an atmosphere of guilt, disappointment and gloom seemed to descend on the project and on the Stoneleigh Bengali community. I personally felt a little confused by the turn of events; partly elated that the young men had, at last, taken a stance against actions which they disapproved of, but would normally have overlooked, but mainly feeling that something was going on which I was missing the point of. While I was not taking things personally, it seemed everyone else was – and was expecting me to.

With hindsight, however, I realized that this incident had opened a rift amongst the ranks of the Bengali young men on the Stoneleigh Estate, which made public and explicit a range of tensions, conflicts and contradictions usually masked through silence and compromise for the sake of a performance[1] of unity and community strength. Where earlier incidents (such as the conflicts in the project or with my car) had constructed clear boundaries of 'outsiders' and 'insiders', often at the sacrifice of individual action, here boundaries were drawn and sides were taken – literally and figuratively – through the heart of the Stoneleigh.

The following chapters are concerned with these two dimensions – interwoven, sometimes competing, at once fragile, resilient and compelling. The next chapter focuses on 'brothers'; on the articulation of notions of family, authority and community, most specifically in their interaction with gendered and ethnic identifications. The present chapter explores peer group formation; its history, its changes, its tensions, contradictions and joys. Picking up on the discussion in Chapter 4, this present chapter returns to the construction of the peer group as 'Gang' and explores the role of friendship in situations of violence. Finally, the chapter explores the articulation of competing notions of 'community' enacted by peer group identifications.

Bad Company: on Family, Community and Other People's Children

As has been argued in earlier chapters, the young men of the Stoneleigh Estate have attracted something of a reputation within the local area – as troublemakers, as a problem group, as a 'gang'. This has articulated racialized representations of Asian young men with notions of 'inner city' deprivation to create and sustain a series of images which position these young men as deviants, marginalized within – or indeed, outside of – both the local community and wider society. This has led to confrontations with local institutions, such as the school and the police, and has legitimated their hypervisibility in terms of surveillance and control. The SAYO project itself can be seen then as at once the concrete manifestation of this representation and a gesture towards what might be termed 'social inclusion'. What these currently fashionable buzzwords – inclusion, participation, empowerment – actually mean for those involved in this process, whether as service providers, workers or users, has proved more contentious and the recent history of the project testifies to the potentiality of their subversion and reimagination. It could be argued, moreover, that what has been defined and legislated as deviant or anti-social behaviour can itself be understood as a form of empowerment or bid for inclusion, however limited, unpopular or occasionally ill-conceived.

Whatever the case, it remains true that studies of youth – and particularly black youth – focus on peer group formation and identification as being distinct, largely autonomous and usually anti-authoritarian subcultures, apart from and positioned in opposition to the dominant cultural community, however defined (Alexander, 1996). The intersection of 'race' and youth, in articulation with notions of masculinity-in-crisis has additionally marginalized black young men from their parental communities and placed them – doubly disadvantaged, inescapably alienated and 'between two cultures' – in the frontline of the popular and academic fascination with dangerous difference, somewhere between apocalyptic vision of post-millenial social doom and rebels with, or without, a cause; what Giroux (1996) has evocatively termed 'fugitive cultures'.

Certainly, some of the drama of these fugitive cultures – within, but not of the community, dangerous and uncontrollable – has staked out the reputation of the Bengali young men of the Stoneleigh Estate. It is the case too that the young men I interviewed felt these images came as much from the Bengali community itself as from others – and perhaps more so. This was one reason for the relative hostility from the Stoneleigh Bengali parents towards the SAYO project over the past years, why a number of local Bengali young men never took part in its activities and why others would sneak in guiltily on a Saturday morning after GCSE revision classes to play football and then vanish. As Shahin commented during the making of the *Heart of the Stoneleigh* video:

> within the Bengali community, when the young people say to their parents that they want to go to the youth club, their parents think it's a bad thing – they're going to go over there and do whatever.

It is undoubtedly true that, until recently, the core members of the project were those same young men who were out on the street, or on the corner of Abbey Street, seen as bunking school, or as out of work, smoking or talking to girls, and who have become a symbol for the perceived problems of the local Bengali community. For many parents, Silver explained, these young men represent most of all a process of change:

> Their children are growing up differently and they find it very hard . . . our sisters are becoming more independent, they're having a voice, they're wanting an education, and our brothers are rebelling against things and they're finding out who they are . . . And that means sometimes doing 'bad' things, to find out themselves and all of that is being misinterpreted . . . You know, someone

is sitting on a street corner smoking, that in itself is a 'bad' act, but you have to look behind that and see what's going on really and our parents don't. (interview, 3 October 1996)

The politics of smoking will be considered later and in the next chapter, but is significant here in symbolizing an absence of respect for the community and a perceived loss of cultural identity. More than this, it is the *visibility* of the act that is important and that points to the significance of visibility – or hypervisibility – in the policing of community boundaries. This is central to the articulation of gender and family relations but is more generally salient in the stigmatization of peer group identities and alliances. As Silver commented to me:

The parents are thinking 'if my son associates with these kids, he's going to have that funny haircut and he's going to have that cigarette behind his ear or he's going to be wearing these sorts of clothes and I don't want that.'

The young men who form the core of this study were then on one level simply the most visible, and therefore accessible, whereas many other Bengali young men on the estate remained invisible, silent and out of reach. This visibility, almost in and of itself, engendered and legitimated a process of disavowal and whispered disapproval from the local Bengali families, matched with the unquestioned assurance that the problems and the blame lay firmly and uniquely with Other People's Children.

This dual process – a homogenizing impulse of sometimes reluctant claiming, surveillance and policing in the name of 'community' on the one hand and the fracturing of this communal identity around family networks, notions of 'good' or 'bad' families and particularly of 'bad company' rendered the position of the Stoneleigh young men highly ambivalent; an ambivalence reflected in their own response to the community and its claims upon them. All those I interviewed thus identified a clear and consistent picture of their group, which focused on the familiar accusations of drugs, sex and unspecified criminality, here potently fused with the image of cultural betrayal. Sayeed, whose family was one of the first to arrive in the area, summarized the image:

The old people think like we're really bad, because they think we're like round every corner taking drugs and all that . . . and like with the older lot they think they're more bad, because they go with girls and everything, some of them run away from home and all that – that's how it is. (interview, 5 November 1996)

Mohammed similarly told me, 'They see them smoking, drinking, staying out till late, late, late, partying, you know, when they hire cars and drive round and that stuff' (interview, 24 October 1996).

This issue of visibility – of *seeing* – is crucial to this labelling process; a perhaps isolated occurrence that is understood, amplified and relayed through a series of common-sense perceptions and assumptions that the young men designated as 'gossip'. Faruk explained:

> they do gossip a lot. Like say you were *seen* in a park, they will be saying, like exaggerating, and they go round to your own house or someone else's house saying 'Yeah, I saw this boy rolling a spliff', then the next time someone says it to him, 'this boy was sniffing cocaine' – that's how it is, like it's exaggerated and when you've got to your own house it's like a big thing. (interview, 22 October 1996, my emphasis)

The power of gossip as a regulatory force was never underestimated by the young men. Most obviously, perhaps, for those young men whose families lived on the estate, the issue of family reputation – and of potential shame – had the most tangible significance and the role of gossip was more immediately threatening. Humzah told me:

> They all know each other, everyone knows each other, so it's harder . . . so everything you do bad, everyone knows . . . *If someone saw you*, that's it, everyone knows. You come home, they know already! (interview, 5 October 1996, my emphasis)

It is worth noting, however, that the status of gossip as a regulatory practice was rendered deeply ambiguous by its very ubiquity. As Faruk commented, 'my parents know these kinds of people, they gossip a lot, how they exaggerate, so they don't take much notice of it' (interview, 22 October 1996). Gossip, then, allows the luxury both of condemning others and excepting those closest to you – a facility particularly useful in blaming misdemeanours on friends and other people's children.

Many of the young men, then, articulated a tension between their families and their friends, particularly focused on the attribution of blame for any wrongdoing – what might be termed the ideology of 'bad company'. Hanif thus told me:

> *Hanif:* My mum sees me hanging about with them lot as an influence on me.
> *Claire:* A bad influence? Is she right?
> *Hanif:* I don't know. I didn't really used to stay with them before, is it? From about the third year I started hanging around. And she thinks I've turned bad since then.

Claire: And do you think you've turned bad since then?
Hanif: Yeah.
Claire: In what way?
Hanif: I don't know. In a way I prefer the way I am now, but I've just started smoking and that, which I shouldn't have done. (interview, 26 September 1996)

It would be misleading to assume that the individual's choice of friends was a source of generational conflict or indeed that the peer group was viewed as a form of escape from the confines of parental culture and control. On the contrary, in fact, the young men not only regarded a primary responsibility of their peer group to be the protection of their 'community' – older and younger – but respect for each others' family was a central condition of friendship. Rather than overt hostility, then, relations between family and peer group were marked by muted parental interest and concern, and occasionally critical comments. Khalid laughed:

She [my mum] thinks they are all influences, all of them. But my mum, she's different: once she would say Shakiel is alright, because he's working, he's studying, all this and the next minute, say he comes and takes me out, whatever, she thinks he's bad! I can't really tell with her. (interview, 15 October 1996)

Shakiel's parents, in their turn, viewed Khalid as a bad influence on their son:

I'm friends with Khalid and Khalid and me got into trouble a lot together and we got caught. My mum doesn't dislike him . . . she just thinks because he dropped out of college and he used to hang around a lot, he ain't doing nothing, he ain't working, and she says 'don't you be like that'. But she thinks he's alright. (Shakiel, interview, 18 November 1996)

Interestingly, and revealingly, the young men were often judged in relation to their families, whether good or bad, which in turn related in part back to family status and affiliations in Bangladesh. Hanif told me, 'My mum sees how the family is' (interview, 26 September 1996). Although the young men themselves were aware of 'caste' status, and this sometimes limited contact between members of the group (for example, visiting each other's houses), all vehemently denied the significance of these divisions in their friendship groups and were, on the whole, reluctant to discuss them in other than general terms. Jamal explained:

It's not bad families, it's bad caste, you know. Some will say, 'don't you know where your friends are from in Bangladesh?' and I don't really care where they're from in Bangladesh, you know, we're not like that – this is the nineties, who cares where they're from! (interview, 17 October 1996)

Hanif similarly commented, 'Some people deny where they're from. It's like they think they're from a bad place . . . but we're all friends, we don't give a shit – maybe our parents would' (interview, 26 September 1996).

The conflation of caste and class status, and their correlation with reputation, do not form part of the present study. Nevertheless, they are mentioned here, firstly, because of the way in which they make explicit divisions internal to an imagined community (whether ethnic or territorial); secondly, because they render visible connections across such boundaries internal to the peer group; and thirdly, because they illuminate continuities between individuals, friends, families and broader notions of 'community'. As I have argued elsewhere (Alexander, 1998) ideas of community exist as fluid and contextual constructions – articulations of often convenient fictions – which allow for processes of inclusion and exclusion, vindication and blame. Recognizing the role of peer group alliances similarly necessitates an acknowledgement of the forms of continuity and contestation with alternative formations of community identification. The peer group does not stand alone, it does not simply rebel against or invert the standards of its wider community, it does not provide an escape; it is rather embedded within a particular space, time and history – a matrix that is constantly undergoing transformation – something which the Bengali young men of the SAYO project were acutely aware of, and enmeshed in.

It is worth bearing in mind that not all, or recently even most, of the young men of the SAYO project actually lived on the Stoneleigh Estate, and that peer group affiliations transcended the tidy, contained contours of family, community and territory. 'Outsiders' such as Hanif and Jamal, Khalid and Shahin thus provided a convenient scapegoat in the labelling of Other People's Children, especially when their families were comparatively unknown quantities. Hanif commented wryly:

Most of them probably think me and Jamal's the bad ones . . . they say, like Faruk's mum would say me and Jamal come from another area and make all these lot fight . . . And Mohammed's mum and that think that like because me and Jamal's hair looks the worsest, she thinks we're the bad ones. (interview, 26 September 1996)

As should by now be apparent, hair was – and remains – a particularly controversial topic in the delineation of community boundaries; an outward, highly visible symbol of wayward individuals. Jamal, whose hair is itself an extraordinary feat of hairgel and hours of loving care, thus told me 'my mum takes the hair thing – like if she sees someone's hair really funky, she would say like "you shouldn't be with him"' (interview, 17 October 1996). Hair can, of course, also be (mis)read as an outward symbol of conformity: one reason why Jamal's mother liked Ifti, for example, was because 'his hair makes him look like a good person'. The notion of 'good', as opposed to 'bad' Bengali youth seems a clearly defined one and was recognized by the young men themselves. Hanif told me, 'the one's you see staying at home and that, they're the ones they would consider as good' (interview, 26 September 1996). Perhaps more accurately, then, it was those you did *not* see who were the good ones; as Sayeed made clear:

Them boys are like – they do the same thing as us, but they would do it in another area, so no people in this area will see them. But the old people think of them as more good than us. (interview, 5 November 1996)

'Good' Bengali young men were then those who, in appearance at least, seemed to embody the stereotypical qualities of Asian youth; what Amitabh described as 'the more hanging on their mother's coat tails type of kids' (interview, 8 November 1996). The young men from the SAYO project generally referred to them, somewhat dismissively, as 'typical'. Mohammed, considered by many in the local community to be a 'good' Bengali boy told me:

Mohammed: I reckon I'm a good Bengali boy.
Claire: What makes a good Bengali boy?
Mohammed: Dressing up neatly, like, that what the community thinks – no smoking, staying on your own or with a few friends and not playing out, staying home a lot.
Claire: And are you like that?
Mohammed: *I do it, but then, they don't see the other side of me,* so they think I'm alright. (interview, 24 October 1996, my emphasis)

For Mohammed, the role of 'good' Bengali boy was performative rather than natural; about being seen to do the right things (which mainly involves not being seen), and not being caught doing anything else. Humzah similarly argued 'People used to love saying that we're the bad group and the other ones, like they're the good group. Well, they're not the good group, they're the *unknown* group' (interview, 5 October 1996, original emphasis).

Although the young men of the SAYO project defined themselves strongly against an idealized image of the 'typical' or 'good' Bengali youth, it is significant that they placed themselves firmly and defiantly at the centre of their community as protectors and guardians, despite – or perhaps in spite of – their many detractors. S. Ahmed commented:

> Most of the Asian people here think that all the boys are corrupted, like they take drugs, they don't do to the mosque, they're bad . . . [but] sometimes it's wrong because like not everyone's the same, is it? Everyone's different. And like it's true, people like us, we should go to the Mosque and pray, because we're not doing nothing, but the problem is, if we wasn't there, the old men wouldn't be allowed to go to the mosque because people would bully them . . . But you know how people think. (interview, 6 November 1996)

Ifti similarly asserted:

> They gossip a lot. I hate that. See we used to have a lot of fights there and everything and Bengali people used to think that we were the boys who cause trouble and they the older people gets the hassle. And they were complaining too much and gossiping a lot. So every Asian youth stopped fighting and we started playing football . . . And they [outsiders] think that we're pussyholes again and they thought they could take us again and they start coming and robbing older Bengali people . . . And still Bengali people gossip that we're bad. I don't think of myself, I'm bad – not that bad – we don't do nothing bad; it's for their own good! (interview, 28 September 1996)

There was then an ambivalent relationship between the peer group and the wider Bengali community, at once fused with the ties of family and friendship and fissured by labelling, suspicion and blame; a process of claiming and distancing, invisibility and hypervisibility, of family, bad company and Other People's Children. Of their generally unfavourable reputation, most were philosophical; as Humzah commented: 'They're always looking for the bad things anyway, they don't look for the good things. That's how Bengalis are' (interview, 5 October 1996).

Circle of Friends: on Peer Groups, Continuity and Change

On Eid day, in the summer of 1996, Yasmin, her children and myself spent the morning in Regent's Park. The park was full of Muslim families, of groups of whispering young women resplendent in new *lehngas, salwar*

kameez and *sarees*, and of young men with new haircuts in designer shirts
and sunglasses. The road around the park was jammed with hired cars,
packed with young men, windows down, blasting out Mark Morrison's
Return of the Mack – that year's anthem – at full volume as they cruised
in the sunshine, calling out to passing girls. In the park we bumped into
the little ones, who were busy dodging the older group, rumoured to be
among the thronging cars, undoubtedly blasting out *Return of the Mack*
and calling to girls. Later that afternoon, as Yasmin and I began a round
of visits to some of the young men's families, we drove down Abbey
Street, and saw clusters of young men gathered by the Nigerian 'phone
box, talking and laughing, while they waited to drive, or be driven in, the
cars hired by the older group for the day.

Eid days, in the time of my fieldwork, have assumed almost mythic
proportions in my imagination. The weeks before were consumed in
continuous discussion of what clothes to buy and where to go – a careful
laying of plans which, almost without exception, were destined to go
awry. While Eid days saw the marking and celebration of community –
religious, ethnic, territorial and familial – through the attendance at
Mosque, the meals at home and in the homes of family and friends, they
also enacted a clearly defined notion of community centred on peer group,
on age and particularly on gender. Eid day as a public celebration was
then an exclusively masculine arena – a chance to spend time with male
friends, to travel outside the area away from the gaze of family and
community, to drive fast cars, talk to girls, stay out all night. The myriad
ways in which these best laid plans were thwarted are by now something
of a communal legend, in which fights with overzealous security guards
vie with hopeful expeditions to Blackpool, which ended up in a deserted
Manchester at 3 a.m., in a role-call of misadventure and frustrated
expectations. Yasmin and I were never part of these activities, although
we sometimes threatened to tag along (much to their horror), and we
would simply wait for the inevitable catalogue of disasters and the final
toll of totalled hire cars, arrests and lost deposits that would emerge over
the following days. And, of course, there was one particularly disastrous
Eid when Mostak crashed his car full of the little ones and we spent Eid
day in the local hospital – the only Eid day I have spent with the young
men to date!

Eid days were crucially structured around two major axes – that of
family and that of peer group. In addition to the few immediate family
obligations, the former was illustrated in the bonds across peer groups,
between the older and younger men, which was manifested firstly, in the
time taken to give the little ones rides in the hire cars (and the reciprocal

obligation to be suitably grateful and appreciative of the driver's skills); and secondly, in the tacit agreement to give each other space – physical and metaphorical – to do whatever they wanted. Most of all though, Eid day was a time for friends; when tensions were forgotten, resources pooled and people who had drifted away in the intervening months were welcomed back without rebuke or recrimination. Eid day plans, then, were centred on a notion of 'community' strongly structured on gender and age divisions, and although a time of solidarity, it was also a time when the boundaries between agesets were most clearly marked. Which group an individual chose to spend Eid day with was, then, a clear statement of status and alliance and, although these choices were not always without friction, they were a clear indicator of group composition and identification. It would be misleading, however, to see these boundaries as fixed and impermeable, and over the years of my fieldwork, Eid day also became a telling barometer of both continuity and change. On the last Eid day, six weeks before the time of writing this chapter, for example, the little ones – now the ones hiring (and crashing) cars – had reassembled in a large group despite the rifts that had appeared since leaving school (although, tellingly, this statement of solidarity seems not to have lasted the day); while the older lot had met for only a short time after morning prayers at the Mosque and then gone their separate ways to study for exams, or go to work, or simply sit in someone's flat and smoke and talk. The middle group, Khalid and his friends, did, however, finally make it to Blackpool!

If Eid day can be seen at once to perform notions of community and solidarity, to mask latent tensions and to highlight processes of continuity and change, it reveals in microcosm the ongoing creation and transformation of peer group identifications. Although from an external perspective, the boundaries of the friendship groups seem rigid and exclusionary – partly a product, I suspect, of the 'gang' label, in which notions of unambiguous and unchanging affiliation are a crucial prerequisite – the picture that emerges close-up is more complex and textured. Over the course of my fieldwork, and after, I learned the history of these groups and was able to observe some of their transformations. It is worth noting, however, that the account that follows reflects at once a process of selection and revisionism on the part of my informants and of reselection by myself, at the time of writing and with the benefit of hindsight. This history, then, reflects a series of standpoints located firstly at the time of interview – and reflecting a number of then current tensions – and secondly, two years later, a more distanced, but no less partial, reappraisal in the light of later developments and present concerns.

The process of change that underpins the history of the young men's friendships was clearly identified by older members of the project, for whom the period after leaving school had been a time of fragmentation and dissonance. Humzah explained:

> I don't know what group to talk about now. If you was to give me this interview about three or four or five years ago, then I would have told you a *different* thing – now, I don't know what to say. (interview, 5 October 1996)

While the younger members, on the verge of leaving school at the time of interview, uniformly resisted the possibility of change or dilution of their circle of friends, it is true to say that the following two years have witnessed a similar process of division, occasional animosity and loosening of group identification. Reading the last chapter, Jamal and Hanif commented, somewhat wistfully, on these changes, recognizing a shift in priorities and of understanding in looking back on the events, but also articulating a sense of loss – of certainty, of focus, of cameraderie.

For the older group too, there was the evocation of a 'golden age' of friendship and solidarity which was centred in the school and forged through the conflicts outlined in the previous chapter. Humzah told me, 'that was the best time of my life then; I was just having fun, fun, fun, fun, fun – and no work!' The older group, as it was constituted at the time of my fieldwork (and as it appears in the present study) was not, however, this group of age – and classmates, although they formed its core elements. Commenting on this change, and on the little ones, Humzah told me:

> I can tell you this, give it another three or four years they're all going to split up . . . because we were like that at one time. There used to be a lot of us – there used to be fifteen, sixteen, seventeen of us . . . *The rest are not our age, they're older*. That's a *big* thing; we joined in a group, like everyone was a different age. That's one thing that was alright, because we wasn't bothered about how old we was . . . *age didn't matter at the time*. That's because of some other things that happened. (my emphasis)

Humzah's account points to the complex matrices of peer group alliances – to processes of change and dispersion, on the one hand, and alliance and solidarity, on the other. He also makes explicit both the significance and malleability of age boundaries in the formation of the older group as it stood then; the ways in which age did and did not matter to peer group formation. As I mentioned in Chapter 2, this older group did not remain static throughout the period of my research, splintering into two distinct factions, partly around issues of age but also of personality. The reasons for the split are considered below. At the time I conducted my interviews, one of these factions, comprised mainly of the slightly older founder members of the SAYO project, including Hashim, had mainly abandoned the youth club as regular users. The older lot now consisted of an amalgam of the remainder of this age set, such as S. Ahmed, and a younger cohort, including Humzah, Shahin, Zohar and Liaquot. This latter group had, with the exception of Shahin, grown up together on the estate and had been friends from primary school. Shahin had joined the group in their third year at Thomas More School, during the conflicts outlined in the last chapter. In school this peer group – the self-invented 'Bengali Bad Boys' – had been formed from a relatively fluid mixture of Humzah's year and the year below, which included Shakiel and Mehraj. However, at the time I started working in the project two years later, this alliance had been succeeded by a fusion with older members of the project, including Hashim and S. Ahmed. Within the period of my fieldwork, a number of divisions within this group also became apparent: Hashim commented:

> Now it's come to a stage where there is a large community and there's different groups with different aims; its all kind of segregated now, you know – like you get Bilal's group, you have Omar's group, and it's all separated, no-one mixes . . . they've all got their different aims and objectives and they're doing their own thing as well. But at our time it was all one group with one aim and I think that used to be really good . . . but now because its so segregated I think it makes the community look a bit weak. (interview, 24 October 1996)

S. Ahmed similarly told me:

> There's more Asian boys – you haven't seen all the Asian boys – there are more of my age group, but like we've moved on. Like, you know Shahin, Humzah, Salman, Liaquot, Jahedul, Mostak – they're younger than me. I used to stay with Hashim and that before and then me, Mustafa, Jahid, Zillul, Zohar and Omar, we've moved on from them because they were too much . . . Like we had backchats and someone will go behind your back and talk about you, this and that, and when it come to a fight they wouldn't stick up for you, they would just leave you and run; that's how it was before. Now like we've moved on and they've moved on, so I like started going around with Shahin and that. I see them lot as much better and they understand more. (interview, 6 November 1996)

Though 'moving on' is presented here as the inevitable and seemingly benign result of different personalities – or what Hashim diplomatically describes as 'different aims and objectives' – the term actually masks a period of intense debate and muted conflict over the boundaries of the peer group and in particular its responsibilities towards younger members of the community. Where some of the original 'older lot' objected to the presence of those younger than them in the same social space, for others age presented less of a barrier. S. Ahmed explained:

> Well to me it doesn't matter, because still the same ones, they're going to grow up, you get me? And they wasn't that younger than me – one year, two years younger than me, that's it. And like when I moved on, some friends from there, they moved on – like Mustafa, Zillul, Zohar, because they knew how the other people were like, so they moved on. But we did have real hassle from the other lot, coming up and saying 'Why are you doing that, why are you making the little ones bad?'[2] because they think I'm taking them to raving and that. And I goes, 'Well, it's up to them, I can't stop them', you understand? . . . so from then it started slowly breaking up and we moved to two groups.

This break up was mirrored by splits within Humzah's peer group, although these seem to have been less acrimonious. The main division was between Humzah's group and a younger subset, including Shakiel, Mehraj and Ashraf, a separation necessitated by their friendship with Khalid, Shahin's younger brother. Humzah told me that, particularly on Eid days, these age/family barriers became most visible and insur-mountable. Where the young men had been usually happy to socialize together on such occasions, Shahin refused to allow his brother Khalid to come along (an unwillingness shared by Khalid himself), so Khalid and his friends made separate arrangements. More will be said on these dynamics in the next chapter, but it is significant that the combination of age and family considerations seems to have forestalled any discussion and alleviated any discontent. The situation was accepted by all as the only possible solution. Shakiel explained:

> We used to hang around with Humzah, Salman and everyone, and play football together and everything, and then Shahin came in and he was alright with us as well. Then we met Khalid and that – we knew Khalid from before, quite long back, but he got more and more close. And, you know, we kind of drifted apart, because we couldn't leave Khalid out, so like we formed our little group. I mean we still talk to each other and that. (interview, 18 November 1996)

From two distinct groups, then, emerged three new entities: an older group, including Hashim; a mixed age group, combining S. Ahmed, Zohar, Mustafa and others with Humzah, Shahin, Liaquot and their agemates; and a third, younger group comprising Khalid, Shakiel, Mehraj and Ashraf. Although the relationships between the latter two groups were close and amiable, the same cannot be said of interaction with the first group, which was initially cordial but became more visibly tense over the first two years of my fieldwork. An exception to this increasing tension was Hashim, who maintained good relations with all the young men and, by becoming a youth worker with the project, effectively extracted himself from this web of alliances and hostilities. Humzah commented dryly, 'so they ended up having about three or four people left and those lot all hate each other!' (interview, 5 October 1996).

These latent tensions were manifest in the summer of 1995 when Humzah's younger sisters, Tahira (then aged fifteen) and Tasnim (then aged twelve) were attacked outside the doctor's surgery on Abbey Street. There had been a minor altercation in the surgery between the girls and a young white woman, and on their way home a car with three white men and two women, all in their twenties, had accosted the girls and attacked them, using baseball bats and an iron bar. Salman intervened, but the attack only stopped with the arrival of some of the little ones and the police, and both girls spent several days in hospital with injuries to their heads and arms. The distress and anger at the incident was heightened when it was rumoured that some of the older group, including Bilal and Aklak (Ismat's older brother), had witnessed the attack and sat by and done nothing. S. Ahmed told me:

> They were just sitting there and only Salman came out of his house and he saw it and only Salman helped, but they were just sitting there doing nothing, that's how it was. (interview, 6 November 1996)

Ifti, Humzah's younger brother, commented:

> They take liberties . . . They wouldn't like it if their sister was getting beaten up like that and we was there watching it – they'd come and diss us . . . No, allow it. (interview, 28 September 1996)

Humzah put it rather more simply, 'I felt like killing them' (interview, 5 October 1996).

By contrast, at least during the time of my fieldwork, the younger group – the little ones – were a relatively cohesive and stable grouping. Like the older lot, most of the group had grown up on the estate, in neighbouring blocks, and gone through primary and secondary school together. Ismat, for example, described his circle of friends primarily in terms of how long he had known them:

Ifti is the closest out of all; I was virtually brought up with him since primary school – before primary school – and then after primary school I got to know Enam who was in my class. Then I got to know Shafiq; I got split from Ifti, he was in a different group . . . so I made new friends, Shafiq, Mintu and them lot, from primary school. Ifti made his friends and then like in school I played with Ifti and we got to know each other, all of us. (interview, 11 October 1996)

Faruk similarly told me:

My closest friends would be Sayeed and Shafiq, because they're really the first people I knew when I lived round here . . . I know Sayeed since I came round, before I came round really . . . because like my dad and Sayeed's dad go back really far, because when they first come here, Sayeed's dad and my dad used to live together in Manchester. (interview, 22 October 1996)

Both acknowledged, however, the expansion of the group and the growth in its internal divisions. Ismat[3] commented of Ifti:

I don't like him as much as I used to . . . He's different now – now when it was us two, that's your best friend, you could tell each other everything and you know not keep no secrets. But now we're in a group and all that, he's changed . . . I preferred it when it was just us two – even though I like being together all of us, but I liked it the way it was when it was just us two. (interview, 11 October 1996)

Like his brothers, Khalid and Shahin, before him, Hanif was a latecomer to the Stoneleigh Estate and only became close to the group in the second year of school. He and Jamal had known each other before this and were already firm friends when they began at the Thomas More School. Hanif told me that initially, as 'outsiders', they were viewed with some suspicion by the others and this led to some early conflict, 'In the first year because they like didn't know us, it's like they were going to fight with us' (interview, 26 September 1996).

The boundaries of this peer group are considered in greater detail below, but it is interesting to compare this experience with Khalid, Hanif's older brother, who on his first day in school got into a fight with Mehraj, now one of his closest friends. Khalid described the events:

Khalid: What happened was, one of his [Mehraj's] friends was on the apparatus and everyone started shaking the apparatus to make him drop, so I thought, why shouldn't I join in? So I joined in and started shaking it as well, and the next

thing I know all of them ... there was quite a lot of
Bengalis in my class in the first year, there was six, seven
of them – and they was chasing me round the gym ...
Then Mehraj goes he wants to fight me, so we started like
dragging each other ...

Claire: So who won?

Khalid (laughing): I think Mehraj did. (interview, 7 October 1996)

By contrast, Shahin seems not to have met with any conflict with his
peer group although, by his own admission, he mainly kept apart from
the Stoneleigh Bengali young men until the third year, staying with his
black friends from primary school and his estate. He told me, 'I used to
talk to them and that – you know someone, you say alright to them, but
you don't really hang around with them, you don't stay with them'
(interview, 26 September 1996).

It is worth noting the way in which each of these accounts reflects the
combination of ethnicity and estate in the formulation of clear boundaries
of the peer group in these early encounters; the sense of a collective
territorial identity founded on a long developed knowledge, a profound
suspicion of 'outsiders' and a strong bond of mutual responsibility and
loyalty. In all cases, however, these bonds proved ultimately more
inclusive than exclusive, and new ties were formed, changes took place
and new groups developed, and perhaps dispersed, without significantly
threatening or loosening these broader emotional and psychological links.

For the little ones, the majority of whom were about to leave school,
the history of the older group served as an object lesson in what the future
might hold and also what they were determined to avoid. As Hanif
commented, 'everyone says they're going to stay together but anything
could happen' (interview, 26 September 1996). In the two years since
they left school, anything *has* happened and the group of young men I
came to know well has splintered into a complex web of individuated
friendships and antagonisms. Pressures of work and college, in addition
to the formerly muted tensions present in the group, have meant that the
little ones have largely gone their separate ways – much more so, indeed,
that the older groups. This last Eid (1999), which took place only a few
days ago, the little ones made no collective plans.

Reinventing the Circle – Constructing and Deconstructing the Peer Group

It is not without a sense of regret and of loss that I think about the changes
of the past two years. While recognizing the inevitability and necessity

of change, it still seems strange to me not to see the little ones sitting together on the corner of Abbey Street, or piling en masse into the project, arguing over the pool list, and then sneaking off with an air of barely concealed guilt to smoke at the back of the building, or of excited purpose on their latest 'mission'. I even miss our sleepless weekends away. What I miss most, I think, is the sense of belonging, of loyalty, of being there for each other, which I came to value most and which made even me feel like part of a family. Sentimentality aside, what was more often viewed from a distance as a threat, as a closing of ranks, as exclusionary, unknowable, uncontrollable, up close seems at once more defiantly enduring and fragile. It is true of course that a more personal perspective tends to focus on detail – on change, conflict and ambiguity – perhaps at the expense of broader continuities, even of its sometimes more negative effects.

Recognizing the fluidity of these bonds over time, the changes in peer group composition and the internal disputes that operate such transformations does not, and should not, lessen the strength and significance of these ties, nor does it ignore the negativity and suspicion with which such ties have come to be perceived. Notions of 'gang' identity are structured crucially around the evocation of absolute divisions and inevitable antagonisms – of internal homogeneity and external antipathy – which needs to be legislated and contained. By the same token, a fascination with hybridity and difference has increasingly positioned any expression of alliance – particularly ethnic/cultural – as The Enemy, regardless of reason or circumstance. While the new theoretical orthodoxy demands the deconstruction of the shibboleths of 'cultural insiderism' or 'ethnic absolutism' – whatever this is taken to mean, and whenever and however they appear – it nevertheless remains true that the emotive power of such appeals remains undaunted, howsoever variously imagined. The young men of the SAYO project felt no such qualms in identifying themselves primarily and unequivocally as 'Bengali', and although this group identity proved fluid and permeable, even transient, in its performance, this sense of belonging – of personal, spatial and social location – remained intact. Silver thus commented of 'the little ones':

> The group is Bengali, fundamentally, and that is the core element of what keeps this group together; that they're all Bengali, they can relate to each other, they can understand each other. (interview, 3 October 1996)

It is certainly true that the little ones, both in school and outside, remained almost exclusively a Bengali group: only one non-Bengali, Adil[4] was a regular part of the group and the only other non-Asians I ever saw with them were a number of white young women from the estate, who dated various individuals for short periods of time. Although most of the young men claimed to have non-Bengali classmates as friends, all acknowledged that they tended not to socialize with them outside of class, a situation made more stark during the conflicts that marred their last years in school. Hanif thus told me that he had dropped his few black friends after the problems with Hansel, adding, 'every Bengali really do stay together in school . . . A lot of our lot, they like keep to themselves, like they won't really associate with no other race' (interview, 26 September 1996). Hanif distanced himself from this position partly because, he claimed, he did not share the same history as the young men from the Stoneleigh Estate. He explained:

> Some of them find it hard to mix in with other races; it's like they can mix with their own properly, but when it comes to another race, like they find it hard . . . I can mix in with any race really. It's like they've all been brought up together and that . . . they went to one school, the majority was Bengali there as well.

Mohammed told me simply, 'it's like you've got to understand at the end of the day you're Asian' (interview, 24 October 1996).

It is interesting to compare this position with the stance taken by the older groups, in particular those in Humzah and Shahin's year group. Like their younger brothers, this group of friends was exclusively Bengali and even though alliances were forged outside its boundaries – particularly with Chinese young men in the Triads – the primary identification was strongly defined by ethnicity and locale. Humzah told me, 'We were walking around, like fifteen of us, having our fun. That time, that was the perfect group – we were all like good friends . . . just Bengali' (interview, 5 October 1996). Being 'just Bengali', for Humzah, was an essential and inevitable part of the group's identity, 'it's natural, innit?' (ibid). This 'naturalness' was, however, more than a simple evocation of 'cultural insiderism', it was rather a combination of shared culture, religion, gender, local history and present troubles. As with the little ones afterwards, the element of conflicts faced and overcome together was a powerful one in welding a sense of communal identity, and one that bound the group tightly; as Humzah explained:

> If it did happen, if everyone was friendly and there was no trouble when we were young, we'd have lots of white friends, lots of black friends. But it wasn't like that.

It bears repeating that these claims to exclusivity did not encompass all their Asian, or even Bengali, peers at school or locally, partly by choice and partly by constraint. Mohammed told me:

> *Mohammed*: Some of them have strict parents – strict, strict, strict parents, and some of them think they can't be bothered.
> *Claire*: Is it because of your group's reputation that they don't come round?
> *Mohammed*: Yes, sometimes it's like that. I don't know, some boys, like Reza, he's Bengali but like we see him in school, he comes around and hangs around with us sometimes but he doesn't come out that much. (interview, 24 October 1996)

The positioning of group boundaries in relation to wider notions of 'the Bengali community', and notably in relation to 'reputation' will be considered in the next chapter. However, the ways in which ideas of shared history and common interests are used to formulate more carefully refined notions of belonging within this naturalized 'ethnic' community are apparent in each peer group. Khalid, for example, told me:

> My closest friends are Mehraj, Shakiel, Ashraf and Moynul; we're like the closest, because we've stuck by each other quite long . . . and the other ones, like they don't come around a lot. It's like we know them and that, they stay with us, but it's not like as close as us four or five. (interview 7 October 1996)

Similarly, Humzah told me of his Stoneleigh friends that, at least during their school years, 'We were much more closer, we were always twenty-four hours together' (interview, 5 October 1996).[5]

Friendship was often posited on the assertion of homogeneity – of history and experience, of growing up together and sharing altogether more prosaic interests:

> We all had one thing in common, every single person that the new group was now – no, two things in common, really – everyone was into fights and smoking . . . Every single one of us used to smoke, every single one of us used to fight. That's how it was. (Humzah, interview, 5 October 1996)

Although it was articulated most strongly in situations of conflict, this ethos of collective identity, of sameness, wielded a strong hold over the individual in more everyday situations. Shahin told me:

> Most of them are alright . . . because you share a lot of the same ideas and everything . . . It's like when we are together, we do talk English, but we mix it with Bengali as well. (interview, 26 September 1996)

Central to this identity, however, is the element of what Humzah termed 'fun'. Shahin explained:

> When we was young, when we was in school we used to go out – it was just messing about outside, trying to create hazards outside; like we would go on the train and get the fire extinguishers and start wetting people on the train and everything; like run from carriage to carriage and someone would pull the alarm and you would run off the train or something – just stupid things really . . . Now we just go out to some far places, and looking for girls as well.

Ifti similarly commented on his friends: 'we're all the same, all ways' (interview, 28 September 1996). Like the older lot before them, the little ones shared a 'plot' – an empty garage at the back of the Stoneleigh Estate. Ifti told me:

> We used to bunk school, kotch in there, play karam, play snooker; we had a snooker table, table tennis . . . it saved us, to get out of trouble, that's why we used to do that.

Also like the older group, the plot was a place to take girls (Shahin, interview, 26 October 1996). Sayeed also laid emphasis on 'fun', 'I go out with them, go trips, go cinema, have a good time and all that – chase girls . . . they're all the same like me, they do all the things like I would do' (interview, 5 November 1996). Likewise, Faruk told me:

> What sort of things do I do with my friends? Well actually it just depends when we do anything – Monday we come to youth club and Friday as well, Tuesdays; and sometimes we don't have nothing to do with it, we just walk around sit, do what friends do – like sometimes we might go places like Trocadero, things like that, visit places around London. (interview, 22 October 1996).

There is perhaps a tension between the assertion of exclusivity, on the one hand, and the seemingly rather mundane, everyday activities through which such exclusivity is often expressed. 'Doing what friends do', whether going to the cinema or the youth club, playing football or just sitting and joking together, is at once a set of unremarkable activities probably common to most teenage boys and yet also the stuff of which boundaries are marked and memories made. Although perhaps obvious, they are recorded here because too often, particularly in the mythmaking around 'the Other', the ordinary and everyday are left invisible and unspoken, and it is the extraordinary, the different, the deviant, which is made to stand, hypervisible and alone, for the experience – pure, untainted, 'authentic'. While the battles of the past few years were undoubtedly significant in welding the bonds of friendship, it was these everyday and unexceptional occurrences which reinvented and sustained them. And it was these events, as much as their more dramatic counterparts, through which the young men viewed and understood their friends. Or as Ifti put it, 'friends are friends – they're good to talk to' (interview, 28 September 1996).

It would be misleading to assume, however, that these boundaries however marked, were drawn in the same way by each individual, nor was each individual positioned identically within these groups. Where the correlation of locale, school, age and gender coincided most closely to unite each group, it is also true that these ties were not so closely knit in each case and not so deeply felt. Shahin, as mentioned earlier, had joined the ranks of the Stoneleigh group comparatively recently; perhaps because of this latecoming, or because he did not live on the estate, his position was less constrained and more critical. Like Zohar, who had attended a different secondary school and made other friends, Shahin maintained alliances outside the group (for example with his Chinese neighbours who had introduced him to the Triads), relied less on their support and negotiated their demands more easily. Shahin told me:

> there's a gym near my house, and I go there as well about twice a week, and I've got a few friends there, like white, Turkish, black and I get on alright with them as well . . . I've got a few friends in Hackney . . . and a lot of my mates from school – some of them are in prison now – they were alright. Some of them come to my house now and then. I mean, when I was with them we used to get into a lot of fights as well, they used to help me out a lot. I had a few problems with some whites when I was in school, with a school over the road, so one day I went with a few black boys and beat them up; and a few weeks later I went with an Asian lot and beat them up again. (interview, 26 September 1996)

Zohar, who lived on the estate, but had attended a different secondary school, similarly told me that many of his friends were from outside the area, mainly black and white school mates, and that he tended to keep the two groups separate. Of his Stoneleigh friends, Zohar commented: 'they're used to it. I don't care what they think' (interview, 22 October 1996). In turn, Zohar had attracted a reputation for being elusive and was somewhat marginalized. Shahin laughed: 'Zohar's . . . usually with his girl' (interview, 26 September 1996).

At the time of my interviews in 1996, the older group had fragmented considerably, and those I interviewed (who, with the exception of Humzah, were perhaps its more marginal figures anyway) were considerably more openly critical of the group dynamics and of each other than they had been previously, or indeed would be afterwards.[6] The younger groups were more reluctant to acknowledge intra-group tensions and were, on the whole, ambiguous about the sources of conflict and disagreement. Recognizing the reasons for either momentary disclosure or concealment, and acknowledging the private, personal and personality-led impetus for much internal tension, many of these conflicts are absent from the following discussion. Certainly, for the most part, the boundaries of the younger group remained relatively fluid and inclusive, and the young men considered themselves open to new influences and new friends – certain criteria notwithstanding; as Ifti commented:

> We get to know them, innit . . . see how they are . . . if they're right idiots I don't want to be with them because if the man cause some trouble we're going to have to back them up and he's not going to be there to fight his own fights. (interview, 28 September 1996)

Although, as Ifti's comment suggests, these boundaries were often oppositional in nature, most notably in relation to non-Bengali peers, they were more often inclusive of occasional members, some of whom came and went, others of whom came and stayed, while others still would pass through when chance arose or disapproving parents could be circumvented, or simply to play football.[7] For one period during my fieldwork, of several months duration, the ranks of the junior members of the SAYO project were swelled by a number of Bengali young men from the neighbouring Amersham Estate. These young men were mainly friends and relatives of Malik, who lived on the Amersham Estate but attended the Thomas More School and had been a significant player in the conflicts with Hansel in year ten. Generally perceived, by 'outsiders' at least, as a 'leader' of the Bengali group, Malik mainly socialized with his neighbourhood friends, who attended other local schools, but he was a familiar – if sometimes elusive – member of the SAYO project and in particular, as a talented footballer, he was valued as a crucial element of the football team – which, indeed, he captained for a time. Malik was the connection and intermediary between the two groups and in the months prior to his exclusion from school and the split from his Stoneleigh friends the following summer, the groups were in regular (if somewhat instrumental) contact. Sayeed told me:

When we were hanging around with a group of girls and things, more people used to hang around with us because we were with that group of girls ... once the group of girls, we split up with them, the rest just split up ... they just come for their good and they forgot about us. (interview, 5 November 1996)

Jamal and Hanif commented, rather more caustically:

Jamal: people like Absul, Tinku, them people, they're useless, they're fools – they come around for one thing and that was when we were with the girls. If they came round for us and like wants to be part of us, then it would be a different matter; but they was only there like idiots for the girls – once we were without the girls, they've gone off.

Hanif: They can't really find girls for themselves, so they came around thinking there's girls there, we might have a chance as well. (interview, 10 October 1996)

Leaving gender relations aside for the moment,[8] the tension between the groups reflects wider concerns around trust and responsibility – that Malik's friends had not been there for them and were therefore not to be trusted or relied on. After a series of incidents in which the Amersham group had tried to blame individuals from the Stoneleigh Estate for a number of muggings that they had themselves committed, interaction between the two areas largely ceased, apart from occasional and thankfully minor flare-ups of hostility (the last of which took place relatively recently). Interestingly, this division was articulated first and foremost as a refusal of 'community' – or at least as a positioning within another community, away from the Stoneleigh Estate. Area and territory served then as a marker of conflicting community loyalties, most notably around the notion of 'respect'. Ifti commented:

Them lot, like they ain't got no respect for olders. Like all of us, all of us smoke, yeah, we can't stop you smoking, but have some respect not to smoke in front of our brothers. They will smoke in front of our brothers, yeah, and at the end of the day, *though they're not us, we will get the blame*, we get told off. (interview, 28 September 1996, my emphasis)

I will return to the issue of community, respect and smoking in the next chapter, but it is significant in demonstrating the expectations both of and within the peer group – firstly, that friends are seen as extensions of the individual, and secondly, that the individual is implicated in, and held accountable for, the actions of his friends. The question of trust then becomes imperative in inscribing a code of behaviour in relation to the wider community and within the ranks of the peer group itself. This tension was clearly demonstrated in the split with Malik in the summer of 1996. As was mentioned in Chapter 4, Malik was excluded from Thomas More School after a series of incidents and accusations ranging from bullying and extortion to the unprovoked attack on a white pupil, Daryl Andrews. This incident provoked a muted dissension amongst his school friends, who disapproved of Malik's actions – a disquiet heightened when Malik told the police that Hanif had also been involved in the attack. Hanif told me:

> He told the police that I hit the boy as well . . . and that seemed a bit bad for me, because my own friend's saying it and the boy [Daryl] isn't saying it . . . My family are like going 'What kind of friend have you got, who stitches you up for something you didn't do?' (interview, 26 September 1996)

Malik's implication of his friend placed Hanif in an increasingly untenable position, called to court first as a prosecution witness, appearing against Malik, and then as a defence witness, backing up Malik's version of events. Hanif finally took the stand as a defence witness, against the advice of most of his friends, primarily because of a still lingering sense of loyalty. Mohammed was also called to give evidence: of Malik's exclusion he told me 'I think he deserved it' (interview, 24 October 1996), but continued:

> You know he went to court and he wanted me to give evidence. I wasn't really up to it but Yasmin, she goes, 'it's like taking liberties because after all he's Asian, and like Bengali, and you can't let him get down' or whatever. So I said 'yeah, alright' . . . He done what he did, but at the end of the day you've got to see that he's Asian; it's like you can't see someone getting done for you.

As with Faruk and Shafiq in the incident described earlier, Malik relied intuitively on the loyalty of his Stoneleigh friends and was rewarded, however reluctantly. Although the young men unanimously disapproved of Malik's behaviour, they were expected to support him and they did, almost in spite of themselves. Mohammed noted this tension, 'he thinks like even if he's doing bad, we are still going to back him up'. This loyalty was crucially posited here on an oppositional articulation of community; that despite his actions Malik was still a Bengali, one of 'us', while the Court system was constructed as 'white' and therefore as threatening and alien. It was on this basis that Yasmin insisted Hanif and Mohammed stand by their erstwhile friend, and primarily on this basis they did so.

What surprised me was that despite what seemed a relatively serious betrayal by Malik the group continued apparently unaffected. It was only several months afterwards, some time after the withdrawal of the other Amersham young men, that Malik was finally ostracized by the group after a confrontation between Malik and Sayeed's older brother, Salman.[9] Mohammed described the incident:

> It's like during the summer holidays we played football, yeah, in the evening quite a lot and like there's other little kids as well; like there's loads of people – about fifty odd Asians from the little ones to the big lots – and we're playing football. And he [Malik] is going around pulling people's trousers down, little kids and they were crying, yeah? And, you know Sayeed's brother, Salman? He comes round and goes 'why you doing that for?' and like he's [Malik] getting feisty to him, so he slapped him – Salman slapped Malik – and he [Malik] goes 'watch, watch' and got his mum and everything. (interview, 24 October 1996)

Several days later the younger group told Malik not to come to Abbey Street or spend time with them. Sayeed explained:

> We all respect our older brothers . . . and like a couple of days after that we met him outside the club and we told him, 'look, if you haven't got respect for our brother, we don't want you to hang around with us, because you're going to put us in trouble just for you'. (interview 5 November 1996)

Like his Amersham friends before him, it was Malik's seeming absence of 'respect' for Salman and, by extension, for all the older group and the community at large which put him beyond the bounds of friendship and loyalty; moreover, where the earlier incident with Daryl Andrews had relied on the strength of peer group ties, of their 'community', this confrontation signalled Malik's contempt of these very same ties – a betrayal of trust. As Sayeed put it: 'like if he ain't got no respect for my brother, then he ain't got no respect for no-one.' Hanif similarly noted that Malik more generally ignored the duties of 'respect' that bound their peer group, in particular by smoking in front of their older brothers: 'Like he will smoke or something in front of the older ones. He has no respect for no-one and when we see one of their older brothers . . . he'll run away' (interview, 26 September 1996). This then implicated the rest of the peer group in Malik's actions, and by extension, in his apparent contempt for community authority – or at least the community of the

Stoneleigh Estate. The only possible response, then, was the unanimous withdrawal of support and the distancing – physically and emotionally – from Malik himself. Mohammed explained:

> If you see we don't hang around with him, you see how we stay away? Because like we know he's not with us, he's not respecting the elders – you know, he's going around smoking with them and so on, and like maybe they think we're doing the same. So we just said like 'yeah, you go your own way'. (interview, 24 October 1996)

Again, as with the wider peer group before this, several of the young men articulated this division as one of area and territory – Malik's family and friends lived on the Amersham Estate and it was there his loyalties lay and his respect due. Sayeed observed, 'he'd be totally different if he lived round this area' (interview, 5 November 1996).

Malik's ostracism from the group was swift and absolute: although he continued to attend the project for a while, the visits became less and less frequent and he eventually disappeared altogether.[10] His erstwhile companions were polite to him in the project, mainly on workers' insistence, and he came with us on a residential to Bradford, but there was little interaction in the club and none outside. Hanif told me, 'he does come by but no-one really talks to him' (interview, 26 September 1996). His exclusion was total and unanimously upheld, and even with the intervening years and the later splits in the group the rift has not healed. Integral to this expulsion was the withdrawal of support, particularly physical 'back up'. Ifti, who was perhaps closest to Malik of all the Stoneleigh group, told me:

> If we're there and we see, if he's getting attacked by five or six, then we'll back him up. I'll feel sorry for him, I'll back him up. But if it's like one to one, that's it, I'll just sit there and watch; because at the end I know that man won't back me up. (interview, 28 September 1996)

Partly, it seems, because Malik's actions were interpreted as a betrayal of the wider bonds of community, his exclusion from the group was formulated similarly on 'community' level, thus extending to a number of his Amersham Estate companions who still attended the youth club. Indeed, because these individuals did not attend Thomas More School and had not shared in the recent troubles, their exclusion-by-association was even more unequivocal and rigidly policed. After Malik's departure, a number of these young men still came into the project and hung around the estate. One young man, Absul, in particular, braved the overt hostility for several months. Rather unfortunately for Absul, in the days after the argument with Salman, Malik had threatened to bring his cousin – Absul's older brother – to Abbey Street to fight Salman and the others. Absul was thus rendered guilty twice by association; firstly, as Malik's friend and cousin and secondly, by his brother's intended actions. As with Malik, this was articulated as an 'area' problem – that Absul refused to abide by the boundaries of the local community. Ismat explained:

> We hate . . . all the Amersham group that used to go to this school, but I hate especially Absul. Malik, he's OK, I can't hate him as much as I hate Absul, because Absul is just plain stupid. I don't know why, but he don't get it, but Malik understands when we don't want him. We don't really like Absul, because Absul and Malik are cousins . . . they feel they have to stick together. But like Musleh and Shamim[11] they're no hassle, no trouble, nothing – they respect our older brothers. (interview, 11 October 1996)

The conflation of individual, family, community and area provided a combination that Absul found insurmountable and he too eventually drifted away from the estate.

The conflict with Malik and his friends illustrates clearly the often finely nuanced imagination of peer group alliances and divisions. Whereas with Malik, notions of family and estate were mapped onto peer group boundaries to articulate and explain present animosities, it bears repeating that these explanations were themselves a product of time and circumstance – convenient fictions rather than a reflection of implacable difference, though with considerable force of action. It is significant, for example, that Hanif and Jamal – both 'outsiders' from the Stoneleigh Estate – were never viewed as such by their friends; partly because of Hanif's brothers' connections with the older young men on the estate; partly because their attendance at the Thomas More School and their central involvement with the group, particularly in times of conflict; but also because of their conformity to the notions of 'respect' to the area and to their friends.

Boundaries of the group were then likely to be drawn and redrawn according to occasion and present need, rather than a broad appeal to less tangible concepts of ethnic solidarity. Although with Malik the division was clearly articulated and maintained, in the majority of cases the marking of friendship was altogether fuzzier, personal and discreet. Thus, although each of the little ones drew the boundaries of their group broadly similarly, each account placed internal divisions in a more individual way, with themselves at the centre and others staged in different positions around them.[12] It is also true to note that these internal dynamics were not usually coherent with an external perspective – even with my own more informed, but still partial gaze – nor, with hindsight, did they herald in any direct ways the more recent fissures.

The drawing of internal boundaries was crucially centred on the issue of 'trust', which was an amorphous concept including not only the willingness and ability to 'back up' each other physically in times of conflict, but also honesty (material and emotional), loyalty (in particular, the assurance that your friends would not 'backstab' or 'backchat'), the demonstration of appropriate forms of respect to family and community (especially older brothers), and support of each other's aspirations and choices – and of course, having fun together.[13] 'Trust' also seemed to involve a tolerance of each other's weaknesses and shortcomings, sometimes for the sake of harmony, but also from a generosity of spirit rooted in mutual knowledge and a strong ethos of caring for 'your own'. The presence or absence of 'trust' could be seen to draw inner circles within the peer group, but curiously these were never visible in interaction and rarely expressed outside the group. Only one individual, Enam, was mentioned, first and without hesitation, by all the little ones I interviewed, as being untrustworthy, yet Enam was always part of the group's activities and though rather quiet and rather shy with me, he often seemed to stand at its centre.[14] Otherwise, divisions were variously articulated around age, around length of friendship, around estate and school, and around participation in the group's activities; however, these standards were never consistently made or applied.

One of the main axes of internal division, which seems to have become a lived reality in the past two years, was articulated around what can be termed, for want of a better expression, 'class' distinctions. This is not to be confused with more family-based notions of 'caste' mentioned earlier, although there is some degree of overlap: rather it was a muted and reluctant recognition of different aspirations and divergent life trajectories. While all denied that this affected their friendships in any way, notes of discord, perhaps even gentle disapprobation, were sounded around a 'traditional/non-traditional' dualism in religion, marriage and especially, in career. These positions cannot be easily mapped onto each other in any direct relation and should be understood more as a shifting matrix of attitudes and beliefs, depending on each individual rather than any generalizable orientation. The focus here is on a rather ill-defined attitude to life – to change and innovation, to adventure, to exploration. These distinctions were broadly articulated around education – a split between those who were going on to college and then university, and those who were going to work. Hanif told me:

Everyone has an ambition when they're small about yeah, I want to be in an office and all this, but I don't think it's going to work out for all of us, because of the way a few of us are heading . . . Half of them will say 'yeah, we're all going to end up in restaurants[15] anyway, so fuck the GCSE's'. (interview, 26 September 1996)

Jamal similarly told me:

It's like I can relate to Hanif better, but with Sayeed and them I can relate to them to a certain point, where they go their way and I go my way and that's what separates us . . . they have different views on things like work and education, stuff like that. (interview, 10 October 1996)

At the time of interview, these differences were visible in the group dynamics, although they were rarely made explicit. They were rather coded in different ways; in particular around leisure choices. Sayeed told me:

Some like doing different things – when some want to go somewhere, the others don't want to go and like the whole day they'll be splitting up into two groups and there's no fun there. (interview, 5 November 1996)

Jamal more directly related these clashes to wider processes of life choice and aspiration:

We used to do quite fun things, you know, we used to go round places, do things, but now it's getting a bit dead, like everyone wants to stay lazing around. That is when you can tell what they are going to do in the future, you know? Sayeed's the type that would want to go places but, I don't know, something in him pulls him back, like keeps him back. And like some of them are strapped for cash, that's one thing. But it don't bother me. (interview, 10 October 1996)

Hanif noted that he and Jamal were generally considered 'boffins' (interview, 26 September 1996) by their friends, both having clear ambitions to go to university. Increasingly, in the months after the interviews, tension in the group became tangible around the choice of sixth form college. All the group (except Faruk and Shafiq who were still in year ten) planned to go to college, but were divided between those who felt the group should stay together and those who wanted to break away, fearing that their friends would interfere in their studies. In a moment of prescience, Ifti told me:

I know if I go with my friends I ain't going to work that much; we're going to start fighting, cause trouble, or they're going to like chirp a girl and it might be someone else's girl, and that boy will come for a fight, and we'll get hassle and I don't want that. And they'll start bunking and everything . . . and if they start bunking, I'll start bunking. (interview, 28 September 1996)

Finally, the group split, with Ifti and Enam enrolling at a local sixth form college and the majority of the others, including Hanif and Jamal, taking courses at a college in North London. Ironically, though not surprisingly, Ifti got into a fight on his first day at college and left shortly afterwards to work in MacDonalds. Of the rest, only Jamal and Hanif remain studying,[16] though they have not entirely avoided the types of conflict predicted by Ifti – and indeed, perhaps tellingly, it was Ifti who was one of the first to offer his help to his friends when this took place. Ifti's comment, however, points to the deeply felt tension within the group between the pursuit of individual success and the loyalty owed to one's friends. Jamal told me:

I would want to be successful, but if that means putting them down then it's like a different matter. I want to be successful for myself but I wouldn't want to say 'yeah, I'm successful and you're dumb, you're a layabout'. I wouldn't want to rub it in like that or nothing. If I was to be successful and they wasn't, like just a loafer, I wouldn't want to rub it in: I'd still be equal with them. (interview, 10 October 1996)

Although unwilling to criticize their friends too severely, several of the little ones looked to the older groups and were able to draw often critical comparisons with their own situation. Hanif commented that some of Shahin's friends had been a bad influence on him at college and noted 'a few of our group will be like that, dossing around, loafing around; but I don't see myself like that' (interview, 26 September 1996). Ifti similarly told me of Humzah's circle of friends:

I know like he's going to get into some fight, I know his friends are going to take him away from college. I know for a fact his friends don't want him to go to college. Like they're not going college, why should he go college, that's how they think. (interview, 28 September 1996)[17]

Ismat also drew the distinction within the older group between those who travelled and socialized away from the estate and the 'loafers' who stayed put, and defined himself against the latter group:

Sometimes I hate them, because they have cars and they sit round the area and I can't believe they have cars and they have transport to go places and they like loafing on the estate! What's the point of having a car and loafing on the estate – you might as well sit on a bench or something . . . so I would not like to be with them. (interview, 11 October 1996)

The older groups in their turn glossed over these perceived frictions; the assertion of internal unity that defied criticism from outside and of even occasionally inescapable reality. The middle group, including Khalid and Shakiel, for example, tended not to draw internal lines – partly, I assume, a product of their smaller number – preferring to 'add on' to their circle on particular occasions, such as Eid. Such tensions as existed were articulated more as a concern for others' wellbeing than as criticisms, underpinned by a determined tolerance. Shakiel, who was at college taking A-levels, and has ambitions of becoming a PE teacher, told me that he sometimes found it difficult to balance college and work with his friends, but continued:

I don't think they make it difficult, but you know you can't blame them, because they're not at college, they probably don't know what it's like – they just think you're just as available as they are . . . If I can't come out I will tell them, 'I can't', they're alright with it. (interview, 18 November 1996)

While Shakiel and Mehraj had moved on to further studies, Khalid and Ashraf had been less focused on their future and were usually to be seen sitting on the corner of Abbey Street.[18] When I asked Shakiel if he thought these differences would lead to tension in the future, he replied:

I don't think there will be tensions, but I think they might regret not going to college . . . We don't argue [but] I mean when the subject does come up I tell them – I tell Ashraf more, I have a go at both of them really, but you know with Ashraf it goes in that ear, through that ear. Khalid thinks about it.

Khalid's perspective managed, interestingly, to be at once supportive of his friends and surprisingly critical. Of Shakiel, he told me:

Shakiel is a more serious person, you can joke around with him, but there's a limit with him, it's like he would take it serious or whatever . . . like he's got his head going, he knows what he's doing and that. He comes out and mucks around but he's got a limit; it's like he knows when to stop, when it's time to study, when it's time to have fun, whatever. (interview, 7 October 1996)

By contrast, Khalid noted of Ashraf:

> He's alright, but it's like he ain't got a care or nothing . . . people probably
> see him on his aggressive side, because he probably tries to show people or
> something . . . but he's not really like that – when he wants to be, he can, but
> like he's got a soft touch as well.

While Shakiel played down tensions within the group, however, Khalid
was more explicit and foresaw greater tensions and eventual divisions,[19]
'definitely, if people's going their own way, different Uni's, some working
there, some of them working there, I think it's going to fall apart'.

As with the little ones, Khalid drew comparisons with the older lot:
'somewhere I reckon they're falling apart. The way they talk it's like
enough people hate enough people.' As mentioned earlier, at the time of
my interviews, the older group had become increasingly fractured and
fragmented. Rather than a group, these young men now constituted more
a loose network of individuals who came together in increasingly fluid
and indefinable knots and then drifted apart. Humzah, for example, had
chosen to spend much of this period away from Abbey Street and with
former school friends amongst whom the ties were looser and demands
more easily negotiated, while Shahin was increasingly involved with his
studies and playwork duties. Of those I interviewed, only Zohar was
openly critical of this group, within which he had always chosen to be an
occasional element. This distance had become exacerbated after Shahin's
troubles at Hammersmith College the previous year, after which Zohar
had also been forced to abandon his studies. He told me:

> I was so screwing[20] that year, I didn't know what to do. I kept saying to myself,
> why did I go to Hammersmith? . . . One big mistake. Because I regretted going
> Hammersmith, I just went for the people pressure – that was silly of me, I
> know, but now I don't listen to no one. I just have to do whatever I have to do
> my way. (interview, 22 October 1996)

Increasingly, Zohar chose to spend his free time with selected members
of the group – Shahin, Humzah and S. Ahmed – of whom he commented
'they're different; they've got their own mind, you know that?' Of the
others, he was more critical:

> I go to them, 'at least I work, I made my money last year and this year I'm
> still making my money and studying. Whereas you just sit on the dole for
> every two weeks, waiting for your dole to come in'. They just shut up; they've
> got nothing to say.

Echoing the concerns of the little ones, Zohar articulated these divisions increasingly in terms of life choices and aspirations: 'It's hard to tell with them lot . . . the people I said that are close I know will end up somewhere and the rest will just be in restaurants.'

Zohar's critique brings together the expression of group loyalty with its implicit coercion, of individual aspiration with collective expectation and of the ongoing negotiation of collective memory with a less certain future. In a revealing, almost prophetic twist, Humzah turned a critical gaze on his younger brother's peer group, contrasting it with his own – perhaps idealized – circle of friends:

> I guarantee you, all of them, I bet, they are not friends properly. They've got their lows and I bet they've got someone they like, they don't like, someone's got a different attitude . . . I bet all of them are not the same. We were much more closer, we were always twenty-four hours together . . . Sometimes I sit in Abbey Street, you know what I see? Sometimes Sayeed and someone else walking this way, Faruk and someone else walking that way, someone else walking that way . . . We never used to do that, never. We were all together. We used to look for each other until we found everyone, then we'd sit down. (interview, 5 October 1996)

Humzah's portrait of a golden age of friendship and harmony – whether accurate or not – provides an imagined baseline against which are measured both the current imperfections of the younger group and of his own more recently redefined circle of friends. It points to a creative lacuna between external appearance and internal imagination; between the performance of unity and solidarity and the masking of dissension, the policing of non-conformity and the divergence of personalities and interests; between the 'community' and the individual. The boundaries of each peer group were at once variously imagined and deeply affective, inclusive and exclusive, redrawn according to time and circumstance and a repository of collective memories and ambitions. Reinventing the circle of friends thus brought together a glorious past, a guarded present and an uncertain future.

Of Friends and Foes

A crucial element in the creation and maintenance of peer group boundaries is their oppositional nature. This was manifested in two distinct, though connected, ways: firstly in the imposition of a collective, usually stigmatized, identity from outside; and secondly through the formulation of notions of inclusion and exclusion from the young men themselves. This latter categorization was posited on a dual assertion of internal loyalty and of external difference – and especially of potential threat. These perceptions were centred on complex and shifting matrix of alliances and antagonisms around notions of community, territory, age and person-ality, but they were also crucial to a sense of individual and collective security. It is this sense, of belonging, of vulnerability, of care and responsibility – of trust – which provides a link between the group and its wider environs, between the assumption and ascription of group identity. Writing in the wake – not to mention the insurgent backlash – of the Stephen Lawrence case and the bombings in Brixton, Brick Lane and Soho, the sense of threat, even of terror, is hard to escape. If race and racism are now firmly – and dramatically – back on the public agenda, it is nevertheless true that its less visible, less dramatic, more recalcitrant manifestations continue unabated and largely unremarked. It is certainly true that for the young men of the SAYO project, the boundaries of friendship were formulated and sustained in the interstices of stigma and danger, and though not fully contained within these parameters, group identity was crucially built on a sense of collective defiance under fire.

A fundamental aspect of 'trust' was, then, the reliance on friends to be there as 'back up' in situations of conflict; and although this often led to private tensions, as in the episode of Malik's court appearance or Shafiq and Faruk's perception of betrayal over the theft described earlier, the marking and defence of friendship groups on occasions of physical conflict was swift and unequivocal. As Sayeed told me, 'they will stick up for me, they always stick up for me' (interview, 5 November 1996). Ifti similarly drew his inner circle of friends around the issue of 'back up': 'You can trust them . . . they will back me up' (interview, 28 September 1996). Ismat noted:

> When one of us is in trouble the rest come back you up, so I say they're good friends . . . It is important because there's a lot of trouble coming along, back and forth, so it is important. Everyone keeps look out for each other's back. (interview, 11 October 1996)

He continued:

> I may not be a good fighter but I stick together; if there's a fight, there's a fight. You know, I don't have to, but I feel alright because I want to, because they're my friends and I need to back them up, they back me up.

Similarly, the reliance on 'back up' carries with it the corresponding responsibility to protect friends from harm; of knowing when not to fight and when to stop. Jamal explained:

> I would like my friends to back me up 100 per cent as possible, up to an extent, but if it means we are going to get beat up, then I expect them to know we should both get out of it. I wouldn't want him to stay there and hurt himself just for me. But if he was in a fight and got hurt, I could understand that he did it for me and he knows what it comes to. But if I could get him out of it, I would get him out of it. (interview, 10 October 1996)

The mutuality of this exchange is important, though it does make allowances for those friends known to be weaker or simply afraid. Ifti, for example, told me, 'I don't like saying it but Sayeed, like he's kinda scared and I don't mind that, because I know he's scared' (interview, 28 September 1996).

The protection of friends or indeed of others in need of help points to a wider ethos of 'community' which will be discussed further in the next chapter. It is worth noting here, however, that the conflation of friendship groups with ethnicity and with gender often invokes a narrowly territorial imagination of community, which has profound implications for the construction of notions of friends and foes. Some of the consequences of this articulation have been explored in previous chapters, notably in the conflict with Hansel, but it is also significant in structuring interaction with other groups outside the Stoneleigh Estate and in particular with Bengali peers from other areas. As I have argued elsewhere (Alexander, 1998), the reification of absolutist configurations of gender, ethnicity, community and territory are crucial to the construction of moral panics about 'the Asian Gang', providing convenient explanations of internal homogeneity and a highly racialized inter-group or intra-ethnic antipathy for situations of 'gang violence'. This has been particularly true of Bangladeshi groups where concern has focused on communities in Tower Hamlets and Camden, conjuring up a rolecall of 'gangs' like the Cannon Street Posse, the Brick Lane Massive, the Drummond Street Posse or the Lisson Green Posse. While it is true that the young men of the SAYO project themselves sometimes articulated this configuration, most notably around the 'reputation' of the Stoneleigh Estate, it is also clear that not only did the 'internal' boundaries of this identification shift, but that the rules of engagement with other 'outside' groups were also complex and enmeshed. Peer group identities became at once a source of engagement and expulsion, often switching status at a dizzying pace. There existed, then, a network of contacts – of alliance or of conflict – between each group on the Stoneleigh Estate and other peers. For the younger group this revolved primarily around family members in other parts of London, but for the older group these contacts also built on networks established in college, or through clubs, *melas*, weddings and other social events. Because of this provenance, the little ones tended, at least at the time of my fieldwork, to mix primarily with other Bengali peer groups, whereas the older lot had a more extensive network of friends and foes from all over London and all Asian groups.

Throughout the period of my fieldwork, the little ones developed a somewhat tempestuous relationship with a group from Tower Hamlets, reputedly part of the 'Cannon Street Posse'. Contact was made initially through Kemal who, as described in Chapter 4, lived in the area and used to attend Thomas More School until trouble with the Triads forced him to change schools. Kemal now attended a school in east London and had made a new circle of friends there. Initially the relationship was cordial, even co-operative – it was these young men who had helped in the revenge attack on Hansel, for example, and in return some of the Stoneleigh young men had earlier helped them in a fight with a group from Shadwell. Mohammed told me, '[It's] not often. Sometimes they call upon us, like Ifti, Hanif and that – sometimes I go down. We rely on each other sometime like that, when there's fights' (interview, 24 October 1996). This tenuous coalition was fractured, however, through a series of disputes and misunderstandings; firstly, when Hanif was chased at Shafiq's cousin's wedding in east London by a group of older men annoyed at his flirting with local girls; and secondly, after a fight at a rave that the project had organised on the Stoneleigh Estate some months afterwards. In the first instance, Hanif and his friends had called the older lot in to help and the incident was resolved partly through this intervention and partly through Kemal's mediation on the part of his peer group the following week. The second incident arose after Kemal had his mobile 'phone stolen during a club session (actually by a group from outside the project) and he had turned up at the rave with a large number of friends to redress this imagined insult. It was rumoured that these friends had come tooled up with knives and other weapons, although they quickly fled from the estate when large numbers of the Stoneleigh young men appeared.

A number of observations can be drawn from these few encounters sketched here, which in themselves are only part of a longer history, before and since. Firstly, it is important that at various times the Cannon Street young men were situated as friends and foes, undermining any straight-forward notion of ethnicized or territorial antipathy and emphasizing the

relational nature of group formation. Secondly, the groups were formulated around a broad inclusive notion of peer group – of shared age-set;
this not only established the parameters of contact and ensured a loose
commonality of status and interests, but also served to defuse tension
after the wedding incident by distancing the Cannon Street boys struct-
urally and perceptually from the older group who had started the fight.
Thirdly, interaction was initiated and mediated by one individual, Kemal,
who straddled both groups, as a former resident of the Stoneleigh area
and part of an earlier formation, and as a current member of the Cannon
Street circle. Kemal was able to vouch for both groups, subverting any
notion of absolute difference and hostility, although his loyalties were
cast in doubt, most obviously when conflict arose. As Ifti observed:

> You can't trust him now because he's like an informer, two ways – but like
> he's known in Stoneleigh and like if we're fighting Cannon Street, they will
> go to him, they'll beat him up. They will turn against him because he's not a
> real Cannon Street boy, he lives around here . . . he's a Stoneleigh boy.
> (interview, 28 September 1996)

Kemal's position is particularly interesting in illustrating the significance and the ambivalence of territorial notions of peer group identity.
Constructed on occasion as both an insider and an outsider to the Estate,
Kemal personifies at once the fluidity of group boundaries – the potential
disjunction of individual, friendship circle, peer group and territory –
and the demand for absolute identification and untrammelled loyalty.
Kemal's circle of friends then formed a subset of a wider peer group
which was fractured along territorial lines – when conflict arose Kemal
was caught between a territorial identification and a friendship expectation, both of which threw into question the issue of belonging and of
trust. Mohammed commented:

> If he had hung around with us, maybe now we would be more close to him,
> but . . . at the end of the day he's with some other boys and like you can't
> trust him that much. (interview, 24 October 1996)

The complexities of peer group networks and boundaries are clearly
illustrated in a series of connected incidents that took place during my
fieldwork, involving Shahin.[21] Throughout these several encounters,
configurations of alliance and conflict, of friendship, peer group, territory
and community, of loyalty, trust and responsibility were reformulated
and contested, deconstructed and reimagined, in a kaleidoscope which
renders any easy or absolute notion of the peer group untenable.

In October 1995, Shahin was attacked outside his west London college as he left to travel home. He and a fellow Bengali student from north London were set upon by a group of twelve or thirteen young men, also of Asian origin, and beaten with baseball bats and iron bars. The incident ended with the intervention of some Asian young women from the college, including Shahin's then girlfriend, who called the police. Shahin spent the next three days in a west London hospital, emerging with stitches on his forehead and a limp that lasted for several months; his friend received treatment for a broken arm and was discharged. It later transpired that the attackers had travelled down from Luton in search of Shahin; they were a group of mainly Pakistani and Sikh origin, although the ringleaders in this incident and main instigators were two Bengali young men, Azmul and Rahul, both long-time antagonists of Shahin.

The incident provoked immediate and angry reaction from Shahin's friends on the Stoneleigh Estate. Immediate revenge trips to west London began the same evening and continued over several weeks, while longer term plans were laid to travel to Luton to seek out Azmul and Rahul.[22] Shahin told me:

> *Shahin*: Obviously I was angry, do you know what I mean, we were after them and then we went to the area – it was like four weeks after I'd come out of hospital, we went to the area and beat a few of them up.
>
> *Claire*: Who is 'we'?
>
> *Shahin*: Just you know, us lot from Stoneleigh, and then what happened, I went to college a few times and we did a couple of them in the college as well . . . We was in their area two, three times a week, just looking for them and some of them were threatened to walk on the streets. (interview 26 September 1996)

Five of the Luton group, including Azmul, were eventually taken to court and sentenced to between three and twenty-one months. Sporadic revenge attacks continued, however, and over a year later, a number of the Stoneleigh young men caught up with the other main ringleader, Rahul. After assaulting him, the group smashed up his car and after a dramatic car chase by police helicopter down the A40, several were arrested. Only one, Mustafa, who admitted responsibility for the whole incident, was eventually charged and was sentenced to six years imprisonment.

The motivation for the initial attack on Shahin, both at the time and even until today, remains unclear and should be understood as part of a series of usually minor confrontations between Shahin and the west London group running throughout their time at college. The feud seems to have its roots, perhaps rather predictably, in Shahin's involvement with a Pakistani young woman from west London, which upset the local young men and caused a lot of backbiting between the two factions. Shahin explained:

> *Shahin*: I had a fight with one of them, this was in my second year . . . he was talking to [my girlfriend] and like this was during summer, some mela in Streatham or something, and I see him that day and he didn't want to talk to me. I was talking to him and he was just walking away, and I goes, 'Look man, it's just me and you now, we can sort this out.' He didn't want to sort it out and like I hit him. I hit him over the head with a bottle.
>
> *Claire*: Because he was talking to your girlfriend?
>
> *Shahin*: Yeah . . . I followed him to the tube station and I goes, 'You can talk to a girl, why can't you talk to me like that?' You know what I mean? And his friends were there as well and they didn't do nothing and when the doors of the train closed he went, 'yeah, I'm going to come back for you'. And then it was about four weeks later he came back. There was about twelve or thirteen of them.

Although it is undoubtedly true that the element of personal competition and sexual jealousy is a significant factor in this series of events, these tensions need to be read in relation to wider understandings of gender, ethnicity, territory and community. Issues of 'community', sexuality and the policing of gender relations will be considered in more detail in the following chapter; here, however, it is worth noting both the inscription and dislocation of group and territorial boundaries around the claiming of the female body. Shahin's girlfriend thus becomes placed as a symbol of both collective identity and its transgression – peer group boundaries are thus at once formed around and subverted by the control and ownership of 'its' women. Significantly, there is a disjunction in this process of claiming between ethnicity and territory – Shahin's girlfriend was Pakistani while the main protagonists in the attack are, like Shahin himself, Bengali in origin.

Both the original incident and the subsequent events should then more properly be read as an encounter between young men, with the young woman placed more as an emblem of status than a motivating cause. More than this, the encounters were between groups of young men – the confrontation of territorially imagined collectivities rather than disgruntled individuals. In the weeks after the attack on Shahin, particularly, action was structured around the imagination of a territorial formation of 'community' centred crucially on the collective identification and responsibility of the peer group. Individuals were then equated with particular groups and with specific areas and the response to the assault was predicated on this collective/territorial basis. Both alliance and conflict were structured around this articulation and were justified through the appeal to group responsibility and 'reputation'. The attack on Shahin was, then, also an attack on the Stoneleigh group and on their reputation – defence was necessitated as much as a symbolic gesture of strength as an expression of righteous anger. By the same logic, an attack on any member of Azmul or Rahul's circle of friends was a valid retribution on the perpetrators themselves – although it was not a sufficient response, as the belated revenge on Rahul illustrates. In the course of subsequent events, alliances were also forged with the north London group on the same territorial basis, forming against an oppositional community that included both west London and Luton.[23]

Despite this rather abstracted description, it is worth noting that these connections – both for and against – were premised on established personal networks. Just as the attack on Shahin was not random, but from known antagonists, similarly the alliance with north London was facilitated through personal connections with individuals from the area. These were formulated through college and social links but also through longer established friendships. Humzah, for example, had previously lived in that part of north London and still had friends and relations there, whereas the Stoneleigh group and the north London group had been involved in other fights together. Interestingly, Shahin told me that on earlier occasions he and his friends had helped Azmul and Rahul in a fight against other west London groups:

We used to see them in raves and that, two, three years ago – we actually helped them once in a fight in the Hippodrome. This was when there was a fight between Bengalis and Sikhs and I think it started off from then . . . all the Bengalis in the Hippodrome got together, so they actually knew us from then.

The boundary between friend and foe then was not always a clear one, with groups shifting status over time, performing alliance or opposition according to the situation. More than this, interaction was structured through networks of known individuals and contacts, mediating and translating any straightforward territorial basis. As I have argued elsewhere (Alexander, 1998), this marks the definition of 'community' formulated through conflict. In particular, it functions through the confrontation of perceived 'peers' – of equals, whether allies or opponents;

peer group can then signify either friends or foes within a particular social location.

If peer group can be used to circumscribe a wider set of social interactions, outside the more closely knit notions of territory and beyond the articulation of 'friendship', it is also true that the performance of local notions of community, peer group and friendship in this encounter was equally fraught. Thus, not all of the Stoneleigh young men were involved in the reprisals – the younger groups being excluded by virtue of age, whilst some members of the oldest group, including Bilal and Aklak absented themselves from the proceedings. It was, in fact, at this point that tensions between these groups became explicit in the project itself and a number of these young men soon stopped attending club sessions altogether. It was then a smaller configuration of the older lot, based on personal friendship and companionship with Shahin, who took up the fight on his behalf.[24] It was for this reason that Zohar, who was otherwise a mild and gentle young man, averse to any form of conflict, took part in finding the addresses of the attackers over the following weeks; and it was mainly for this reason – for loyalty – that the others became involved. Humzah thus recalled of the initial attack:

> I went to the hospital and I could see he was like damaged. There was blood everywhere and I couldn't look at him. I looked at him for a minute . . . I knew what he was thinking and what he was saying. (interview, 5 October 1996)

Later in the interview, he put it more simply: 'I didn't know how to show my face to Shahin . . . if I didn't do nothing'.

Perhaps the most extraordinary example of this loyalty is demonstrated by the actions of Mustafa, who the following year assumed responsibility on behalf of the group for the attack on Rahul. His motivation in the aftermath of the attack was to protect his friends, especially Shahin, who was about to begin a law degree at university. Mustafa then put his friend's wellbeing, and that of Shahin's family (especially his mother), above his own; interestingly, he was especially concerned that Shahin's ambitions to become a barrister should not be damaged by the fallout from the events.

Conclusion

The discussion above has focused primarily on the imagination of peer group in which ethnicity has been a primary, if not exclusive, marker of collective identification and action. Where a defining common-sense feature of 'gang' identity is the belief in rigid and absolute affiliation, 'the Asian Gang' provides a double inscription of these notions through the evocation of naturalized ideals of 'cultural difference'. This chapter has attempted to show how these fictions of community are themselves fractured and translated through alternative performances around age, gender, territory, history, geography and personality. It is important to stress, however, that peer group identities need not privilege ethnicity as a motivating force and that other axes of identity often proved equally potent in both formulating and transcending peer group boundaries.

This reimagination of community as extended peer group was clearly demonstrated in the aftermath of the incident involving Faruk and the African-Caribbean young men from Clifton described in Chapter 4. A day after the initial encounter, a number of young men from Clifton returned to the Stoneleigh Estate looking for revenge. Unable to find any of the Bengali young men, the Clifton group accosted a mixed group of black, Asian and white young men, who lived on a neighbouring estate but were unfortunate enough to be on the Stoneleigh at the time. Unable to receive the satisfaction they desired, they attacked Jason, a white young man, inflicting head injuries that kept him in hospital for several days. The next day the Clifton group returned again and this time caught up with Khalid, who had not been involved in the earlier incident, but was Asian and on the Stoneleigh and unable to run fast enough to get away. They beat Khalid with bricks and a pick axe, leaving several nasty lesions on his back, although his leather jacket prevented worse injury. Over the next few days it was rumoured that a large group from Clifton were to descend on the Stoneleigh Estate and during a general club session one Tuesday evening a large number of young men gathered apparently (though not explicitly) in expectation of the onslaught (which, as usual, never happened). What struck me was the number and range of young men who had shown up in defence of their friends and their estate. Not only was a large group of Bengali young men of all ages (many of whom had disappeared off the estate in recent times) present, but there were Chinese friends of Khalid's from his estate, and many black young men from the Stoneleigh and the neighbouring estate, as well as black, Asian and white friends of Jason.

Throughout these events, as with the Shahin incident, peer group was fused with territory to subsume these conflicts' more individualistic origins and create area-based allegiances and antagonisms. However, it is significant that ethnicity was not a mobilizing force here, except perhaps during the attack on Khalid. Rather, individuals were constructed primarily on an area basis and constructed themselves into a complex network of motivations and loyalties which transcended simple lines of friendship, peer group, ethnicity, age or, indeed, area (though not gender), welding a temporary, but undoubtedly compelling, defensive force.

It is nevertheless true that on a day-to-day level peer group formations were at once simpler and more complex, more coherent and yet also more fluid, more clearly bounded and more individuated, certainly less dramatic yet no less compelling. What Mustafa's actions, in particular, demonstrate most dramatically and poignantly to me is the affective power of friendship ties and loyalty, which survive the many transformations and occasional tensions of his peer group. What emerges from the previous discussion is then two opposing movements – towards change, fragmentation and dispersal, but also towards endurance, solidarity and belonging. While perhaps not reconcilable descriptively or theoretically, these two movements nevertheless co-exist in a creative tension, marking at once continuity and change, sameness and difference, safety and danger. It is certainly true that the formations described above have themselves necessarily undergone further change: the little ones have left school, moved on to work and college and their circle of friends has fractured, first into opposing factions and later into loose clusters of confidantes and passing acquaintants; the older groups have dispersed further into a more occasional network of long-time friends and selected companions. If the boundaries of these peer groups have become less visible and less coherent, it is nevertheless true that the connections and the sentiment remain intact, and the space for performance, for re-imagination and for reclamation is always present.

What is clear, moreover, is that notions of 'gang' identity, formulated around absolutist notions of identity and belonging, together with the conflation of ethnicity, gender and territory in the invention of the alienated 'other', exist more as convenient fiction than reality. The imagination of peer group and the performance of friendship are at once more complex, textured and subtle, and stubbornly resilient, more exacting and compelling, and more important than such notions allow. More than this, as the discussion above demonstrates, the imagination of the peer group is inseparable from wider notions of community, of which it forms one aspect. It is to these broader alliances and alternative performances that I now turn.

Notes

1 Performance is used here as drama and enactment.

2 The 'little ones' refer to Humzah, Shahin and others who form part of the present study's 'older lot'. This ambiguity reflects partly a difference in standpoint but also a shift in status from junior to senior members. The interaction of age barriers and responsibilities will be considered in the next chapter.

3 Ismat was a more marginal member of the group at this time, mainly because he attended a different school and was often not part of the events taking place with his friends.

4 Ifti told me that Adil had grown up with them on the estate, although he had more recently moved away, and that his family had close ties with Bengali families in the area. Adil drifted away from the group during the troubles of their final two years in school and eventually disappeared.

5 This situation was very different at the time of interview, when Humzah had drawn away from the group. However, he was unwilling to discuss the reasons for this and has since rebuilt bridges with at least some of his friends on Abbey Street.

6 Reading the last chapter, Humzah, for example, was unhappy with some of the criticisms of his friends that he voiced at this time; for this reason, many of the comments made do not feature in the present discussion.

7 Football was an important arena in which barriers of ethnicity/community were transcended and one of the few occasions when non-Bengalis joined the group.

8 Gender relations will be considered in Chapter 6.

9 I chose this name after famous Bollywood actor Salman Khan, in recognition of this young man's dreams of superstardom.

10 Malik spent some time working in restaurants in Wales and then returned to Bangladesh, where he was recently married. He occasionally visits Yasmin and myself in the project but has never returned to the estate.

11 Two other young men from the Amersham Estate. Shamim is also Malik's cousin, but continued to be part of the group, at least in school. This would suggest that Absul's position was more a personality and 'respect' issue than a simple area-based hostility.

12 Such positions did not of course remain static, but were constantly shifting and being reinvented according to situation, opportunity and occasion.

13 Being around to take part in daily activities was considered an important aspect of group loyalty – those such as Adil and even Mohammed, who were not around for trips and so forth were the more marginal members of the group.

14 Indeed, I have a special fondness for Enam, who early on in my research was vocal in his support of me to some of the older young men. On one occasion, during a disagreement with Bilal, Enam defended me, telling the older young man I was 'safe'.

15 Restaurant work is read as stereotypical Bengali employment and seen as the ultimate sign of personal failure, although many of the older lot did work in this service for differing amounts of time.

16 Others, such as Ismat and Mohammed have drifted away but plan to return next year.

17 Humzah did indeed give up college soon afterwards, although it is unlikely that he would lay the blame on his friends. By so doing, I lost a bet with Zohar that Humzah would, this time, see out his year of studies.

18 Khalid has since moved into playwork and also works as a teaching assistant in a local primary school. He has undergone a range of training in playwork and youth work as part of a local youth training initiative.

19 The first draft of this chapter included an extended discussion of this group's dynamics and tensions, which Khalid asked me to remove.

20 Frustrated/angry.

21 Some aspects of these encounters have been recounted in 'Re-imagining the Muslim community' in *Innovations*, No. 11, Vol. 4, 1998, pp. 439–50.

22 The young men were apparently waiting for the police to carry out an identity parade before making this trip which, at least to my knowledge, never took place.

23 The week after the initial attack, a group from north London – friends of Shahin's fellow victim – arrived at the SAYO project to meet with Shahin and discuss reprisals. Although a joint expedition was planned, it never took place and the groups acted independently over the following weeks.

24 It is worth noting that on some occasions, including the later attack on Rahul, some African-Caribbean schoolfriends of Shahin's were also involved, again mediating the assertion of absolute peer group identifications.

–6–

Brothers

In October 1997, only weeks into their first year of A-level studies, a number of the little ones were involved in a fight with a group of local Bengali young men at the north London Further Education College that they all attended. Tension had been building over the previous weeks and the conflict started early in the day when some of the local young men began to insult and jostle Jamal. Once college was over, this group, swollen with support from friends from their area, waited outside the college gates for Jamal and about twelve of them attacked him, then turning on his friends, Hanif, Sayeed, Ismat and Liton, as they came to his defence. Jamal escaped more serious injury only by flagging down a passing car, whose driver, it later transpired, was a cousin of Adil, one of Jamal's former schoolfriends. The others made their escape by bus and returned to the Stoneleigh Estate bearing several bruises, a gashed lip, a cut eye and a chipped tooth as testament to the encounter.

As with many such similar incidents, some of which were discussed in the previous chapter, the salience of peer group formation in this skirmish is clearly evident. The conflict was, then, internal to a peer group, broadly defined by age and gender (and also, in this case, by ethnicity) and the motivation for the fight seems to have been based in the intersection of this social field with a localized notion of territory and control. Although the Stoneleigh young men were unclear about the trigger, it was speculated that the tension originated in the north London group's jealousy of Jamal's popularity with the young women at the college, although this was never explicitly stated. The correlation of area-based chauvinism, sexual competition and an imagined peer group served to create an arena within which competing notions of community were enacted; at once a local/territorial notion of 'insiders' and 'outsiders', a performance of sexual ownership linked to highly gendered perceptions of 'community' and the establishment of a community-through-conflict based on shared age sets, gender and environment (the college). The initial attack on Jamal was then the articulation of peer group concerns centred around the notion of territory, friendship and ownership; the widening of the attack onto Jamal's friends was similarly legitimated through the extension of this matrix of alliances and loyalties to his circle of friends and, by extension, to the Stoneleigh Estate itself. By the same token, Hanif and the others responded to the attack on Jamal firstly, and immediately, as friends, but later as a broader peer group clearly located within the estate. Offers of help came at once from Jamal's wider peer group, including Ifti, Enam and others who had moved on to work or to other colleges and had started to drift away from their former school-friends.

In the following days and weeks, however, the response to the attack came not from this group but from two alternative sources. The first of these was the intervention of Ibrahim, a Bengali young man who had grown up and still lived in the area of north London where the college was situated and had strong links with his peers in the local community. Ibrahim was also a cousin of Yasmin and, through her, had spent the previous summer working for the SEPA project as a volunteer playworker, when he had established links with Jamal, Hanif and the other junior members of the SAYO project. After the attack on Jamal, Ibrahim offered to act as mediator between the two peer groups and in subsequent weeks opened a dialogue aimed at resolving the situation. Ibrahim[1] thus straddled the boundaries of the opposing factions and was able to occupy a position of limited trust with both – a position strengthened by his relationship to Yasmin, who herself was part of the same north London community and had strong personal links with both areas.

At the same time as Ibrahim's intervention, dialogue was also opened at another level. This was initiated by Shahin, Hanif's older brother, who had been called after the attack and who assumed responsibility for the protection of his younger brother and his friends. Gathering a number of the older lot together in their role as 'elders' of the estate, Shahin travelled to north London to meet with the older brothers of the attacking group, to discuss the events and, hopefully, prevent further incidents. It was subsequently agreed by these older groups that hostilities would end and that this tenuous ceasefire would be guaranteed by the 'elders' of both communities.

This intervention by Shahin functioned on two significant, and interconnected, levels. Firstly, within Shahin's peer group, both in mobilizing his circle of friends from the estate and in using long-established ties of friendship with the group in north London. As was noted in the last chapter, these ties had been forged through college, clubs and other social events, and also through shared struggles against other groups. Indeed, it was these same young men who had offered assistance after the attack on Shahin by Azmul and Rahul. Secondly, and perhaps more significantly, the intervention was structured through notions of family and community – a hierarchy of responsibility and authority that transgressed peer group identifications. Shahin's role was premised crucially on his position as *bhaya* (older brother), not only to his younger brother Hanif, but also to all Hanif's friends. By extension, Shahin's wider peer group also stood as *bhayas* to Hanif himself and to all the younger members of their local community, both male and female, with the duties of protection and care that this entailed. Moreover, in his position as friend and contemporary of his north London peers, Shahin also stood, provisionally, as *bhaya* to his brother's attackers and was able to use this position of authority and respect to negotiate a settlement, particularly through establishing a fictive kin association – a bond of brotherhood – that enabled and constrained the younger groups to cease hostilities (however unwillingly) without loss of credibility on either side.

A number of dynamics within this encounter are worth highlighting. Firstly, the position of Shahin with the north London assailants was contingent not on an unmediated sense of ethnicity or community, but specifically on his ties with his north London peers. Secondly, Shahin's role as 'brother' did not function within either his immediate circle of friends or the wider peer group, although these peer group ties legitimated and sanctioned his authority *across* age sets. Thirdly, the intervention by the older groups in the dispute effectively placed the younger combatants in a position of obligated conformity – to continue the conflict would be to disrespect the older groups of both communities who had assured its resolution. Fourthly, and by the same token, the failure of the older groups to control the actions of their younger brothers would be read as a sign of disrespect to their corresponding peer groups and could lead to an escalation of the conflict, although now at a 'higher' level. Either way, matters no longer rested with the initial protagonists of the incident, who now stood as the subjects of legislation rather than the vanguards of action. Fifthly, it is important to note the enactment of family and community links across these peer groups and age sets. This can be seen not only in Shahin's reponse, and that of his circle of friends, but also in Ibrahim's links with Yasmin who was part of the north London community and who also knew a number of the older men in the area. Yasmin thus stood in the position of *apa* (older sister) to both sets of young men and was able to use this position, with its linkages of respect, authority and protection, to influence events backstage. Humzah had also lived in the area for several years and still had family there, while Shahin himself was a well known figure locally. Indeed it was reportedly commented by one of Jamal's assailants that 'had he known Hanif was Shahin's brother he would never have got involved'.

The relationship between peer group formation, family and community is a complex one and cannot be easily fitted into neat categories and predicted outcomes. In this incident, as with the theft discussed at the beginning of Chapter 5, the articulation of bonds of authority and responsibility mediated and eventually overtook the bounds of peer group loyalty. It would be misleading, then, to view peer group identities as autonomous and self-absorbed, as apart from wider processes of community formation and imagination, just as it would be misleading to pretend either that peer group bounds are coterminous with community boundaries or that familial loyalties and hierarchies can completely control or define other forms of identification. Thus, although Shahin's intervention above served to mute hostilities between the younger groups, it would be naïve to suggest that tensions did not remain and did not threaten to explode despite these constraints.

Where Chapter 5 focused on peer group formation, change and alliance the present chapter explores the role of family and community in mediating these identities. In particular, it looks at 'brothers' – at the articulation of authority, hierarchy and respect between the peer groups and the relationship to wider notions of community, howsoever variously imagined. The chapter takes issue both with simplistic holistic notions of 'community' and with the current fascination with Asian youth subcultures – the new 'Asian cool' – which reifies hybridity and commodified rebellion at the expense of continuity and contestation. It also implicitly critiques unscrutinized assertions of patriarchal overdetermination in the formulation of Asian, particularly Muslim, masculinities, by exploring the shifting and contested notions of respect and gender hierarchy. The chapter focuses first on relationships of ethnicity, authority and masculinity between 'brothers', exploring notions of family and community encapsulated in the performance of 'respect'. It then turns to the role of gender, sexuality and power in the discourse around 'sisters'.

Of Brothers . . .

On the evening of the cricket World Cup Final between Pakistan and Australia (20 June 1999),[2] another titanic cricketing clash took place on the Stoneleigh Estate. The match was between the older lot and the little ones, a nine-a-side, three-innings tournament, which lasted for nearly four hours. The challenge had been made a week earlier, coming from several weeks of intense cricketing practice in a local park and it attracted a considerable crowd of spectators, comprising mainly local Bengali young men of all ages, including the teenies (thirteen to fifteen year olds), several slightly bemused black young men who were passing and stopped from curiosity, and myself, who had brought refreshments. The atmosphere was good natured and affectionate, but intense, particularly as the little ones – the definite underdogs – drew the first innings. Unlike the World Cup final itself, the favourites were here triumphant – and jubilant – while the little ones merely shrugged philosophically and vanished onto the estate.

The match was a significant event, partly because it brought together a large number of the Stoneleigh young men – as it had on many summer evenings in the preceding weeks – who had otherwise gone their separate ways and who mainly no longer attended the project. It thus embodied a spontaneous expression of 'community' that existed outside institutional structures and beyond family organizations; a visible and informal articulation of 'belonging'. It also manifested the boundaries of this community-within-a-community – all those present were young men, almost all were Bengali, there were no older members of the community, no children and, apart from myself, no women. At the same time, within these boundaries, there were clear divisions of age and peer group status; the match itself was structured with the older young men competing against their younger brothers and the spectators were similarly grouped around age and friendship groups. Unlike other evenings, the Teenies were excluded from the game (to much muttered grumblings and quiet criticism of the style and skills on display), and tensions between them and the older groups were occasionally manifest, with the little ones particularly complaining that the younger boys were 'feisty' and 'lacked respect'.[3] On the other hand, links across these barriers were also apparent, not only within the match itself but in the presence and support of onlookers of all ages; in the time taken by S. Ahmed to talk to and encourage the younger boys; in Ismat's younger brother's implicated joy and embarrassment at the older's successes and failures; in the – perhaps somewhat self-satisfied – concern of the older lot not to humiliate the little ones *too much* when their third innings total reached 124 runs and seemed it would go on forever.

It is in these everyday, unexceptional acts of social interaction, rather than their more dramatic counterparts discussed earlier, that constructions of authority, respect and community are created, traversed and transformed. It was, indeed, these taken-for-granted performances that first caught my attention and held my fascination most during the research, and which continue to intrigue, sometimes bewilder and occasionally amuse me. For the young men themselves, these structures were a recognized but naturalized part of their daily lives, a facet of 'how things are' or 'how things are done' that was accepted, but went generally unremarked and was, for the most part, unexplainable. For me they constituted a minefield of '*dos*' and '*don'ts*' which I observed and became enmeshed in, both personally (due to gendered expectations and the pursuit of an easy life) and in trying to avoid implicating the young men through my own ignorant comments or actions.

To some extent the present chapter is an exercise in navigating these pitfalls – by making visible and explicit dynamics, opinions and activities that are either left implicit or masked through careful negotiation, silence and discrete mutual distancing, the material explored here runs the risk of exposing positions hitherto overlooked (by default or design) to scrutiny, reaction and, perhaps even retribution, amongst the young men. Humzah once commented to me that he was looking forward to reading about the little ones because he knew so little about them; the present chapter, in particular, has to negotiate the provision of this knowledge (however mundane or minor it may seem) and its implications. More than this, although the little ones know much more about the older lot's activities, which are less shielded by the constraints of 'respect', the issue of articulation – of making this knowledge *visible* – is potentially equally problematic and uncomfortable, for them and for me. Although my instinct is to declare an amnesty for all – myself included – in what follows, and hope for the best, the reality remains to be seen.

The boundaries of the SAYO 'community' were clearly manifest during sports and other social events, although sometimes in unexpected ways. Until relatively recently, the older lot were reluctant to engage the little ones in competition, considering them too young, inexperienced and generally untalented to be taken seriously.[4] The little ones were, for their part, initially disinclined to approach the older lot, preferring to give way to the senior members in any confrontation, sporting or otherwise. This would give rise to situations where brothers would refuse to play on the same football team and would avoid tackling each other in opposition, or where the younger group would yield up pool games or table tennis to older members on demand. It was for these reasons that Yasmin decided to split the evening sessions between junior and senior members, allowing the younger group to develop confidence and skills away from the constraints imposed – consciously or not – by the older groups' presence. The senior members, to their credit, used this time to re-evaluate their responsibilities toward their younger brothers and over the following months and years many of these barriers were removed, or at least mediated. As S. Ahmed commented:

> I wasn't happy, because then we'd just get one day, Friday, and they get more days, but then I thought, what's this, they're little, they need more time and I know like if they were to do something and we are here, it can't be private because we are their older brothers, so they like have respect for us. (interview, 6 November 1996)

As S. Ahmed makes clear, the relationships across age groups were defined by a dual axis of rights and obligations – a marking of both distance and familiarity that constituted a complex web of prohibitions, responsibilities and allowances, which were at once hierarchical and profoundly implicated in relations of negotiated mutuality. Over the time I worked at the SAYO project, these relations underwent modification, eliding some of their more rigid manifestations – a recognition perhaps of the move towards shared 'adult' status, along with the remarcation of divisions with the Teenies, who now occupy the 'junior' position. As the football team developed and particularly as the first fashion show proved such a success, the groups reintegrated on more 'equal' terms – a mutuality finally publically demonstrated in the second *Independence Day* fashion show which combined both junior and senior walks and – perhaps our major triumph – the 'brother's walk' which brought together the three sibling age groups on stage in a public statement of solidarity, mutual respect and affection.

These changes signalled less a breaking of boundaries that a reformulation, some of the contours of which are considered below. It is worth noting, however, that these performances of respect work both as a marker of distinction from others and of continuity with the wider imagined community. Playing football one evening in the schoolgrounds during a mixed-age session of the project, Cavanagh[5] kicked the football onto the roof of one of the school buildings. The match ground to a halt as the young men watched Cavanagh scale the building to retrieve the ball. Sher Khan, watching with me from the sidelines, leant towards me and observed: 'see, now if he'd been Bengali, one of them would have fetched that for him'. As if to reinforce the point, when S. Ahmed also kicked the ball onto the roof several minutes later, Shafiq ran without hesitation or request to collect it. The performance of 'respect' was then here closely bound up with notions of 'community' defined through a combination of ethnicity, territory and familiarity. Although the young men had all known Cavanagh for many years and liked him, in this situation he was positioned as an 'outsider' and therefore exempted from the obligations of 'respect'. S. Ahmed, by contrast, was considered an elder of the community, a *bhaya*, and the respect paid to him by the little ones amounted almost to an instinctual response. The imagery of family was used then to define the boundaries of an ethnicized communal identity, which could be used to include those from outside the estate, such as Farhan, or exclude those who lived or worked locally, such as Cavanagh, and even those, such as Amitabh, who were Asian but not Bengali. By the same token, the young men could choose to include individuals within this fictive kin network irrespective of these requirements and by general unspoken consensus. It is significant that gender was not a primary definer of this status: as already mentioned, Yasmin was positioned as *apa* to the young men, though she lived in north London, while the same duties and care were extended to me over time by virtue of my closeness to the young men in the project.

It is important to view this boundary creation as part of a wider matrix of community allegiances and alliances. As noted in Chapter 5, although the young men perceived themselves as often positioned at the margins of the local Bengali community, they also placed themselves at its heart in terms of responsibilities to, and protection of, its members. Respect was thus due to, and legitimated by, a network of family ties rooted locally and spanning beyond this territorial base to a wider imagined community. S. Ahmed thus told me that his position as *bhaya* to the little ones had its origin in his relationship with their older brothers and, by extension, with their families:

> I know most of their older brothers, I know their parents as well; they know me really well and like all these Asian things – it's like respect that they have.

Despite their misgivings about community 'gossip', all the young men, whether locally-based or not, told me that it was important to show respect to older people in the community – men and women. Humzah thus explained:

> In our culture you have to respect the elders, that's the rule – it's like a *big* thing. Even if they're wrong, you have to. (interview, 5 October 1996)

Ifti similarly told me:

> If you're mucking around over there and they walk past you and you saw them . . . that will be like a smack in the face, you don't do them stuff. (interview, 1 October 1996)

Ironically, this in turn meant that the young men were in no position to challenge the dominant perceptions outlined in Chapter 5. As Shakiel noted:

> They just get that media thingy, that you hang around there doing nothing, but you know they could be working all day, just come out for a little chat with their friends and that, and they don't see it that way. We could say that about *them* when they come out of the Mosque and just hang around in the street all day, but you can't say that to your older ones can you? (interview, 18 November 1996)

The performance of respect, as argued earlier, is a two way process, structured on a hierarchical but reciprocal series of obligations which positioned each individual and group in relation to their older and younger 'kin' within a wider community. For the older lot, respect was payable to the adult community, and their role towards the little ones was articulated in terms of a combination of protection on the one hand and discipline on the other. This was in turn inseparable from the performance of respect from the little ones, which endowed them with the status and responsibilities of *bhayas*. Humzah told me, 'I know they do respect me, but mostly it's like I protect them a lot. I protect them all' (interview, 5 October 1996). Similarly, the expression of authority without the concomitant duty of care was rendered illegitimate. S. Ahmed told me:

> *S. Ahmed*: I look after them, that's true. When something goes wrong they will come to me or someone else, tell us what's happening. Like when Jamal had a fight, Hanif told me that Jamal had a fight in school – the next day he's telling me. It's like they tell us what's going on and that. And like sometimes I'll catch them – once I caught them with some girls, all of them run except for Ifti, Humzah's little brother, and Enam. They stayed, so I caught them ... I beat them up and I sent them home but they wouldn't say nothing. They could have turned around and said 'you do the same thing, why can't we do it?' you understand, but they didn't do that.
>
> *Claire*: Why do you think they didn't say that?
>
> *S. Ahmed*: Because the one thing is the respect and another thing, I know their brothers as well. (interview, 6 November 1996)

S. Ahmed's account highlights a number of important features: firstly, his role as protector of the younger group; secondly, his corresponding role as disciplinarian; thirdly, the acceptance of these roles by the younger group out of 'respect'; fourthly, the unequal nature of this encounter, in particular the recognition of double standards of behaviour; fifthly, the connected, but implicit, notion of the greater *visibility* of the older group's activities vis-à-vis the *invisibility* of the younger group (which also connects to the comparative lack of knowledge of the little ones by the older lot); sixthly, the relationship between visibility and disrespect – thus S. Ahmed commented on his encounter with Ifti and Enam above that 'they was wrong [because] like I caught them *blatantly*'; lastly, the grounding of the duties of respect in the relationship of brothers – both 'real' (S. Ahmed's friendship with their brothers) and fictive, 'we're all like brothers, all of us; it's good to have responsibilities'. It is these later relationships – between friends and between brothers – which provide the parameters of this community of 'respect'. As noted in the previous chapter, respect for brothers carries with it the incumbent obligation of respect for his friends, while friendship brings with it the concomitant unstated demand for respect for brothers. Similarly, the duties and authority of protection and care are more often rooted in family connections mediated through friendship links – either as a friend's brother or a brother's friend – than in any more abstract imagination of community. Ismat explained:

> It's the way of respecting them, because they're our older brothers, you have to respect them. Even though some of us might not respect them, but we respect them in other ways, because it might be our friend's brother, so because we are hanging around with our friend, we have to respect his brothers. (interview, 11 October 1996)

Mohammed thus noted of his circle of friends:

> To my brothers and sisters, everyone I know they will try to set a good example . . . My friends, some of them tell me 'if you see my brother out, tell him to go home'. Now when I see him, I just give them a slap and say 'go home, you plonker' and like they don't really mind. And it's the same with my brothers and sisters. (interview, 24 October 1996)

For the little ones, these relationships had clear cut duties and expectations in relation to the older groups, 'we keep out of their way and they keep out of our way, or they may tell us to do things – basically they keep a look out [for us]' (Ismat, interview, 11 October 1996). Ifti similarly commented of their relationship to the younger children on the estate:

We take care of them, like see how they're going on and if they've got trouble we tell them to fight, defend themselves . . . If they're like losing or something, we stop it and tell them to go home. (interview, 28 September 1996)

It is important to note that not all of the young men articulated these responsibilities in the same way. Zohar, for example, told me that although he was happy to help and support the younger group, he chose not to adopt the role of disciplinarian, particularly over the always contentious issues of smoking and girls: 'We done that ourselves . . . They're over 16, if you smoke, you smoke . . . They see me, so what makes them so different that they can't?' (interview, 22 October 1996). Hanif likewise drew the boundaries rather differently than some of his friends, 'I would look after them, even though they're not my own brothers. It's just them lot [his peer group] go a bit overprotective of them' (interview, 26 September 1996). For Hanif, the boundary between care and discipline were sometimes too blurred, leading to the type of bullying which was characterised in the events leading up to Malik's confrontation with Salman discussed in Chapter 5. It is interesting that both Hanif and Zohar are the youngest in their respective families and although they were subject to, and performed, appropriate forms of respect to their older siblings, they themselves viewed the bonds of respect due more loosely than some of their contemporaries. Zohar thus told me of his older brother, 'he's like the head of the house, whatever he says goes, isn't it?' (interview, 22 October 1996), but stated that he was himself more flexible in his attitude towards his nephew, Shay, a friend of Khalid:

I don't expect him to give me all that respect as being his uncle because it's hard out there . . . I know a lot of Bengalis, like my friends, will say 'oh, he's your nephew, you shouldn't allow him to do that' but I think, I say 'it's up to you to think' . . . I can't tell him something. I can act that older [role] but it won't make a difference, he'll still go behind my back again.

Implicit in Zohar's comments is a distinction between his role and responsibilities as Shay's 'real' uncle and the roles and rights of his wider circle of friends towards his nephew. Thus although articulated as 'brothers', there was a recognizable qualitative difference between 'real' and 'fictive' kin networks.[6] Humzah, for example, told me that although he helped Ifti's friends whenever necessary he had different expectations of them: 'They respect me more than anyone . . . [but] I haven't been the big brother type. I have, but not like I've been to Ifti . . . I've been more free' (interview, 5 October 1996). Shahin similarly expressed his responsibilities solely in relation to his two younger brothers, Khalid and Hanif:

> For my younger brothers, I feel like I'm responsible for their wellbeing and everything ... I don't know if I'd call it a role model, it's just like you can call it that – like if I'm behaving in a bad way they might think, 'my brother's doing that, so I should be doing it as well'. (interview, 26 September 1996)

In Shahin's case, unlike Zohar's, setting a good example mainly involved distance and discretion – in not being *seen* by his younger brothers:

> Like when we're outside, if they see me somewhere they don't come, they stay a few yards, they don't really come within my group and . . . like if they're doing anything, it's in their own little space away from me.

The duty of care and protection can be seen then as largely inseparable from the maintenance of authority and discipline – two sides of the same familial coin – though differently weighted according to individuals, time and circumstance.[7]

On one occasion, Khalid was attacked[8] during a rave in east London, where he had gone with a number of his friends, including Shakiel and Ashraf. Khalid told me:

> It was near Cannon Street, and it was just total rubbish ... I was leaning against the wall with my leg on the wall and some boy walked past and moved my knee and I just looked at him; and after he went into the other room and I saw enough boys coming in and just looking at me ... That boy come up to me, yeah, he goes he wants to fight me ... Shakiel and that saying 'look, he don't want to fight you' and then after, I got up and there's a next bloke at the back – I didn't even see him. He's saying in Bengali 'Is it the one?' and he come out of the blue and he just punched me and then I think they started punching and they started pulling me out . . . [then] the same one that punched me first, suddenly he jumped in the air and whacked me with a belt, he whacked me about three or four times with a belt ... When they rushed me the first time I was like really angry, I was telling Shakiel to call my brother. I don't know why I did that, because it was like a split second thought, I just goes 'call my brother, call my brother', and I think one of them went and called my brother. And after that I hear my brother's here. (interview, 15 October 1996)

By this time the police had also arrived and Khalid's attackers had vanished into the local estates, and Shahin and his friends were unable to do anything. Perhaps partly because of this, Khalid then became the focus of Shahin's frustration and anger:

> By the time he got there he'd softened down, just kicked me in my leg and Salman and that stopped him, going 'what are you doing that for' and I went home in the car, and Salman and that's saying 'take him to hospital' and my brother goes 'no, let my mum see him first, let's see what he's going to say to my mum', and he was like shouting at me all the way through the car and Liaquot was going 'shut up Shahin you fool, leave him, leave him' and all this; and then I went home . . .
> *Claire*: So why was Shahin so angry with you?
> *Khalid*: Because it was in the rave.
> *Claire*: And you shouldn't have been there?
> *Khalid*: No.

Of this incident, Shahin told me:

> The thing that got me mad was that they were in some party or something and like when they phoned me up they said they went to Cannon Street to buy some meat! (interview, 3 October 1996)

Three connected dynamics are of particular significance to the present discussion: firstly, Khalid's almost instinctual reliance on his older brother for protection during the attack; secondly, Shahin's immediate response to this call and the coalescence – and confusion – of the roles of care and discipline in the aftermath of the incident (and which were accepted without question by Khalid himself); and thirdly, the intervention of Shahin's peer group in these events. The latter dynamic points to the more complex mediation of heirarchical relations in this encounter. Salman, Liaquot and the others were present as Shahin's friends and thus as Khalid's protectors, but they were able to use this role to intervene in the sibling relationship, notably on Khalid's behalf. In many instances, then, the fraternal blood relationship also facilitated a greater familiarity across the age groups with the wider circle of friends. On the one hand, boundaries of respect were more rigidly defined and enacted where 'real' brothers were involved and, on the other, these relations allowed for spaces of intimacy and ease with fictive brothers. It was noticeable, for example, that Hanif's interaction with Shahin and Khalid's peer groups was marked by greater warmth and mutual good humour than was afforded Hanif's friends. Khalid thus commented of his friends:

I reckon the way they treat my little brother is like different to what they treat the others . . . it's like they joke around and that, play around with him. (interview 15 October 1996)

The duties articulated by the older groups were not, of course, always interpreted or experienced in the same way by the little ones. As mentioned in the previous chapter, the younger group did not always regard the older young men uncritically, nor see them as role models – sometimes quite the opposite. In addition, a number of the little ones I interviewed resisted the idea that the older group were there as protectors, except as a last resort, preferring to sort out their own disputes whenever possible. This aspect was, indeed, something of a bone of contention amongst the little ones; as Hanif explained:

They think like, they always want to fight with the older ones – let's not sort it out, let's get the older ones to beat them up. It's like the boys are our age, we should deal with it ourselves. If they're bigger than us then why not get them, but if we can deal with it, deal with it. They're always getting the older ones into it. And they get a bit fed up thinking 'can't they do anything for themselves?' (interview, 10 October 1996)

It is important to recognize that the notion of 'fighting with' is actually lived out as 'fighting for', and that it was only on rare occasions that the young men of the SAYO project stood, regardless of age, side by side in any confrontation. Indeed the duties of protection necessitated also the exclusion of younger individuals from situations of conflict or potential harm.[9] Where peer groups constituted a first line of defence, they also strongly bounded the fields of confrontation; thus, when Shahin was attacked in Hammersmith and Khalid visited him in hospital, he told me:

I was just looking at him and thinking shit. I got really angry, but you can't really do nothing . . . I told him sometime once just for a joke or something, I said 'just say you're going up there to get them back, let me come with you' and he goes 'you fool'. (interview, 15 October 1996)

Paradoxically, Hanif expressed his concerns in terms not of part-icipation, but also of protection – this time of his older brothers by him 'I don't really like calling them; I don't really want them to get involved, because say the police get them for something, I'd feel inside it's because of me, innit?' (interview, 10 October 1996)

Hanif's comment points to the reciprocity of the relationship between the groups of Bengali young men on the Stoneleigh Estate; the exchange of ties of affection and care that underpinned the superficially top-down authoritarian structures, which validated and sustained them. As mentioned earlier, these duties of discipline and protection were themselves rooted in a notion of imagined community, which was recreated through the performance of responsibility on the one hand and 'respect' on the other. 'Respect', in particular, was articulated through minute, taken-for-granted formulations of behaviour that constituted a series of prohibitions, distances and silences automatically adhered to and, almost of necessity, invisible. Although over the past several years I have learned to recognize such structures and accommodate them almost as a matter of course, these complex manoeuvrings still fascinate and occasionally confuse me. The young men themselves found it difficult to express the rationale behind 'respect' although they could all recognize its concrete demands and demonstrations – it was, put simply, the way things were done. As Shahin told me, 'I think it's just the way the culture is' (interview, 26 September 1996). The most significant, and one of the most potent, symbols of 'respect' is smoking and it is mainly on this issue that the following discussion focuses.

In November 1998, Farhan, one of the SAYO project's workers, married. A number of the young men from the Stoneleigh Estate, along with Yasmin and myself, went to the wedding in east London, travelling in a three-car convoy. Each car divided almost automatically into separate peer groups, with Shahin and his friends in the lead car, Yasmin with Khalid and the middle group in the second car, and myself with the little ones bringing up the rear. As I struggled to keep up with Shahin's speed driving, the little ones lit up cigarettes and the discussion centred around who was going to 'twos' the others and, more urgently, whether or not they could be seen by Khalid from the car in front. At one point Ismat threw a cigarette butt from the car window and Hanif cussed him angrily for making so obvious a gesture. I pointed out that Khalid was probably more concerned whether Shahin could see him smoking in Yasmin's car than with what was going on behind him, and from Khalid's slightly nervous laughter when we arrived it seemed that this was a reasonable guess.

The issue of smoking was one of the most concrete examples of a wider notion of 'respect' and one that had powerful effects. It is worth noting, for example, that when the little ones expelled Malik from their group for disrespect to Salman, this was validated through the appeal to a more general disrespect symbolized by who he smoked with. This was read as a lack of regard for at once his immediate peer group, the older group and the larger Stoneleigh community.[10] Jamal told me:

I could choose to smoke around here if I wanted to, in front of everyone's parents, but if I'm smoking, even in front of my mates, like Sayeed . . . he gets the bad reputation; even though they'd be talking about me, they don't know me, so I wouldn't get the reputation. (interview, 10 October 1996)

As Jamal makes clear, smoking marks the boundaries of the immediate peer group, while 'not-smoking' defines the extent of the wider community of respect, though imagined strongly through a familial and territorial basis. It is significant that for Jamal these community limits are strongly tied to 'reputation', which in turn links to knowledge of the individual and hence to the individual's family: 'the thing is they don't know my parents, so it's OK for me.' It is also important that Jamal performs respect in these circumstances as part of his duties of friendship. He thus smokes with his friends and joins with them in 'not-smoking' as a sign of friendship and a symbol of respect to their families and their local community.[11] Smoking or 'not-smoking' needs then to be read against a broader backdrop of 'community' loyalties and obligations rooted strongly in family connections. As Hanif noted, 'most of it's to do with respect and that . . . it's like when your mum or someone finds out, it's like a bit shameful' (interview, 26 September 1996).

On a day-to-day basis, the main focus for issues of smoking (or not-smoking) were the various hierarchically structured peer groups and, indeed, a main indicator of individual or group status was who one chose to smoke with, or who one avoided. For the older lot, at least within the auspices of the project, smoking was less of an issue – they smoked openly and were only concerned that the younger groups did not smoke in front of them.[12] This was sometimes articulated in terms of the mixture of protection and discipline discussed above and of setting examples (whether good or bad was less clear). Shahin thus told me:

Actually I don't even smoke in front of my younger brothers . . . say like if me and my brother were in the room, I'm not going to like sit there smoking . . . because he might think 'he's doing it so I might as well'. (interview, 26 September 1996)

Humzah by contrast explained to me:

Humzah: Smoking is not good for you.
Claire: But you smoke though.
Humzah: But that's it – I don't want *him* [Ifti] to smoke . . . I don't want him to be like me. I didn't want him to get involved in anything. (interview, 5 October 1996)

More generally, however, smoking was seen as a symbol of the presence or absence of respect and consensus on the response was unequivocal:

Claire: What would you do if they did smoke in front of you?
Shahin: Beat them up. (interview, 26 September 1996)

The boundaries between the little ones and the older groups were clearly demarcated. Ismat told me:

None of us smoke in front of our older brothers, even if they're not our brothers but our brother's friends, we don't smoke in front of them . . . It's the way of respecting them. (interview, 11 October 1996)

The articulation of this respect led to often elaborate manoeuvring for space, where the little ones would disappear *en masse* at regular intervals during mixed club sessions and reappear looking slightly guilty, or lurk watchfully on street corners taking furtive drags on barely concealed cigarettes, ready to cast them aside at the first sign of the older groups' approach. On one occasion, Enam sat in a tree near the club building, where he had gone for a quiet cigarette, for nearly the whole session because the older group had arrived unexpectedly and he had been afraid they would see him and guess what he had been doing!

As Malik's expulsion clearly demonstrated, the younger group was particularly strict in policing the boundaries of respect within their group vis-à-vis their older brothers. Sayeed, for example, told me that responsibility for reprimanding Malik after his confrontation with Salman lay with him, as Malik's friend, rather than his older brother:

I should have done something instead of my brother because he was giving the lip to my brother and I should have said 'don't give the lip to my brother'. (interview, 5 November 1996)

Similarly, Absul was excluded from the group for failing to observe the bounds of respect, especially in regards to smoking. Faruk explained:

See our older brothers, yeah, it's like we can't smoke in front of them and things like that ain't it, so he like goes off with them and stuff, smoking and things, and like they think 'if he smokes the rest of them must smoke as well' ain't it, and then that's how we get caught. (interview, 22 October 1996)

The little ones were able to avoid implication in this disrespect by redrawing their boundaries and excluding Absul. Faruk commented, revealingly, 'our brothers don't know Absul, do they, so they can't say nothing'. Absul was then positioned as a stranger to the community and outside its restrictions (but also beyond its reach of care and protection). Age and ethnicity are not, then, in themselves sufficient factors for the expectation or attribution of respect, which is rooted in more personal relationships and family networks. Humzah, for example, told me that who he socialized with depended less on age than on the individual's connections with other members of the local community, which defined the forms of interaction:

Claire: If it was a friend of Ifti's, that would be different wouldn't it?
Humzah: That would be different because that's *his* friend and because its *his* friend, he will look to me as a big brother, because I'm his friend's big brother; so I can't really mix with him that much. But if he didn't know my brother, then it's a different case. (interview, 5 October 1996)

As with the duties of care and discipline, the performance of respect was inseparable from these more personal considerations. There was, for example, a distinction between those in the younger groups with older brothers and those without; the latter having, theoretically at least, more freedom to move across groups, mediating the forms of respect or ignoring them accordingly. Mohammed thus explained:

Some of them [his friends] have big brothers, so like when they're smoking and that you've got to hide and so. But for me it's like alright because sometimes I go round with the bigger groups and sit around and they don't say nothing, because like they know I ain't got a big brother, so like there's no-one to boss me about. But with the other lot, my friends, it's like they've always got to stay in corners and stay out of the way and so on. (interview, 24 October 1996)

Mohammed acknowledged, however, that the actual situation was less clear cut: firstly, because of his obligation to his friends; secondly, because of his acquisition of honorary *bhayas* such as Hashim, Mustafa and S. Ahmed, who assumed responsibility and care of him; and thirdly, because of his need for that older support base: 'As I don't have any older brothers, yeah, I do rely on them quite a lot.' Mohammed also told me that although he and Enam were ostensibly more free floating, a choice of allegiance was enforced and lines of respect were established accordingly:

I think of my friends, isn't it? I think if I smoke with them [the older lot] they might be thinking I might be smoking with them [the little ones] and I might be giving them the habits . . . [Enam] used to smoke with the older lots and then come with us and once we just told him, 'If you keep on doing that yeah you might as well hang around on your own because you know we don't like that' . . . so now if he does hang around with them, he's no-smoking, just quiet, talks and so on, but he don't smoke with them now.

The question of choice was then a constrained one, bounded part-icularly by the duties owed to friends but also by the demands of the local community and the needs of the individual for support. In practice, however, these choices were less clearly lived through, incorporating a series of exceptions and exclusions, which mediated and temporarily translated these seemingly absolute hierarchies. Within the SAYO project, for example, there were a number of freefloaters, moving between peer groups and withholding allegiance to any – and thereby exempting themselves from the duties of respect. Although these young men were generally perceived, if not with suspicion, at least with amusement and sometimes barely concealed contempt, they were an accepted feature of the community. Mujib, who is Khalid's age, spent his time primarily with the little ones, who tolerated him but paid him no tokens of respect; thus Ifti commented, 'he gets dissed by them [the older lot] he gets dissed by us' (interview, 1 October 1996). Similarly, Tarek, Shafiq's older brother, a married man in his late twenties with children, who used to spend his time with the senior group was also viewed as outside the bounds of respect.[13] Shakiel commented:

He's like coming on to thirty and he's hanging around with eighteen, nineteen year olds and he's got about four kids – I think that's stupid really . . . he still thinks he's a little kid and everything. (interview, 18 November 1996)

Humzah described Tarek:

the thing he's thinking is he's missed everything so he wants it. So we understand as well (interview, 5 October 1996).

The position of Tarek and Mujib points to the disjunction of age, peer group and the attribution of 'respect'; a potential disruption within the apparent coherence of the narration of community. While the attitude towards freefloaters seems to indicate at once a desire for coherence and an acceptance of its impossibility, it also makes tangible the contextual and malleable nature of group identification and the ordering of respect. This was reflected more widely through the patterns of smoking. Shakiel thus told me that he would on occasion smoke with Shahin and the older lot, though not when Khalid was present:

I did, or I do smoke with him [Shahin], Humzah, well, not all of them[14] . . . I did used to smoke with Shahin. I just thought it weren't right. He don't ask me not to, nothing like that; but I don't really do it no more. (interview, 18 November 1996)

Shakiel's greater familiarity stems from the time when he, Shahin, Humzah and the others formed part of the same peer group, while his redrawing of the boundaries of respect around smoking indicates the split in this group primarily – and most significantly – because of his friendship with Khalid. Similarly, Ashraf did smoke with some of the older lot though not, revealingly, with Shahin. To make matters more complicated, while smoking cigarettes was considered relatively unproblematic in these cases, smoking other substances was an altogether different issue. Khalid thus told me:

Shakiel does smoke with my brother . . . but like once Ashraf was smoking weed with Liaquot and that and my brother was there as well and Liaquot gave Ashraf a two's and Liaquot told Ashraf the next day that like Shahin was shouting, saying 'you might as well give it to my younger brother' . . . It's the same with Shakiel, I don't think Shakiel will smoke all that – he will smoke cigarettes but not the other. (interview, 15 October 1996)

Interestingly, Khalid also commented that while it was acceptable for the older lot to smoke tobacco in front of the younger groups, drugs were considered unacceptable – a source of potential disrespect from the younger men. Khalid said of Shahin:

I think he smokes weed and all that, and once I see him in the park burning up and I was walking past and he like hid it . . . He'd smoke in front of me, but that's like different; *ganga*, that's different to cigarette.

Shahin's reaction to Liaquot in this instance points to the reciprocal nature of these relationships of respect. Rather than constituting a simple trade off between top-down authoritarian structures for a bottom-up tribute of respect, the relationship proved a more complex and shifting dynamic. As already noted, not all the older group were figures of respect, and 'respect' was reconfigured according to time and circumstance (and substance). Relations of respect were then created mutually, and came with strings attached, for the older as well as the younger men. The emphasis on mutuality as a condition of respect was a common theme; as Faruk put it, 'you have to respect someone to get respect off them, innit?' (interview, 22 October 1996). Of the older lot, Ismat explained:

The way they treat us I like them, they treat us with respect. When we were young and all that they respect us, keep a look out for our backs, not to get in trouble and all that – even if we are in trouble they help us out, but most of the time I wouldn't like to get in trouble with them. (interview, 11 October 1996)

A strong contrast was drawn with the other older group, consisting of Bilal and Ismat's brother Aklak. Ifti told me:

See the older people, our brothers and them lot yeah, they give us respect, we give them respect back, but *them* lot [Bilal etc.], they just want respect from us, they don't give us respect back . . . They're right idiots. (interview, 1 October 1996)

This condemnation extended even to Aklak though friendship to Ismat precluded any public demonstration of disrespect, 'Ismat don't respect none of them except for his brother and he *has* to'.

Bilal, in particular, was prone to insisting that the younger groups, including the older lot, pay him the respect due simply by virtue of age. His failure to enact the obligations of respect, however, rendered his claim illegitimate, notably after his failure to protect Humzah's sisters from attack. Shahin told me:

I mean to get that respect man, you can't really say to someone 'respect me', you have to earn that respect. It's the way people see you, you can't just say to someone 'I want respect, you respect me' you've got to earn that respect and you have to give respect back to people as well to get respect – it's not that he's older than them so they've got to respect him. (interview, 26 September 1996)

Bilal's position as *bhaya* was then viewed as illegitimate and his demands as spurious. Faruk was harsh in his assessment: 'I reckon he's an idiot, a total idiot. He ain't saying nothing, don't know what to say' (interview, 22 October 1996). His quest for respect had, moreover, brought him into conflict with the older lot on a number of occasions:

He really picks on the little ones, he really picks on them, because all the time he had a fight, yeah . . . it was always about picking on someone little. Like S. Ahmed had a fight with him because like Bilal was hitting Shafiq and he [S. Ahmed] was going 'what you hitting a little one for, idiot, look at you, why you hitting someone younger than you' and that's why they had a fight.

Shakiel and Khalid took special delight in teasing and mocking Bilal during club sessions – what Shakiel saw as a fitting response to Bilal's lack of respect for them, 'they don't respect you that way either . . . and you think 'you idiot' . . . them lot are sad cases' (interview, 18 November 1996). Shahin summarized this reaction succinctly, 'he's just a joker; you look at him, you have to laugh' (interview, 26 September 1996).

If Bilal was effectively excluded from a 'community of respect', it is significant that the younger groups still paid formal lipservice to some aspects of this duty, notably in the observance of 'not-smoking' in Bilal's presence. The issue of the illegitimacy of claims of respect, particularly around smoking, were however also brought into play in other circumstances with individuals not so excluded. Ismat, for example, claimed that he would smoke with Ashraf, Faruk's brother, even if Faruk was there, though only at Ashraf's instigation: 'He makes me smoke with him, I don't know why – he knows that I smoke and he asks me for a cigarette and I sit down and smoke with him' (interview, 11 October 1996). At other times, however, and seemingly at whim, Ashraf would take issue with the younger group about smoking. On one occasion during a club session, Ashraf caught Hanif smoking and slapped him, claiming, firstly, that Hanif was disrespecting him and secondly, that as his brother's friend, he had the right to discipline him. Although Hanif did not respond to Ashraf, the little ones were generally agreed that Ashraf had overstepped the boundaries of respect. Hanif told me: 'The thing that got me angry was because he ain't nothing to me, innit? What gives him the right to come and punch me?' (interview, 26 September 1996). Hanif acknowledged his error on being seen by Ashraf, and the respect due to him as Khalid's friend: 'It's because he's my brother's friend, I guess . . . he thinks he's got the rights of a brother'; however, the consensus was that the appropriate course of action would have been to tell Khalid and let him deal with it, a feeling made stronger by the recognition that Khalid himself would not have dealt with the issue the same way. Ismat said:

> That wasn't right; it was none of his business basically. He should have told Khalid and Khalid do something about it – it wasn't right, I know for a fact it wasn't right for Ashraf to smack Hanif. (interview, 11 October 1996)

Ashraf's brother, Faruk, was condemnatory but circumspect:

> *Faruk*: I thought it was out of order, because his own brother wouldn't do that. That was stupid, but if he catches me now I know, if he catches me.

Claire: He's going to treat you the same way?
Faruk: He's going to treat me worser! (interview, 22 October 1996)

If 'not-smoking' did not always fully correlate with the attribution of respect, it is also true that smoking did not always signal an absence of respect. Indeed, for the little ones particularly, a number of careful exceptions were drawn around whom they would smoke with. In the first few weeks of their split sessions at the project, the junior members would skulk off to the back of the building to light up, until Yasmin confronted them and gave them permission to smoke – a breaking of barriers that soon translated into other areas of activity and facilitated a closeness between the young men and female members of staff more akin to their relationships with their older sisters. As Ifti commented of Yasmin and myself: 'You let us smoke . . . it's different' (interview, 28 September 1996). Things were less straightforward with male staff, who were all Bengali and who were also, until recently, mainly from the local area. When Hashim arrived, in particular, a rather fraught stand-off ensued over the issue of smoking: Hashim was a much respected elder of the community, a friend of Ismat's *bhaya,* Aklak and senior even to the older group. Ifti told me:

Hashim's safe. Hashim deserves respect. I don't know why everyone smokes in front of him in the youth club . . . because before like when he used to walk past us, yeah, we used to hide the cigarette and everything . . . we didn't want to do that anyway [smoke openly], we was trying to hide from him and smoke, but we couldn't do that, he was everywhere!

Hashim similarly expressed his concerns about maintaining the boundaries of respect within the project:

When I first started working here, it was the main thing for me, I thought oh my god, if I mixed in with them, then from outside – because obviously they're really young and I might be with my older friends . . . and they might talk to me like *they're* my friends, and I don't mind that but my friends would think 'What's the younger guys talking to you like that for' . . . But they've never had a problem with me outside and you know it's all going fine . . . Outside it's different, that's why the respect is there, you know, in the club it's like more friendly. (interview, 24 October 1996)

An arrangement was then tacitly agreed and understood whereby the junior members would joke with and smoke in front of Hashim in his role as youth worker and redraw the boundaries of respect as their *bhaya* outside the project. Hashim continued:

I know that they respect me, the younger lot. They were a bit hesitant at first to smoke in front of me, thinking I might go and tell their brothers and everything, and I've caught a lot of them smoking in front of me and they're thinking 'oh shit, he's going to tell my brother' and that and they see me with their brother, but their brother never come back to them . . . and that's because that's totally different, because what they're doing in the club is our problem here.

For Hashim, then, respect was due in recognition of his different roles: 'In this place I'm a worker, and you have got to respect me as a worker'. This distinction was sustainable, however, only because the little ones maintained their respect for Hashim *as a brother* outside the project. Ifti, for example, stated:

When he's in the club and the man comes out sometimes we're there and like he catches us blatantly and sometimes, like when he's not in the club, that's when we give him respect. (interview, 28 September 1996)

What this peculiar, but mutually satisfying, arrangement points to is the constructed and contextual nature of hierarchy within this imagined community; it thus allowed for the maintenance of respect both within and outside the project, recognizing and accommodating the differing demands of each. These shifting boundaries highlight at once the artificiality of such notions and also their enduring significance. Boundaries of respect could then be redrawn, by unstated but mutual consent, or unilaterally to exclude individuals or groups, or indeed, as in the incident with Ashraf and Hanif, contested in terms of rights and obligations. The maintenance of respect was crucially founded on a mutuality which bound the young men into a structure, seemingly rigid and authoritarian, yet the strength of which lay in its flexibility, allowing for intimacy and distance, support and autonomy, control and surveillance but also for freedom and the capacity to 'turn a blind eye'.

The symbolic power of the act of smoking, rather than the act itself, was clearly apparent; that is, there was a distinction between smoking, being *seen* to smoke and *knowing* you have been seen to smoke. Khalid thus explained of Hanif:

Khalid: I would like him to respect me like I'm his older brother and that.
Claire: So what sort of things would show that?
Khalid: So like don't talk about – like smoking and all that. I don't know if he smokes or what, but I think he does . . .
Claire: He wouldn't smoke in front of you?

Khalid: No.
Claire: What would you do if you saw him smoking?
Khalid: If I see him and he probably never see me, I reckon I would just ignore it, but if say I was walking past and he's got a cigarette in his mouth and I walk past and he see me and I see him – I wouldn't do nothing if he was with his friends, I wouldn't really do nothing there, because it would be distressing for him, I would probably go home and sort it out. (interview, 7 October 1996)

The issue of respect around smoking is, then, inseparable from the question of visibility; as in the previous discussion around what constitutes a 'good' or 'bad' Bengali boy, the definition of respect pivots crucially on a disjunction between doing and seeing (or being seen), or between forms of knowing. Thus, while the older lot acknowledged privately that they were aware of the little one's actions (or most of them, anyway!), the lack of visibility gave them space to 'not know' and therefore 'not act'. Shahin stated pragmatically:

I . . . give them advice and that, you know, it's really up to them if they want to follow it. As long as they don't do whatever they're doing near me. (interview, 26 September 1996)

Similarly the little ones knew that the older group had this knowledge and that the performance of respect therefore lay not so much in the act itself as in not being caught. Ifti thus noted of Ashraf:

Ashraf knows that all of us smoke, he knows even that his brother smokes, but he ain't going to say nothing; he just wants his brother not to smoke in front of his face. (interview, 28 September 1996)

Ismat put the issue clearly:

They are strict. How do I put this? They know that we do things and like they don't want to think that we are doing it, so they pretend to be strict and all that. They pretend not to know that we're smoking – because Ifti's been smoking in the house and like he smokes in his bedroom and his mum knows that he smokes and all that, his brother knows, but like when he's out he still keeps away from his brother, not to smoke, not smoke in front of him, even though his brother knows that he smokes. My brother knows that I smoke and I keep away from him. (interview, 11 October 1996)

If part of paying respect is to maintain this screen of invisibility, the other crucial element is to sustain the act of 'not knowing' by the older groups – allowing space to the younger individuals. This again points clearly to the centrality of mutual interest and goodwill in the creation of respect. Humzah thus explained:

> If you were smoking and an old man was to come along, you'd hide it. And if he's stupid and he comes looking and checking and that, that's wrong for him, that's wrong because we've hided it from him . . . next time he's walking past you smoke in front of him, you know what I mean – he's lost his respect. (interview, 5 October 1996)

The enactment of mutuality was not, however, always clear cut, leading to some unexpected and ambiguous encounters. On one occasion, the junior members left their Monday club session to go to the local cinema to watch *Striptease*; about half an hour later Sayeed returned, alone and disgruntled, apparently because some of the older group, including his brother Salman, had also turned up at the cinema. The younger ones had attempted to hide, to avoid being seen, but had been spotted, and Salman had ordered Sayeed to 'go home'. The others did not arrive back at the project, however, and it turned out that after some disagreement and attempted bribery, the older group had left the cinema and the younger ones had stayed to see the film. Jamal explained:

> *Jamal*: It was *Striptease* and they [the older lot] came later and Mustafa's going 'we might as well go, let them stay'. That was the first choice, but them lot, they don't know nothing, they don't know shame . . . Mustafa has like a bit of dignity.
> *Claire*: But I don't get it. Why can't you all be in the cinema at the same time to see this film?
> *Jamal*: It's like the way they see it is 'we are watching naked ladies and so are our younger brothers over there, so that's stupid, isn't it.' So Mustafa tried to avoid it by saying 'let's get out of here, if we're not in there then we won't feel the same way and when we're out of there.' (interview, 10 October 1996)

Interestingly, in this case the moral high ground (if that is the appropriate term here) was occupied by the little ones; partly because they had arrived first and partly because of the content of the film, it was incumbent on the older group to maintain their respect by vacating the space[15] – and in particular to extract themselves from its sexualized implications:

> *Claire*: Who would feel more uncomfortable in that situation, you or them?
> *Jamal*: Them, because we wouldn't think nothing, we would be like 'We're

young we don't care about that stuff, we don't care if they're watching us.' They're thinking 'We're older, look at them, they're younger than us and they're watching this' . . . it's a bit disrespectful.

It is perhaps the idea of implicit participation in this scenario that decided its outcome, although obviously not all the older group agreed. Though they did agree that it would be unacceptable for both groups to remain in the cinema to watch Demi Moore taking her clothes off, some obviously expected the little ones to leave, as indeed Sayeed, at his brother's behest, did. However, they were not able to exercise this degree of control over Sayeed's friends and, when bribery failed, they – to maintain respect – were forced to leave themselves. The issue of 'setting an example' seems to have been central to the debate, particularly around the policing of sexuality. Unlike smoking, the constraints around sexual activity were more mutually prohibitive (as perhaps with the use of drugs) and the older groups were keen to sustain an aura of invisibility, through distance and discretion, towards both their younger brothers and the wider community. This raises questions about the role of wider gendered relations in the imagination of community and it is to these issues that I now turn.

. . . and of Sisters

One week in February 1996, it snowed in London. The snow lay only an inch or two in depth on the Stoneleigh Estate, but it was thick enough for snowball fights and ambushes, of which there were many. Closing the gate to the project building one Monday evening after a junior session, Yasmin fell victim to such an ambush, as the little ones pelted her mercilessly with snowball after snowball, while she exchanged laughing threats and curses. As I passed through the gate to reach my car, Hanif called to his friends for a ceasefire: 'It's Claire, we can't get her, *she's a woman.*'

The comment made us laugh – though I think Yasmin was a little taken aback – but it did reveal a significant difference in the perception of the young men concerning Yasmin and myself at that time. Where in the months after her appointment Yasmin had established a close and informal relationship with the junior members of the project, I was still viewed with some reserve and distance; where I was a recipient of polite and dutiful care and protection, Yasmin was seen almost as 'one of the boys'; where I was a 'woman', as I commented to Yasmin at the time 'I'm not sure where that leaves you'. Where it left Yasmin, at least at that time, was in a different category from me – or perhaps more accurately, it left me in a different category from her: I was 'a woman' and as such was marked out as distinct from and outside the young men's immediate imagined community. Yasmin, on the other hand, formed part of that community; the barriers were down and she had been accepted, embraced (and ambushed) as a 'sister'. The distinction was an important one, pointing to a crucial dichotomy in the articulation of gendered relations; that between 'sisters' and women, insiders and outsiders, family and community on the one hand, and 'strangers' – friendly or otherwise – on the other. These categories are not absolute and incorporate distinctions based around age, ethnicity, family position, locality, marital and sexual status, and personality, but they do reflect a similar performance and negotiation of notions of 'community' as relationships between 'brothers'. In particular, the relationships with 'sisters' point to the complex artic-ulation of layers of gendered authority and hierarchies that challenge any simplistic assumptions of homogeneous and antagonistic patriarchal relations within Asian (particularly Muslim) communities, which position women uncritically as victims and subjects of control and men as always already the villains of the piece.

The young men of the SAYO project at the time I started my research had long been cast in this role, and had a clearly defined reputation as not only sexist but overtly hostile to women. The early confrontations with Shopna, outlined in Chapter 3, had singled the young men out for anti-sexism training courses and the image remained vivid and seemingly ineluctable in the minds of Shopna and Julia, and a symptom of general social and cultural dysfunction amongst their other detractors. While not wishing to rehearse this history here it is, I think, significant that neither Yasmin nor I have ever encountered the forms of gendered hostility met with by Shopna or imagined by others. That said, it is certainly true that our positions within the project and in the local community were deeply gendered, though in different ways, and in different forms, depending on the young men concerned. However, this positioning clearly illustrates the considerable variety and flexibility in the imagination of gendered relations, which reflects more widely on the creation of community identifications. It should be noted that because of the gender-specific parameters of the project and wider community constraints on (visible) interaction between young men and young women, it was comparatively rare to see the young men in interaction with women, other than youth and community workers. Although I have come to know several of the young men's sisters well over the past few years and have known of, advised on, and occasionally met or seen their girlfriends, these constraints and my own discretion demand that much of the texture of these personal, private and often intimate encounters and knowledge is absent from the present work, although it does inform its more general insights.[16] For these reasons, the perspectives of the few young women I met are also absent, and the comments that follow reflect very much my own viewpoint and edited highlights from the young men – a young woman's perspective on these issues would, perhaps inevitably, differ.

The role of Yasmin and myself within the youth club, and hence in relation to the wider community, was an unusual – and hypervisible – one, a position that elicited scrutiny and comment, and demanded discretion and circumspection. As a Bengali young woman, and worker-in-charge, in particular, Yasmin's employment was a matter of close examination and comment from the young men themselves and seemingly from the wider Bengali community. This was generally seen as a positive attribute and articulated in terms of a broad notion of 'community', imagined in terms of shared ethnicity (especially language, religion and 'culture'). Shahin thus commented:

> It's just the communication thing, you know, that's the way the Bengali thing can help, because you share the same – you know, what an Indian person will share won't be the same as what a Bengali person shares, it will be similar but different. (interview, 3 October 1996)

Khalid similarly told me:

> It's like Bengalis are different; it's like if it's a white person you couldn't muck about the way you're mucking about with Yasmin. It's like it's really different. (interview, 15 October 1996)

Yasmin's position was undoubtedly mediated (especially in contrast to Shopna's) by her status as a married woman and mother of two, which offset her appearance of youth and somewhat unorthodox manner and career choice. Mohammed expressed some of these reservations, although interestingly he was the only one to make such observations:

> *Mohammed*: First of all, she's not properly dressed – she's not always dressed like a woman, head covered and everything, and secondly, if my sister was to work, my mum would never like one woman with all these boys, it's quite awkward.
> *Claire*: But it doesn't make you feel awkward?
> *Mohammed*: It does really sometimes, but you know the way she treats everyone she's like a friend . . . [but] she's married and got kids so she's got responsibilities. (interview, 24 October 1996)

The adoption of Yasmin by the little ones almost as an *apa* (older sister) – in behaviour, if not in name[17] – facilitated a familiarity and affection which served to assuage any doubts held by the older groups or their parents, establishing a basis of trust and aura of 'respect' in work and outside. Although the young men themselves did not describe Yasmin as a sister, with all the obligations this entailed, they clearly placed her within the boundaries of their community; as Ifti asserted: 'She's like us, she's like a girl to us. She's old yeah but when she gets along with us we think she's a girl . . . we joke around with her innit?' (interview, 1 October 1996). Most described Yasmin simply as a 'friend', yet this had clearly familial overtones. Ismat, for example, told me:

> She looks very young, she likes to have fun and all that, so I wouldn't think of her as married with children; I'd say she's outgoing and all that, likes to have fun . . . a worker and a friend, someone that – not keeps an eye – someone that sees how you're doing and things at school; *basically a sister's friend*; so I'd say yes, she's a close friend . . . *I try to respect her.* (interview, 11 October 1996, my emphasis)

Hanif similarly decribed Yasmin as a 'good friend', (interview, 10 October 1996), while Jamal explained the difference between this role and that of a sister:

> A sister wouldn't let us smoke. She lets us do things, she takes us as we are . . . our sisters would say 'You're too young to smoke, don't smoke in front of us or with us.' (interview, 10 October 1996)

As Hanif commented in response to Jamal's statement, however, this distinction still incorporated the performance of 'respect':

> If she kind of said we can smoke in front of her then it's not disrespectful. But if she had not kind of said it then we wouldn't do it. (interview, 10 October 1996)

Yasmin then occupied a seemingly ambiguous – if convenient – space; at once a worker and a friend, and yet more than this, part of an extended family network that entailed the duties and obligations of 'respect', but which were freely given. Ismat's description of Yasmin as a 'sister's friend', or indeed a 'friend's sister' shows clearly the distinction between familial blood obligations and these fictive, more consensual ties. Although this freed the young men in terms of the duties of 'respect', for example, around smoking, it also illustrates the element of potential obligation – that the young men were *allowed* to smoke and that Yasmin could request them not to and they would comply. The issue of smoking here also clearly illustrates a crucial distinction between brothers and sisters – that concerns with sisters centre less explicitly on discipline and control than on care and protection,[18] and are more easily negotiated. Yasmin's status can partly be accounted for by virtue of an ethnicized notion of community, by being Bengali, but also by virtue of age, marital status and most crucially, by personality. It is interesting to contrast Yasmin's relationship with the young men with Shopna's in this regard; where the latter insisted on the more formal relationships signified by the use of familial labels such as *apa,* in an attempt to constrain and control individual behaviour through the conjuring of 'respect', this attempt at compulsion served only to alienate the young men and add to their already substantial discontent at her organization of the project. Hanif told me:

You can relate to her [Yasmin]. Like Shopna, she was more *typical* . . . Once I tried to joke around with her and she looked at me in a funny way. (interview, 10 October 1996)

Where Shopna had attempted to make use of the duties owed to older sisters – and failed – Yasmin tended to personify the elements of care, of indulgence, of familiarity and of fun that the little ones especially valued in their older sisters and the older young women in their community. Being Bengali was then not sufficient to ensure this position as *apa*, just as not being Bengali did not necessarily deny this role. From a position of careful reserve and polite protection that guarded me from snowballing assaults, the past four years have seen me move from the position of friendly stranger, of a 'woman', towards the category of 'sister friend'. By the time of the interviews, the young men cast Yasmin and myself in similar roles as 'friends', though with allowances made for differences in temperament – as Hanif, rather delicately, put it: 'We know you're a bit more, you know – take things a bit more seriously.'

Perhaps a central distinction between Yasmin and myself, personalities apart, was in marital status; Mohammed commented, 'they don't see you in the same way [because] firstly she's married and she's got kids so she's got responsibilities' (interview, 24 October 1996). Interestingly, this meant less that I was seen as young, free and single than as vulnerable and in need of protection. Where Yasmin was seen as a sexually mature, unshockable married woman and mother, I was seen as a naïve, infinitely shockable and rather vague individual whose years in education meant that I was respectable and 'nice' but unworldly in an ivory-tower sort of way, most especially about men.[19] The little ones would then delight in trying to fix me up with any eligible (or especially ineligible) man we came across, would offer to beat up any man who showed an interest in me and would give me concerned advice on how to behave with the few men they saw me with. Recently, meeting me with a male colleague, several of the little ones called me aside, asked me – somewhat incredulously – if I was going on a date, where I was going and then advised me earnestly to make sure I did not invite him back to my flat for coffee. They have even offered to arrange my marriage for me and are actively seeking a Keith Sweat lookalike – preferably a Bengali one – to fill the position. As I mentioned in Chapter 2, this categorization worked to position me as a 'respectable' Asian woman, who could be relied upon and trusted, who was an acceptable – if sometimes temperamental – part of their community.

Ironically, though Yasmin and myself were often positioned as extreme opposites, the inclusion of us both within this community was founded on a careful control – and denial – of any sexual identity. The role of 'sister' almost by definition precluded any recognition of autonomous sexuality – a division of gender and sexual identities that allowed for intimacy without danger. For Yasmin, this was achieved easily through her position as wife and mother, and although the little ones in particularly would often turn to her for advice or information about sex (in a way, interestingly, they would not turn to male workers), this was in the safe and certain knowledge of this circumscribed sexual identity. I, on the other hand, was a different issue altogether, and a position of safety was achieved through a dual process of denial – a practice made easy by my advanced age (in relation to fifteen year olds, anyway) and professional status (I was not interested in men because I was too busy studying)[20] – and an assumption of ownership; that I was to be looked after, advised and eventually disposed of to a 'suitable' man, carefully vetted by them. During a day trip to Birmingham for a football match with an Asian youth project, Majid[21] asked me jokingly about my love life. When I told him I did not have one, and could not even get a date for dinner, the young men – who had been listening attentively – remarked indignantly that *they* had just taken me for lunch (to a local kebab shop) and anyway since I had them, who else did I need? Sher Khan added, only half-jokingly, 'anyway, we couldn't bear the thought of you being with anyone else', and the young men nodded gravely, then offering to arrange my marriage for me. The little ones would never ask me for advice about sex or relationships, since I obviously did not have either, although they would often try out pick up lines, or flirt with me, if only for effect. This was also true of some of the middle group, especially Khalid, who recently told me that he was 'saving himself for someone exactly like me – *but older*'. It is significant, however, that the older group never flirted with me and tended to maintain a greater distance with both Yasmin and myself. Although I suspect we were often the subjects of discussion and speculation, this never entered into our interaction and was carefully screened from visibility; by the same token, there was none of the physical contact or personal jokes which were a constant feature of our interaction with the younger groups. As mentioned in Chapter 2, this was probably because we were seen potentially to occupy the same social and sexual matrix; it is also true that the older lot tended not to place Yasmin or myself in the safe, but hierarchical, category of 'sister' – unless they needed a favour. The positioning as 'sister' not only depended on the denial of autonomous sexuality, it also rendered male–female relationships non-sexual and therefore innocent. On the occasions that the young men did see me with male friends, they assumed automatically that these were colleagues or 'friends from Oxford', never boyfriends or potential partners. This allowed close relationships to develop and 'respect' to be maintained almost irrespective of circumstance – a mutually satisfactory arrangement in which I was happy to collude.

These dynamics – of mutual care and protection, of 'respect' and authority based on closeness and support (rather than distance and discipline), and of carefully maintained and policed fictions of desexualization – were constant features of the relationship with sisters, real and fictive, which marked individuals as part of an imagined community. One of the primary considerations in the formulation of these relationships was, however, age: as with their brothers, the position as dispenser or object of authority with women was strongly structured through age hierarchies, which in most cases outweighed gendered privilege. Although, as with their younger brothers, younger sisters were subject to the control of the young men, and their protection, this was not so clearly the case with *apas*, who were often the repository of familial power. Shahin explained:

> If they're younger than you, you have to look after them more than if they're older, because when they're older than you, if you turn round to them and say do something, they say 'look man, shut up', you know what I mean, if they're older than you. (interview, 26 September 1996)

Shahin and his brothers have three older sisters, all of whom wielded different forms of authority over their brothers. Shahin told me:

I'm mainly closest to my older sister . . . sometimes I tell her that she's like another mother . . . with the other two when I was younger like they used to help me out with money and that, so they're alright as well. We were more like friends, but my older sister, she's like, you know – there's things I can talk to my other sisters about that I can't talk to my older sister about. I'm more open with my other sisters, but like my older sister, it's more like respect and things.

Although as the eldest son, Shahin had more leeway than his brothers the lines of authority were clear, 'when they're older than you it's like they've got more power over me, you know what I mean, and you yourself have to pay that bit of respect as well.'

Shakiel, who is the only son in his family and has five sisters (three older, two younger), similarly told me:

The thing with me and the sister that's immediately older than me, me and her got a more friendship kind of relationship, and the oldest one's like more adultish – she's the one that sometimes gives me lectures and that. But she's alright at times, we joke around . . . she don't tell me what to do but if I do something wrong she is the first to have a go at me out of all of them . . . [the others] like to, you know, if they want to tell me something they're not always serious, they tell me jokey, have a good laugh about it and that, cuss me, why do I make a fool of myself like that. It's not really them, you know, give me a lecture – that comes from your older sister. (interview, 18 November 1996)

The disciplinary role of *apas* – and particularly *boroapas* (eldest sister) – is, then, clearly acknowledged; in claiming us as 'daughters', for example, Shahin's mother gave Yasmin and myself the right to 'beat' her sons, should the occasion arise. It never has, but Yasmin assures me that if it should, Shahin, Khalid and Hanif would submit to this familial power! What also emerges from the above accounts, however, is the very strong bonds of affection and support that bound these young men to their older sisters – a closeness which was not as obviously present in the duties of protection expected of brothers – and in which much of their authority lay. Ismat, for example, told me that he saw his older sisters, rather than his brothers, as role models: 'My dad wants me to follow them, I do as well – I'd like to grow up and get a good job,[22] settle down close to my parents' (interview, 11 October 1996).

For the young men, then, sisters were a resource and support, more often fulfilling the roles of confidante and ally than of disciplinarian. Where age hierarchies tended to impose a formal distance between brothers around particular issues – for example, smoking or sex – these gaps were filled by the closeness to older sisters.[23] Sayeed thus told me that of all his family he was closest to his only sister, Sultana, who is a year older than he:

> *Sayeed*: Because I can tell her stuff that like I can't tell my brother and like she keeps it a secret and all that.
> *Claire*: What do you tell her that you think you can't tell your brothers?
> *Sayeed*: Smoking, and like girlfriends and all that . . . If she were a boy I couldn't tell her things because like she'd beat me up.
> *Claire*: So what's she like as a sister?
> *Sayeed*: She's friendly, kind, when she's got money she gives me money if I ask her, she looks after me and everything. (interview, 5 November 1996)

Ifti similarly placed his older sister Tahiya in this role as confidante and financial support, with an unquestioning assumption of her duty and his right: 'She gives me money. And I rob her every time' (interview, 28 September 1996). For Ifti, the relationship was simple: 'She's my *boroapa*.'

In several cases, it was to older sisters that the young men would turn first with problems, particularly of a romantic or sexual nature; Zohar's sisters, for example, were the only members of his family to know about his long-standing girlfriend, Humaira: 'I'm more open to them, they know how it is . . . [they] know everything about my problems' (interview, 22 October 1996). Tahiya often acted as intermediary and messenger with Ifti's many girlfriends: 'She's safe with it' (28 September 1996) and Ismat's sisters knew of his previous relationship with a local Turkish girl. Shakiel told me that his sisters would be the first people he would tell if he were to have a serious girlfriend and that he would rely on them to broach the subject with his parents should he decide to marry: 'I'd tell my sisters, they would tell when the time comes, they'd probably say – if I was serious about someone I would introduce her to my sisters' (interview, 18 November 1996). Several of the other young men said it was their older sisters who would play a key role at the time of marriage, either in arranging it or in smoothing the path for a love marriage. Sayeed thus asserted:

> If I was told to pick, I'd tell my sister to pick for me . . . I'd rather let Sultana find somebody than my mum . . . that's the only sister we've got, it would be better if she picked for me. (interview, 5 November 1996)

Ifti similarly told me: 'I will make my sister and brother sort it out . . . I told my sister blatantly that I want a pretty woman' (interview, 1 October 1996).

There is, moreover, a strong degree of reciprocity in these relationships, especially in the older sister–younger brother dynamic. While older sisters were placed in a pseudo-maternal role, younger brothers fulfilled a double role of protection and also of more indulgent support. Ifti told me of all his sisters: 'I back them up if they're in trouble and my big brother would do the same.' Of his *apa*, however, he recognized limitations in this role, a gap of authority which was filled by his older brother, Humzah: 'If my sisters were to do [something bad] I don't need to do nothing, my big brother would do something.' 'Not needing to' actually translates here as 'not able to' and all the young men acknowledged the greater freedom accorded to their older sisters by virtue of age. This was particularly salient in the discussions around boyfriends – just as the younger brothers would tell their older sisters of their relationships, so too would the older sisters often confide in their younger brothers, secure in the knowledge that they would do nothing and tell no one. Ifti, for example, said of Tahiya:

> If she had a boyfriend, yeah, I'd try and back her up; if the boyfriend really likes her and they want to get married, I'd try and back her up . . . I'd cover up, like I would chat to my parents, 'yeah, I know a good boy'... I'd make out that *I* know him.

Sayeed similarly explained of Sultana:

> My reaction would be, if she's got one, she's got one, I do the same thing . . . I'd really do nothing. If she were younger I would tell her 'don't do it, you're too young for that'. (interview, 5 November 1996)

Ismat put it even more clearly: 'There's nothing I can do really, she's my older sister' (interview, 11 October 1996).

Shakiel drew a clear distinction between his roles as younger and older brother; of the older sisters he asserted a constrained concern:

> *Shakiel*: It would be fine if she had a boyfriend – I would probably go behind her back, find out about him, if I don't like him I would have words with him.
> *Claire*: But if you did like him, then what?
> *Shakiel*: I wouldn't say nothing, I wouldn't approach him. (interview, 18 November 1996)

His role as *bhaya* to his younger sisters was rather different:

> *Shakiel*: The one that's a year younger than me, I know for a fact she's going to give me a lot of problems . . . I'll probably end up having to hit her.

Claire: Do you think that's OK in your role as a big brother to do that?
Shakiel: It might not be OK, but if you ain't got no other choice.

Jamal similarly told me of his younger sister: 'If I knew my sister had a boyfriend that would be a different matter – I wouldn't want her to . . . she's my younger sister, I should look after her'. (interview, 17 October 1996)

As with 'brothers', the category of 'sister' extended beyond the bounds of immediate family to encompass the sisters of friends and other young women in the local community, along with its incumbent rights and responsibilities. Jamal commented, 'your friend's sister is like your sister'. Mohammed similarly told me:

It's just like good friends – I know them, if I see them, I say hello, if they need help – like sometimes they go 'can you go and get me a bottle of Coke' and I quickly run to the shops and that. (interview, 24 October 1996)

Ismat also explained that his sisters' friends also assumed the same position of care towards him as a younger brother:

Ismat: They may treat me like a younger brother and I might treat them the same as I treat my sisters basically . . .
Claire: So what sort of things would they do to treat you like a little brother?
Ismat: [Tell me] 'come, sit down, eat', tell me to do things, like you know, 'read a book, get your head stuck in a book' . . . like they'd do it like my sister, they take it nice and gently . . . because they're like my blood sisters. (interview, 11 October 1996)

It is significant that when Tasnim and Tahiya were attacked, the little ones ran immediately to their defence and in the aftermath of the incident young men of all ages were involved in finding the attackers – one of the rare occasions when action was mobilized on a 'community', rather than peer group, level. By the same token, Bilal and Aklak's failure to enact their duties as brothers in protecting the young women placed them irrevocably outside this community.

One important consequence of the categorization of 'sisters' as a collective, community identity was the desexualization of local young women. All the young men I interviewed were adamant that they never considered local Bengali young women as sexually available – as Humzah put it: 'there's no girls on the Stoneleigh' (interview, 5 October 1996). He explained:

The girls that are there, they're either someone's sister, someone's cousin or something, so we don't even notice them – we don't *want* to notice them, you get me? . . . It's like you look at them, you go no, because it's someone's sister or someone's friend or someone's this, and you don't want to take liberties.

Hanif similarly commented: 'that's not on . . . your friend's sisters are like your own sister . . . if they were nice, I probably would look at them, but I would never go out with them' (interview, 10 October 1996). Zohar also noted: 'I know everyone around here . . . I just know them, sister's friends, my mum's friends' daughters' (interview, 22 October 1996).

Interestingly, the young men justified these constraints firstly in terms of 'family', and secondly in relation to their immediate peer group – to the respect due to friends and to brothers. Hanif, for example, told me: 'there's only one family round here I'd say the girls were nice . . . *they haven't got brothers that come round here*' (interview, 10 October 1996, my emphasis).

Young Bengali women from the area were then doubly restricted, as 'sisters' at a general community level and, more specifically, as the sisters of friends. Ifti, for example, told me that he would never consider dating a friend's sister:

That's liberties, no way . . . If it was a friend's sister, no way, I'd never do that . . . That's stupidness. If I'm going with my friend and I'm trying to go with his sister, you think my friend likes that? . . . I'd be like an idiot. (interview, 1 October 1996)

Jamal also stated:

Your friend's sister is like your sister, but in a different sense . . . when you think girls like no-one knows it's your girlfriend and like you go round to your mates and say 'yeah I done that, I done this' – if you go out with your friend's sister, how can you say that, it's a bit stupid. And anyway, I wouldn't feel nothing for my friend's sister. (interview, 10 October 1996)

More than this, however, local young women formed part of a broader notion of community that conflated area and ethnicity in a combination claimed by most of the young men as being simply 'too complicated' (Hanif, interview, 10 October 1996). Shahin told me, 'I don't pay much attention to them' (interview, 3 October 1996), whereas Ismat expanded the category to preclude even the formation of friendships:

Ismat: They wouldn't be seen with us and we are not supposed to be seen with them because our religion is strict – you're not supposed to be with girls and girls are not supposed to be with boys; I don't know why.

Claire: So it would be too awkward to spend time with them?

Ismat: Round this area . . . We have to like dodge all the older lot, all the older people, our parents, our cousins, everybody we know – even if we don't know them, if they go to the Mosque, we still have to dodge them, because they probably know our parents. So we kind of like run, try and hide from everybody. (interview, 11 October 1996)

It is worth noting that although the young men desexualized the local Bengali young women as 'sisters', this did not mean they did not recognize the potential for sexual behaviour by the young women with young men from outside the area. Many of the little ones, for example, knew of romantic liaisons involving their older sisters (real or fictive), but were unwilling or unable to interfere. Ifti, for example, told me that he had once seen Sayeed's sister Sultana with a young man, but had promised not to tell her brothers: 'I knew she used to go out with someone, I didn't tell . . . I was shocked' (interview, 1 October 1996), while Jamal had reluctantly been caught up in its rather untidy conclusion:

One of the problems was she had a boyfriend that come on to her a bit strong and everyone was pressuring me to tell my mate . . . [so] I just told him about the boy . . . I was really just listening to her problem and they all thought I spent too much time with her, everyone thought I had a thing with her . . . so I had to tell him at least a bit of what's happening, to let him know I'm not with his sister. (interview, 10 October 1996)

Amongst the older group too, there were many stories of young women who had run off with boyfriends – usually with disastrous consequences – but most were reluctant to talk more openly; interestingly, to protect the feelings of their friends. Khalid thus told me:

I wouldn't cuss them if they were like somebody's sister . . . you know you have to respect them – if you knew their brother obviously you wouldn't say nothing about their sister because the brother would get offended. (interview, 15 October 1996)

Humzah commented:

Some girls in the area are so bad . . . Everyone knows and no-one says anything. There's one blatant one . . . *but I'm not going to say*, you must have heard, *she's my friend's sister.* (interview, 5 October 1996, my emphasis)[24]

Such cautionary tales occupied the status of 'dark, dark secrets' and the present work respects this discretion. They are mentioned here, in passing, to demonstrate: firstly, the divergence between the fictions of asexuality within the local community and its more fraught reality; secondly, the acknowledgement by the young men of this sexual identity – however publicly denied; and thirdly, the limitations of any notion of control over women's sexual identity, particularly over that of older sisters. It is worth noting here also that, at least in one notable case, the young men themselves did not always live through their public stance of carefully self-policed sexuality as regards local young women. Salman, then, was infamous amongst the young men for dating Asian young women on the estate; however, even he had drawn the line at sisters.

The overarching fiction of family and community in relation to young women meant that for the young men, too, sexual activity was severely constrained and largely invisible. The discourse of 'community' in this respect was however articulated rather differently by the older group and the little ones. For the latter, this meant dating young women from the local area but outside of the Bengali community. For a few months during my fieldwork, a number of this group dated some white young women from the Amersham Estate; though these relationships soon became rather difficult. Jamal, who was involved with one of the girls, told me:

Jamal: At the time I didn't know how she was, you know, and everyone just put us together. It was alright, she was alright, she liked me and that, and then as the relationship went on everyone started finding out she wasn't – that's when the other girls started telling how she was.
Claire: So, how was she?
Jamal: She was a tart, innit. (interview, 10 October 1996)

Hanif was uncharacteristically harsh, 'they're just good for one thing' (interview, 10 October 1996), and Ismat told me:

I don't treat girls differently but white girls you get more advantage of because in their religion boys are nothing – parents tell them go and get a boyfriend or something . . . it's more advantage of getting them basically. (interview, 11 October 1996)

By contrast, Asian, especially Muslim girls, were viewed as a more difficult option; Ifti observed to me: 'I don't really go for Muslim girls . . . they're too tight, let's keep it like that . . . they won't even give you a cuddle!' (interview, 1 October 1996). Although they did on occasion meet and make dates with Asian young women from other areas, these choices were constrained by lack of transport and money. Sayeed thus confided to me:

> *Sayeed*: I've been out with white [girls], that's it.
> *Claire*: Why is that do you think?
> *Sayeed*: (laughs) I don't know – whites are easier to get!
> *Claire*: What about the Asian girls in this area, don't you like them?
> *Sayeed*: Yeah, I like them a lot, but they've got like a lot of respect in themselves, they're like into religion and all that, they wouldn't really go out with a boy unless they're married.[25] Like all the Asian girls you find is on Eid day, or you go to a local Asian area, you find them there . . . We go round for Asian girls, we look in schools and all that; sometimes we find them, sometimes we don't.
> *Claire*: But the Asian girls round this area, you don't really think of them?
> *Sayeed*: No. No, because we think of them the same like our sisters. (interview, 5 November 1996)

Ismat similarly stated:

> There's not much Asians round here to go out with. They're not nice or nothing, but if I grow older I may have a car and then I may go and get to know more Asian people . . . We want to get cars and meet Asian girls, not white girls – get cars, go places where there are Asian, Pakistani, Indian girls, because there's not much round here. (interview, 11 October 1996)

It is significant that Ismat excludes Bengali girls from this statement, and several of the young men asserted that although they would prefer to date Asian young women, they did not want Bengali girlfriends. Jamal commented: 'The Bengali ones are dibby in every way, they don't know nothing, you can't relate to them . . . I don't see nice Bengali girls' (interview, 10 October 1996). Ifti claimed, in a perhaps more accurate reflection of the young men's perceptions: 'If you go out with Bengali girls . . . they will expect you to get married' (interview, 1 October 1996). There was then a correlation between notions of ethnicity, family and imagined community, which worked to exclude sexual relationships with Bengali girls. Interestingly, although the older groups primarily dated Asian young women, met in college or in clubs, they echoed these sentiments about Bengali girls. Khalid commented, cynically: 'most Bengali girls are all ugly, that's what I reckon' (interview, 15 October 1996), while his older brother Shahin – of whom Zohar commented 'Shahin goes out with anything'[26] (interview, 22 October 1996) – similarly drew the line at Bengali girlfriends: 'most of the Bengali girls from the area, they're just not my type . . . with Bengalis they might know someone you know, whatever' (interview, 3 October 1996). Several of the young men had longstanding Asian girlfriends, mainly of Pakistani origin, although they were rarely seen together and never on the Stoneleigh Estate. This invisibility was explained, as with their younger brothers, in terms of 'respect' to their families and the local community. Humzah thus stated:

No one will come with girls in this area, *we* don't even come with girls round the area . . . that's a big thing. One person sees it, the whole person knows, you get it? It's already done. We never used to hang round with girls in our area in the first place, they just made it up from somewhere, 'yeah, they're fighting and they're hanging around with girls in Abbey Street', and like bloody hell, what do you mean, girls, there ain't no girls in bloody this area . . . if they was to see us, then it would be like madness – no, no way! (interview, 5 October 1996)

Humzah's statement makes clear the role of sex in drawing the boundaries of community: firstly through the issue of (dis)respect and (in)visibility; secondly, the recognition of these boundaries by the young men; and lastly, the drawing of alternative boundaries of community which allowed for sexual contact. Dating Bengali girls would be to muddy these divisions – the convenient split of 'sisters' and 'women', that facilitated sexual and romantic liaisons. 'Women' were, then, by definition, outside of community and therefore potentially available for sexual relationships, whereas Bengali women, as fictive sisters, were considered part of a wider imagined community and therefore unavailable – or at least potentially too difficult. However, most of the young men I interviewed said that they expected to *marry* Bengali women, whether the marriages were arranged or not. Humzah thus told me, 'if I was to have a [serious] girlfriend, I wouldn't just have any girl, I'd look for a girl that my parents would approve of' (interview, 5 October 1996). Shakiel also stated:

I reckon I wouldn't go for someone my parents would really hate or something like that – like someone who flirts around too much; I wouldn't go for that. I want someone down to earth, like normal, someone who my mum and dad know could really fit in. (interview, 18 November 1996)

The criteria of 'fitting in' was particularly significant since most expected to remain in their parental home after marriage. Wives, like sisters, were then imagined as part of the family group and internal to the community. If not Bengali, all without exception, insisted their wives would be Muslim. Khalid asserted, 'I'm a Muslim person and I would like my wife, my children, everyone, to be Muslim as well, to be brought up the same way as I have' (interview, 15 October 1996). The role of religion in defining a wider imagined community around gendered relations was placed as a primary boundary marker in the marriage stakes, although most acknowledged that there was, in reality, a smaller actual marriage circle, defined through a narrower definition of 'culture' – Bengali culture – that carried with it the added weight of family ties; as Ifti put it, unquestioningly, 'you're going to get married to a Bengali girl anyway, your parents are going to sort it out' (interview, 1 October 1996).

For women, the constraints were even more strongly applied; Ifti thus commented of his *apa*, 'if the boy ain't Bengali, no way, no way – if he ain't a Muslim, no way she's going to get with him.' Ifti's strictures illustrate the collapse of the categories of religion and ethnicity in which Muslim and Bengali are assumed to be interchangeable, but also exclusive, notably defining out Pakistanis as potential marriage partners.

There were, perhaps inevitably, exceptions to this position: Jamal, for example, told me that he would prefer to marry a Pakistani woman (interview, 10 October 1996), and, indeed, the majority of the older group's serious girlfriends were of Pakistani origin. Zohar had been dating his Pakistani girlfriend Humaira for two-and-a-half years at the time of interview;[27] interestingly, the couple had met through Shahin, who had dated her friend for a short time, and Humaira was a constant presence with Zohar – the only young woman I ever saw the older group with. Zohar told me that Humaira was perhaps the only young woman accepted by his Stoneleigh peers and was treated with the respect normally accorded only to sisters:

That's the only girl they treat with respect, no other girl gets that treatment . . . They give her respect, you'll see, they chat to her, they wouldn't cuss her or nothing, because she's so safe[28] with them. And they go to me 'you should marry her . . . because you're never going to get another woman like that'. (interview, 22 October 1996)

Perhaps because of Zohar's undoubted, and overt, commitment to Humaira, and vice versa, Humaira was accorded family status – she was seen, in effect, as Zohar's wife. Zohar continued: 'She's not that flirty type . . . the way she treats me with respect, I treat her with respect, so them lot think she's my wife.' Humaira was the accepted by Zohar's peers as part of their imagined community, as a 'sister':

She treats Shahin like a brother . . . [Liaquot] treats her like a sister, you know that? He wouldn't look at her no ways. Like when she goes out and I'm not there and she's round the area, he'd look after her and everything. He'll just look after her like a sister.

Interestingly, Zohar contrasts this relationship, with its familial connotations of respect and care, with the girlfriends of the other young men, who were, according to Zohar, 'really Westernized Asian girls' and thus were placed outside this community. Humaira was a 'respectable woman', who behaved and dressed appropriately, was religious and perhaps most importantly, 'she can cook like a Bengali girl . . . She can do everything the way we do it.' Zohar acknowledged, however, that this relationship would inevitably lead to conflict with his parents when/if they chose to marry, because of the difference in origin:

They would blow up probably, innit . . . it's going to be hard, man . . . I would love to marry Humaira if it carries on . . . If it does I will fight for it, though, I'd leave home.

There is then a potential conflict between these articulations of community – a blurring and slippage of boundaries between peer group, family and territory, religion and ethnicity, women, sisters and wives, which renders any absolute correlation of sexuality, ethnicity and community highly ambivalent and often contradictory. It is worth noting, further, that although most of the young men expected to marry within 'their' (Bengali) community, the formulation of even this community was itself highly contested.

Most of the young men I interviewed thus drew a distinction between young Bengali women from Britain and those from 'back home' in Bangladesh. Shahin commented:

Like a lot of Bengali girls in this country, they get married back home because their parents think the Bengali boys in this country are useless, so they take their daughters back home to get them married there, and vice versa, the parents of the boys think the girls here are useless, see what I mean, so they take them back home. (interview, 3 October 1996)

The young men themselves generally demurred from this view, preferring to marry young women from Britain. Shahin, for example, told me, 'I can't really see myself going back home and getting a girl from there – I would have communication problems, man, number one.' Hanif similarly reflected:

You don't know how your partner is, you might have nothing in common, plus you're from here, she's from back home, she will see things different from you and you can't really relate to her the way you'd relate to someone from here. (interview, 10 October 1996)

Jamal elaborated:

She'll have to be from this country . . . [otherwise] we're different peoples, have different views on different things – I'll tell her to do something but she'll be like into cooking and washing – I wouldn't want my wife to be like that! (interview, 10 October 1996)

A number of the older men on the estate had married women from back home and several young men commented that although they preferred to marry from Britain, their friends or family were expecting to look for wives in Bangladesh. Sayeed's oldest brother had married a woman from Bangladesh and Salman was expected to (indeed, there had been a rumour in the summer of 1995 when Salman went home for a visit that he would marry there), but Sayeed himself claimed that he wanted something different: 'it's OK for my brother, but I wouldn't like that' (interview, 5 November 1996). Others amongst his circle of friends, however, drew a clear division within the group between those who would go 'back home' to marry and those who would not – a division which correlated almost exactly with the other hot issue of debate – whether or not the marriages would be arranged. Many of the young men felt strongly opposed to the idea of arranged marriage; Jamal noted: 'That ain't following the Prophet. The Prophet chose his own wife and done everything his way, you know' (interview, 10 October 1996). Khalid stated:

I wouldn't like to get an arranged marriage . . . I reckon it is totally stupid if you don't even know each other or whatever and you're just getting married and sleep in the same bed. (interview, 15 October 1996)

This issue also reflected a broader traditional/non-traditional divide, mentioned in Chapter 5. Where Shafiq, Enam, Ifti and perhaps Sayeed, were viewed as most likely to have arranged marriages with girls from Bangladesh, the others defined themselves strongly against this image. Hanif told me:

Everyone says Ifti's going to get married first . . . And they started saying to us who was going to get arranged marriage – I goes no, Jamal goes no as well. And it's like we started asking them lot, like Shafiq, and they all started getting moody, like shouting out: 'So what if we're going to have arranged marriage, if our parents want us to have arranged marriage we will have one, we don't care.' It's like because they know they probably won't have one – a love marriage – it's like they're really taking it out on us. We're going like 'there's no need to bite our heads off, it's only a question'. (interview, 10 October 1996)

Where those so defined resisted the implications of this role of 'typical' Bengali youth, it is interesting that the young men who embraced the ideal of 'love marriages' also felt constrained, or even conflicted, by the demands of family and of community. Jamal noted: 'My mum expects me to [have an arranged marriage] but she knows I ain't going to have it' (interview, 10 October 1996), and Ismat acknowledged:

Ismat: My parents want me to have a traditional arranged marriage; I would like to do it my way basically, fall in love with someone.
Claire: Can you see a time where there will be rows with you and your parents?
Ismat: Yes there will be. I can see it in my head now, if I was supposed to get married with someone I liked and my dad didn't like, yeah he would have a go at me. (interview, 11 October 1996)[29]

These incipient dilemmas can be seen to encapsulate processes both of continuity and change around the issue of marriage that reflect less a rupture than a reformulation of community boundaries. Where girlfriends or sexual partners were perceived as outside the boundaries of this familially imagined community, wives (along with sisters and mothers)[30] were firmly and unequivocally placed at its heart, although perhaps the route there was increasingly contested, not only across the generations but amongst the young men themselves. How these issues are raised, confronted and resolved as yet remains to be seen.

Conclusion

For me, the undoubted highlight of the *Independence Day* fashion show – apart from the triumph of our *Men In Black* routine – was the 'brothers' walk', partly because, I think, at one time it seemed like it would simply never happen. Teaching twenty embarrassed young men a five-minute dance routine was a walk in the park in comparison to getting our nine brothers[31] in one room at the same time to practice walking down a catwalk together. The result was, however, visually stunning and while some obvious discomfort remained, the public expression of affection and solidarity – of brotherhood – was deeply touching. At one point, in an unexpected and spontaneous gesture, Shahin embraced his younger brothers, Khalid and Hanif – a small but significant act of claiming and of care that stands, unstated and unremarked, at the core of the SAYO project and the Stoneleigh community.

The brothers' walk, as much with its many discomforts and delays as its eventual success, served to focus and mediate many of the issues explored in this chapter. The reluctance of the young men to even rehearse with their brothers – at least openly[32] – illustrates the salience of 'respect', of distancing and of the recognition of authority, which marked out the public interactions of both individuals and peer groups. At the same time – and almost in spite of themselves – the central elements of affection and care were also inescapable.

The 'brothers' walk' was an expression of family, but beyond that, it was part of a broader performance of 'community'. As noted earlier, this performance of community was often centred on an age- and gender-specific grouping with clearly recognized (though often shifting) internal and external boundaries. These boundaries brought together different friendship and peer groups in a complex web of obligations and duties which were mutually recognized and enacted. As noted in Chapter 5, rather than constituting an autonomous and freefloating generational entity, this 'community' is enmeshed in, and legitimated by, a broader matrix of family relationships. Community ties thus functioned horizontally, between friends and peers, and vertically, between brothers (and sisters), each deeply implicated in the other.

This is not to suggest, however, a rigid and stultifying enactment of community, inseparable from, and suffocated by, the demands of a reactive ethnicity, nor is it, by contrast, to deny the embedded nature of these forms of community identification. It is rather to highlight the performative nature of community formation, its deeply gendered imagination, its negotiation and contestation of structures of age, territory and family, its powerful affectivity and its enduring strength.

Along with Chapter 5, this chapter has attempted to unravel some of the complexities of masculine identifications amongst the young men of the SAYO project. Where the earlier chapter focused on friends, and sought to challenge the pathologization and criminalization of Asian peer group identities encapsulated in the symbol of 'the Gang', the present chapter has two main foci. Firstly, it explores the re-imagination of 'community' through the lens of gender and generation, examining processes of continuity and change, which challenge absolutist notions of 'the Asian community' or of 'Between Two Cultures' anomie. Secondly, it has sought to challenge racialized constructions of Asian masculinities, which counterpose uncritical assertions of ethnicized patriarchal authority with assumptions of 'masculinity-in-crisis', captured potently in the spectre of a reactive religious fundamentalism, to position Muslim young men in the firing line as Public Enemy Number One. In the relationships with 'sisters', in particular, the aim has been to explore some of the complex negotiations of gender, age and sexuality, which are too often ignored or too easily vilified, and to recognize, as with brothers, the role of love.

Notes

1 In particular, Ibrahim was able to exemplify the moral error of the attack – as a friend of Jamal, the attack could be interpreted as an attack on Ibrahim himself and thus a sign of disrespect to Ibrahim, his family, peer group and local community. Ibrahim thus wielded considerable moral authority in preventing further escalation of the conflict.
2 Two days prior to the time of writing.
3 A complaint often levelled at them by the older lot when I first arrived at the SAYO project.
4 A situation replicated with the teenies and the older groups now.
5 Cavanagh is another full-time youth worker who was covering for Yasmin that evening.
6 This was marked by, for example, in the substitution of terms of respect for proper names with 'real' brothers and older kin by most of the young men.
7 There is also an important distinction to be drawn between private and public relationships; Khalid, for example, told me 'all of our three brothers we go on quite close and that, joke around, have little fights' (interview, 7 October 1996).
8 Khalid, who is a gentle spirited young man, seemed to become a target for an unwarranted amount of violence during the years of my fieldwork.
9 As was the situation with the Triads outlined in Chapter 4.
10 see chapter 5 for greater detail.
11 As noted in Chapter 5, it also points to the salience of collective identification and judgement, of being judged by one's friends.

12 However, when Hassan ran the project, smoking was a major source of conflict; Hassan styled himself as *bhaya* to the young men and saw smoking as a sign of disrespect toward him.

13 The older group would smoke with Tarek etc., although the little ones did pay him respect in his role as Shafiq's *bhaya*.

14 The exceptions were S. Ahmed, Mustafa etc. who had previously formed part of a senior group.

15 Leaving the cinema also allowed the older lot to 'not see' the younger group in the situation and therefore 'not know'.

16 Although a number of the young men were surprisingly open about their romantic and sexual lives during interview, I have decided it would be inappropriate to make use of the material here.

17 The young men never employed the term *apa* in reference to Yasmin; by contrast, Shopna had attempted to force the young men to refer to her in familial terms as a way of enforcing authority, although this had served ultimately to undermine the relationship.

18 Although the results are often the same – I have seen both brothers and sisters order their younger siblings to 'go home' and both have been immediately obeyed, without question or comment from the individuals concerned or their friends.

19 There was one notorious occasion at a Bangladesh Independence Day celebration when a Bengali musician asked me if he had seen me somewhere before, and I replied I didn't think so. Ifti pulled me aside and told me the man was trying to chat me up, and asked if I wanted him to beat the man up. The rumour flew round the project, to the young men's great delight, that a man was trying to 'chirps' me and I had not even realized!

20 On one occasion, during lunch at MacDonalds, Ifti asked me if I knew how to 'flirt', and seemed shocked when I told him that I did and had even been quite proficient in my younger days. I later realized that what he and I meant by 'flirt' were not necessarily the same thing.

21 Majid had recently moved to Birmingham to act as Head of Youth Service and had invited us to meet with a local Asian youth project that was experiencing difficulties. The project's had come together on several occasions, of which the football match was the latest event.

22 Ismat's sisters both work for banks.

23 Younger sisters were less likely to fulfill this role in the interests of maintaining respect.

24 Where the young women had no such personal connections, judgements were considerably harsher – and often vocal; thus Ifti commented of one local young woman: 'She goes with anybody.

She's an idiot. She's a disgrace to Bengalis' (interview, 1 October 1996).

25 Sayeed's depiction of local Asian young women demonstrates his fiction of desexualization rather than fact.

26 Shahin's comment to me was typical: 'Last year was really good for girls, man' (interview, 3 October 1996).

26 Zohar and Humaira are still together.

27 Gets on well with them.

28 Ismat's oldest brother had had a love marriage and his father had cut him off, though the rest of the family maintained contact with him.

29 Although this chapter has not mentioned mothers, it is worth noting that all the young men, without exception, told me that their mother was the most important woman in their life.

30 The brothers were Shahin, Khalid and Hanif, Humzah and Ifti, Salman and Sayeed, Ashraf and Faruk.

31 There was apparently a great deal of practice at home!

–7–

Conclusion

Over the course of the past five years (since 1995), I have collected hundreds of photographs of the young men of the SAYO project. My favourite photos are laid out in three albums, starting with some pictures of the little ones sitting on the wall outside the youth club building and ending, to date, with the summer cricket match discussed in Chapter 6. The pages between record two fashion shows, several Eid days, four weddings (including Farhan's), countless football matches, occasional pool, table tennis and badminton competitions, the Duke of Edinburgh's award work (including two notorious camping trips), an NRA day, several residentials and training weekends, the first AGM of the Senior Member's Management Committee and a whole lot of hanging out, doing very little, smoking, striking poses and trying to look cool. There is a silent narrative in these albums, beyond the events or non-events they capture; a progression from a wide-ranging, rather unfocused desire to capture everything and everyone to a narrowing of vision, in which fewer individuals and groups appear and reappear (the longest phase in the story), and latterly a more sporadic, occasion-centred set of images that seem more disjointed and unconnected. Interspersed with pictures of the young men are photographs of several families – mothers, fathers, sisters, nieces, cousins; project staff (there are a whole range of photos of Sher Khan, usually asleep, in different settings); and there are the walk-on photos of other young men – school friends, visiting youth projects, individuals from local estates drafted in for football matches or who passed through the project for only a short time. Looking at the albums several months ago, Jamal commented that I had caught 'all the years of our growing up'.

In some ways Jamal was right: the albums do reflect a specific time and a sense of progressing, of 'growing up', growing together and eventually growing apart. For the little ones, in particular, the past five years have been a period of transformation, from fourteen-year old schoolboys to adulthood, from school to college, university and work, through the occasional stresses of puberty and sex and driving. On another level, the pictures reflect a more personal story, which charts my own development in research and with the project members, from its broader, more encompassing beginning (otherwise characterized as total confusion and a terror of missing anything), to its intense period of focus on the young men who form the core of this study (along with a broadening of connections, in some cases, with their families and other friends), and then to its later, current position of both distance and familiarity; of more occasional contact with some and a familial ease with others. At the same time, what is presented is a far more selective and subjective photo-story than Jamal's comment suggests. What is absent from the albums are the myriad photos that were badly focused, or jumbled, or of people I did not know (or like), or that I decided were irrelevant or simply boring. What the albums constitute, then, is a carefully edited portrait, with photographs selected at the time of taking and again at the time of mounting. Although they are *a* reflection of those years, the albums are crucially *my* reflection of those years, at events where I was present (for example the trip to Tunisia in 1998 is not represented), with subjects of my choosing and composed, usually in dialogue, though sometimes not, with the individuals contained therein. They reflect, therefore, a set of preferences, of encounters and of interpretations that are my take on those years, which are a recognizable but not definitive portrait, and that by default do not represent events that I was not a party to. They reflect, then, a partial gaze, one that renders other accounts or other events invisible; at the same time, I am largely absent from the representation – there are very few pictures in which I appear, though I am the author of all those in which I do not appear. There are, of course, other collections of photographs, which tell different tales and represent different events and different encounters – but those are someone else's stories.

In many ways, the photographs show the story that I would like to have told, that I had planned on telling. They capture the fun, the affection and the energy of those days and those young men, they tell stories of adventures and experience, of change and growing, of the everyday and the new and the triumphant. The story as it has emerged, as much to my surprise as anyone's, is in some ways much darker and less forgiving than I had expected, more focused on problems and issues and debates than I would have wished – more haunted by the folk devil of 'the Gang'. Perhaps there is less to be said about the positive and the ordinary, and perhaps that says something about the ways in which black communities in Britain are understood. Perhaps that is why a newspaper article I wrote in 1996 on Black History month and the *Style and Culture* fashion show was rejected by the features editor for being 'too celebratory' and 'too subjective'. No burned out estate cars, I guess.

Conclusion

These happier, more ordinary moments nevertheless form an important perceptual and emotional baseline for the study, one that may have been lost in the process, but still a significant one in setting the scene. On a broader level, the albums also represent a version of the research process captured in the preceding chapters. The portrait painted in these pictures is, then, time and place specific, more a series of snapshots that a full-fledged documentary; the events are located within a particular geographical and temporal space, enacted through a particular group of individuals within a bounded period of their lives. While I have tried to make these boundaries and internal changes explicit whenever possible, it must be borne in mind that these young men have already moved on from these positions, and even at the time of writing are still moving on. Similarly, in the course of the two years this book has been in the making, my relationships with the young men and the material have also changed. From the relationships outlined in Chapter 2, for example, I went on to develop closer and stronger links with members of the older group, particularly those on the Senior Member's Committee, and these have informed much of the writing of later chapters. Over the past year, my links with the project have lessened, though my interaction with some individuals has grown much stronger; several have been integral to the writing process, commenting on drafts and providing sounding boards for ideas, or acting as *aides memoires* to half-remembered events or histories. Rather than treating these relationships as bounded and static, I have attempted to incorporate comments and changes in the text, which explains the sometimes erratic timescales from chapter to chapter; similarly, I have included events that happened outside the scope of the initial fieldwork period to capture the sense of process and of continuity in the research and writing dynamic. There are also, of course, the discontinuities – the ruptures in writing, which has made the move from the Open University to Southampton and, finally, to South Bank, through three homes, five computers and two summers in the Caribbean (where admittedly not much writing was done) – which have left their mark, apparent most of all in the time it has taken to complete the manuscript. I have resisted the urge to make the text more coherent and seamless; though it would perhaps be neater, the process of writing has itself been an untidy and sometimes jagged experience – one that I have chosen not to make anonymous and distant and smooth.

One of the main aims of the book when I started it was to make the process of writing more transparent and more dialogic, to construct it with the young men as fully included in the process as possible. The final result has, I think, been more authored than I had hoped or envisioned, although the text has been formed in discussion with, and seen by, a number of the young men as well as by Yasmin and other workers. Although it is not always apparent in the finished product, some changes were made in accordance with comments or criticisms; some quotes were left out, some stories amended, some interpretations re-thought. At some points, it seemed impossible to please everyone and compromises were made that pleased no one: for example, the history of the SAYO project in Chapter 3 was seen by Majid as too negative in its portrayal of the young men, while Silver argued that the description of Shopna was unjustifiably harsh. In the end the issue remained unresolved: I was not there during that phase of the project's development and was unable to weigh up the different accounts, so I made some minor changes and could only acknowledge the contestation of perspectives. The young men who read the chapters, and discussed them with their friends in cars on Saturday nights, were less critical and were, I think, remarkably open-minded about my presentation of their lives and opinions.[1] However, they did not always agree with my version of events and although some details were taken out or altered in discussion, it still remains my interpretation rather than a transparent reflection of their experience.

For myself, throughout the writing process, there was a constant and conscious editing of material that went beyond a simple selection of stories and quotes to illustrate my arguments. The text contains, then, a number of silences and omissions; it excludes the voices of those young men I did not interview, many of whom feature in the text with parts scripted only by me; it excludes young women and parents; it renders invisible the young men who were the combatants in the conflicts described; and it has overlooked, to a large extent, institutional perspectives. There are also, of course, the sections of interview I chose not to include; the details that the young men chose not to tell me (or told me later, in the strictest confidence) and the many things I will never know (but perhaps might still miss). Much of the material I collected or the knowledge I accumulated over the past five years is not present in the book, perhaps because it was intensely private and I had either been asked not to use it, or knew it to be sensitive; because it was irrelevant or tangential to the subjects on which I finally decided to focus; because the details or personalities involved were too easy to identify; because there were some doubts about who might finally read the book and learn, to quote Humzah, 'dark secrets' (interview, 5 October 1996). For the young men, these potential readers were envisioned as people they knew, part of their imagined community, whom they would feel uncomfortable in providing this hitherto carefully screened 'knowledge'; I myself was more concerned with my role and responsibilities in relation to the young men in the study *vis-à-vis* a wider audience, engaged in the construction or legislation of Asian/black youth identities.

In the Introduction to *DisOrienting Rhythms*, Sharma, Hutnyk and Sharma (1996) point accusingly to – or perhaps I mean *at* – a burgeoning literature on South Asian communities in Britain and Europe, which, monolithically and inescapably, reinscribes an Orientalist gaze. The authors argue:

> These cultural forms continue to be imbued with an exoticized, othered status in the West and our primary goal has been to break out of the Orientalist tradition of making knowable these cultural productions for an ever-eager academic audience and other agencies of control. (Sharma, Hutnyk and Sharma, 1996: 2)

The process of 'knowing' or 'understanding' is inseparable from the inscription of relations of power and control, most particularly in relation to the surveillance of black youth. They continue:

> We recognise interest in a sociology of South Asian culture in Britain, and especially youth cultures, as having close ideological connections with the disciplines of command that police inner-urban neighbourhoods, close down Black clubs, collude in immigration control and so on.

Top of their academic Hit List are 'exercise(s) in meticulous descript-ion, or authoritative ethnography, or insider "native" accounts' (Sharma, Hutnyk and Sharma, 1996: 1–2); a list that encompasses most work on South Asian cultures (see Benson, 1996 and Chapter 1 of this book) and, perhaps justifiably, reveals the researcher as 'innocent' (or not) assassin.

In its defence, I would argue that ethnography, at least at its theoretical margins, has developed a highly critical self-reflexive gaze that has undermined its claims to 'truth' and to making known 'the Other', and made explicit the relations of power that create and sustain it (Clifford, 1988; Clifford and Marcus, 1986; Rosaldo, 1989). Nevertheless, it remains the case that very little ethnographic work, still less the wider range of empirical studies, actually takes the time to acknowledge these tensions and even less bother to make the dynamics visible, except in occasional footnotes (a recent exception is Back, 1996). It is true, moreover, that the ethnographic gaze still predominantly defines research on South Asian communities in Britain and still – in spite of its critical edge – stubbornly inhabits the domain of 'Truth', of the 'authentic' voice of 'the Other'. In many ways, the central claims of empirical research to an unmediated pathway to 'reality' – and, perhaps more importantly, to policy formation – has continued largely unaffected by theoretical critiques; indeed, it could even be argued that the increasing separation between theory and empiricism has allowed the latter to largely ignore the strictures of critical reflexivity, while dismissing theorists in their turn for having become abstracted from any empirical base. Ethnography may no longer be fashionable, it may have been exposed as a hopelessly flawed enterprise, but its power – even as an emblem of 'Truth' – remains undiminished.

The present work finds itself rather between a rock and a hard place; in seeking to create an ethnographic piece of work that makes no claims to objectivity or 'Truth' but which, at the same time, is involved in the construction of a portrait of a group of 'real' people, it runs the risk of being dismissed by some as 'too subjective' and by others as writing for 'the Enemy'. A colleague of mine, also an anthropologist by training, once told me that it would be better for me to 'write fiction'. My dilemma has become perhaps more acute by the changing focus of the book as I wrote it; as it transformed from what I had initially – and rather naively – imagined to be a relatively benign, or even positive, piece of work exploring Asian youth identities[2] to a more closely focused engagement with the notion of 'the Asian Gang'. While I had been hoping to move away from the folk devil after the events described in Chapter 4, it seemed that any framing of the discussion of peer group, friendship, community and gender were inseparable from the ascription of pathology and incipient criminality that defined 'the Gang'. Like black youth identities, it seems that Asian youth have become synonymous with crisis and with threat. It became impossible, then, to frame my account either through the dominant problem-oriented representation of 'the Gang', or apart from it. By the same token, it was impossible to write the narrative thread as either simply about constraint or simply about creativity (though my heart still leans towards the latter). Sharma, Hutnyk and Sharma (1996) have criticized both the sociology-as-social-control and the increasingly fashionable cultural-studies-as-celebration approaches to ethnic minorities, particularly in the light of the emergent focus on Asian youth cultures, as silencing the contradictions and ambivalences inherent in this positionality. Crucially, they place politics explicitly back at the centre of academic research, and have thrown down the gauntlet to others:

> We are interested in both diversification and consolidation of the possible points of resistance to such imperatives of disciplinary control, and in a critique of the celebration and substitution of 'difference' for ensuing socio-economic

inequalities and racial terror . . . against simplification, against anti-politics, against victimologies. (Sharma, Hutnyk and Sharma, 1996: 2)

The challenge is one that the present work takes seriously – perhaps more so in the light of the suspicion of collusion and treachery-by-default in which ethnography is already mired. Although it was not what he meant, I have followed my colleague's advice and chosen to write 'fiction' (Clifford, 1988); moving away from an authenticist account towards one that is explicitly subjective, partial (in both senses, as fragmented and affectionate) and situated. Rather than making 'the Other' known, its aim has been to contest this possibility, to argue for a knowledge that is both highly located and shifting, structured through an unequal dialogue between researcher and subjects, and unavoidably compromised in the act of writing. The material contained here does not make claims for autonomous data revealing an unmediated 'reality', but constitutes a dialogue with and between alternative forms of representation; my own, those of the individuals in the study and the hegemonic discourse around 'the Asian Gang', in its popular and academic manifestations. In place of a structure/culture, representation/reality, constraint/agency dichotomy, then, the study posits a dialectic in which each is enmeshed in, and constitutive of, the other – or, indeed, 'the Other'.

A claim to partiality, to 'writing fiction', should not, however, be seen as a convenient escape route for those who prefer their academic writing more opaque and their 'Truths' unmediated. In making the dynamics of the research more explicit, the aim has not been to deny its wider significance in the understanding of Asian youth identities, nor to undermine the importance of representation and resistance in the lives and experiences of the young men of the SAYO project. Nor should the small- scale, personal approach adopted here obscure the wider implic- ations of the work regarding the construction of racialized representations of black communities in Britain or the demonization of black youth. Acknowledging the present work as 'fiction' is also to insist on the implication of all writing and research – theoretical or empirical – in the power relations that underscore the production of knowledge, in the inescapably political and partial nature of academic discourse, and in the lived effects of that discourse, however contested.[3] This is not, then, to reinscribe the notion of a top-down, labelling-theory production of identity, nor is it to champion the notion of a bottom-up, subcultural approach to resistance, but to argue for the ongoing – and unequal – intersection of multiple discourses of identity in the imagination of 'the Asian Gang' and, beyond this, of other folk devils.

In making these dynamics as explicit as possible, the aim is not to give the reader a get-out clause. Rather, I have aimed to explore the ramifications of bridging theory and empiricism, of fleshing out abstract assertions of complexity and ambivalence on the one hand, and of contesting fictions of objectivity and Truth in empirical research on the other. This is not to retreat to a position of absolute relativism or anthropological navel gazing – the issues are too important for that: however, it is to insist on the location of *all* research within an explicit historical and geographical space, with agendas – personal, political, theoretical – laid clearly on the table and with an eye on the stakes as well as the prize. More than this, I have taken seriously the agency of its subjects, *as subjects* rather than objects to be 'discovered', analyzed and contained. Rather than the more usual parachute-in-interview-and-escape route to empirical research, I have been lucky enough to spend time with the young men in this study, getting to know them in all their complexity and richness – their histories, their lives, their experiences – over nearly five years. The result is, I think, a more open, mutual encounter; one that defies ownership and disrupts certainties (even mine). In moving beyond the quantifying, categorizing *Whiskas*-cat-food approach that characterizes so much empirical research, particularly on Asian communities ('eight out of ten Asian girls told us . . .'), I have tried to sketch a portrait of people I know well and care deeply for and about. If the book is not about giving them voice – and it is not – it *is* about acknowledging their presence and their impact in the research process, and their existence beyond its confines. At the same time, the aim has been to place these individuals within a broader canvas of representation, structure and inequality; using their stories as a study of social process writ small. It is, after all, at this small, individual and personal level that social processes assume immediate, often devastating effect, are resisted, and, sometimes, meet a triumphant, if fleeting, defeat.

Re-imagining 'The Asian Gang': Ethnicity, Masculinity and Identity

In the midst of the current obsession with South Asian culture in Britain, and indeed worldwide,[4] it seems British Asian youth have finally arrived – belatedly perhaps – in a blaze of bindis, nosestuds and henna tattoos. Increasingly, urban youth culture has become entangled with notions of the 'Asian underground', now coming fast overground, and into the spotlight. As Sharma, Hutnyk and Sharma comment, 'Finally, the "coolie" has become cool' (1996: 1). This hypervisibility, as the *DisOrienting*

Rhythms collection importantly argues, has rendered invisible the enduring processes of racial violence and social exclusion, and left untold the longer history of Asian cultural practice and resistance (Kalra, Hutnyk and Sharma, 1996). There is, however, an additional dimension to this hypervisibility, perhaps best characterized as 'the Other' to 'the new Asian cool' – the 'uncool', the dangerous, the threatening 'Other' – also newly discovered, equally visible, equally under scrutiny, but hardly celebrated. This 'Other' is best captured in the image of 'the Underclass', 'the Fundamentalist' and, of course, 'the Gang'.

'The Asian Gang' has emerged as a relatively new phenomenon, at least in the minds of the media and more latterly, of academics and social researchers. Its 'discovery' has brought Asian communities to the forefront of public concerns over crime, urban decay, poverty and civil unrest, increasingly taking the place of Britain's African-Caribbean communities as scapegoats amidst renewed prophecies of millennial social doom.[5] 'The Asian Gang' has particular potency, fusing longer established fears of 'the Underclass' and 'the Fundamentalist/Terrorist' with the physical presence of young men on the imaginary landscape of the city. Concerns over 'social exclusion' then seamlessly become translated into the marking of boundaries of 'social inclusion' in the imagination of society or nation, defining out the marginalized, the alien, the Othered.

As I argued in Chapter 1, the imagination of 'the Asian Gang' marks the redefinition of Asian communities in Britain in three closely connected areas: ethnicity, gender and generation. These have combined to place Muslim young men under the spotlight as the new folk devil, marking a transition in the perception of Asian communities from passive victim to aggressor – a reformulation increasingly predicated on the reification of perceived religio-cultural divisions, which draw on common-sense notions of cultural and gender dysfunction to transfix Muslim identities as Threat. The present work has sought to explore some of these notions as they impact on, and are contested by, the young men of the SAYO project, and to examine their broader implications for the understanding of identity construction. While not necessarily offering any solutions, the study does pose some challenges to the current theorisation of ethnicity, gender, generation and identity, which argue for a re-imagination of 'the Asian Gang'.

Ethnicity

As the Introduction to *DisOrienting Rhythms* points out, the 1990s saw a resurgence in the popularity of 'ethnicity', 'Ethnicity is in. Cultural difference is in. Marginality is in' (Sharma, Hutnyk and Sharma, 1996: 1). As a mode of consumption, the 'ethnic' has never been so fashionable, nor so profitable, while as a theoretical concept 'ethnicity' has been rescued from the 1980s culturalist scrapheap (CCCS 1982), given a cultural studies makeover and released as the 'new' identity politics.

Of course, despite its 'new' reincarnation, old-style ethnicity has never quite left the scene. This is particularly true of studies of Britain's Asian communities, which are still largely framed and made known through traditional anthropological concepts such as 'culture', and 'community', themselves imagined primarily as bounded and static ideals. As Banks (1996) has argued, the term 'ethnicity' has been additionally reinvented and given common-sense status as defining 'cultural difference' in an increasingly primordial sense, providing explanatory power to 'ethnic' conflict abroad and hostility at home. Ethnicity has thus become inseparable from its synonyms – community, culture and nationalism (Banks, 1996: 171); however, while it has never quite escaped its links with racism and colonialism, it has been reinvented and reclaimed as the champion of 'the Other' – taking the perspective of the subject, giving voice to the 'actor', celebrating the positive, collective aspects of identity: what Modood (1992) refers to as 'one's mode of being' rather than 'one's mode of oppression'.

Modood's reification of 'the mode of being' conflates the sense of ethnicity as an essence of identity and the more conventional anthropological notion of ethnicity as a performance of culturally demarcated boundaries (Barth, 1969; Anthias and Yuval-Davis, 1992). This current of primordialism does, however, mark out the ambiguity of the concept of ethnicity in its 'old' incarnation; that in placing static notions of culture and community at its centre, it fixes identity and reifies 'difference' behind the barricades of ethnic absolutism, and becomes, in effect, the equivalent of 'race' (Gilroy, 1992). The central symbol of 'old' ethnicity is 'community', which evokes ideals of bounded cultural entities defined by internal homogeneity and external difference, real or imagined. The assumption of collective identity facilitates processes both of solidarity and resistance, and of labelling and pathologization (Anthias and Yuval-Davis, 1992), and which marks out individuals as the repository of these cultural practices, whether valorized or demonized.

The symbolic currency of 'community' can be clearly traced in the emergence of the notion of 'the Muslim community' in the past decade. Celebrated as the emergence of a new consciousness, whether religious (Lewis, 1994; Baumann, 1996; Modood et al., 1997), philosophical (Sayyid, 1997), cultural (Jacobson, 1997; Baumann, 1996) or political

(Gardner and Shakur, 1994; Glavanis, 1998; Halliday, 1999), the term 'Muslim' has become to stand for people of particularly Pakistani and Bangladeshi descent, and increasingly to supplant alternative identifications (Modood, 1992; Modood et al., 1997). The reification of 'the Muslim community' has brought with it, however, its own set of demonologies – the underclass, the terrorist, the Fundamentalist, the book burner, the rioter – which have served equally to pathologize these groups *as* communities. Notions of cultural anachronism, of pre-modernity (Sayyid, 1997), of alienness have promoted a 'culture-of-poverty' approach to British Muslims, which is blamed for the problems faced by those of Pakistani and Bangladeshi origin. This pathologization is of particular significance for youth, who are seen either as the heirs of this cultural disadvantage or the victims of a doomed 'between two cultures' bid for freedom (cf. Modood et al., 1997: 147). The insistence on boundaries places youth either inside or outside 'community', which in turn is seen as the primary – if not the only – factor in the construction of identity. To be inside 'community' is to become an emblem of all the perceived ills of that cultural community; to be outside is to be without identity and on a course for social and cultural anomie: a lose–lose situation.

While 'old' ethnicity lost favour with many theorists in the 1980s, particularly under attack from the neo-Marxist writers on 'race' (CCCS, 1982) who saw the focus on 'culture' as ignoring structural inequalities and playing into the hands of New Racist ideologies of cultural difference, the 1990s have seen the reinvention of ethnicity as the new politics of identity. With the decline of the political salience of the inclusive term 'black' throughout the 1980s, and dealt its death blow, according to Modood (1992) with the Rushdie furore and the growth of Islamophobia, 'cultural difference' has been seized upon as the foundation for a new identity politics. Unlike its 'old' counterpart, however, the 'new' ethnicity is concerned not with fixed notions of 'being', but with the shifting, contingent and constructed notions of identity, what Hall has termed 'Not an essence, but a positioning' (1990: 226). Challenging unidimensional notions of 'black' identity, 'race' is seen not as *the* primary marker of identity but formulated through, and sometimes against, other structures, such as ethnicity, gender, class, sexuality – increasingly, religion – and so on. Hall argues:

> What is at issue here is the recognition of the extraordinary diversity of subjective positions, social experiences and cultural identities which compose the category 'black'; that is, the recognition that 'black' is essentially a politically and culturally constructed category, which cannot be grounded in

a set of fixed transcultural or transcendental racial categories and which therefore has no guarantees in Nature. (Hall, 1992: 254)

Hall places 'ethnicity' at the centre of these new identities, but seeks to uncouple it from its colonial legacy and replace it with 'a positive conception of the ethnicity of the margins, of the periphery' (Hall, 1992: 258). Rather than the traditional anthropological concept of ethnicity as a cultural possession or birthright – language, religion, ritual, dress, food – it becomes part of a socially, historically and politically located struggle over meaning and identity:

> Cultural identity, in this second sense, is a matter of 'becoming' as well as of 'being' . . . Cultural identities come from somewhere, have histories. But, like everything which is historical they undergo constant transformation. Far from being eternally fixed in some essentialised past, *they are subject to the continuous 'play' of history, culture and power.* (Hall, 1992: 225, my emphasis)

While Hall's analysis is aimed as much at dislocating hegemonic discourses of 'race' and nation as at the margin, it is on the latter that the concerns with cultural difference have congealed, most notably in the field of cultural studies. The emphasis has thus moved away from the contestation of the narratives of the centre (Bhabha, 1990) towards a celebration of the margin in and of itself, almost as an autonomous and inherently positive site of resistance. Marginality then becomes valorized, commodified and incorporated into the multi-cultural centre, part of a Benetton-style celebration of difference that silences the structures of inequality, renders invisible historical location and denies political action except as a feature of style (A. Sharma, 1996). Ash Sharma comments:

> The debate about marginality itself is becoming a politics, and not a discursive site from which to intervene into the functioning of cultural violence. Instead, the margin is the place from which dominant structures exercise their disciplinary control . . . the power relations between centre and margin remain intact. (Sharma, 1996: 18)

This neutered version of the 'politics of difference', which has forgone 'politics' in the pursuit of 'difference' alone, ironically shares its margin with the old style anthropological ethnicity, which similarly reifies 'the mode of being' as distinct from 'the mode of oppression', and which celebrates 'culture' as the core of identity formation. It also, paradoxically, shares the same obsession with 'authenticity', though defined here by hierarchies of marginality, and by the valorization of 'hybridity' as the new essence, the emblem of 'reality' and 'Truth' – unless, of course, it is tainted with commercialism. The aim for ethnicity, old and new, is then to render knowable 'the Other', whether from behind the cultural barricades, or across the (level) playing field of cultural production.

It is interesting to reflect on the implications of these two versions of ethnicity for understanding black identities. Firstly, it is worth noting that 'new ethnicity' has been more comfortable with the construction and play of African-Caribbean identities than it has with Asian or African identities, defining 'diaspora' as crucially a Caribbean experience. It has then played down the emphasis on continuity, imagination, history and memory (for example, in Hall's 1990, 1992 work) for a reductive fascination with change and disruption and difference in the definition of primarily contemporary black identity and cultural production – with the 'new' at the expense of the 'ethnicities'. At the same time, it has proved uncomfortable with the more 'culture-rich/tradition-bound' Asian communities and has tended to consign them to the 'Fundamentalist' fringe, left to the mercy of 'old ethnicity'. The exception would be the interest in the work of Salman Rushdie and Hanif Kureishi, but perhaps the reaction to *The Satanic Verses* proved an unexpected, decidedly un-hybrid, empirical obstacle to the theoretical celebration of difference. Secondly, the concern with representation has focused attention mainly at the level of culture as cultural production – music, film, theatre, literature – and ignored empirical research, while 'old' ethnicity has continued, unabashed and un(der)theorized, in uncovering 'the real'. There has been, with the exception of my own study (Alexander, 1996), little recent empirical work on black identity creation in Britain and a total absence of work on Asian cultures from a theoretical perspective until *DisOrienting Rhythms* (Sharma, Hutnyk and Sharma, 1996). Thirdly, the result of these divergences has been the absence of recognition of processes of continuity, of solidarity and of community in recent theoretical work on black communities, and a corresponding denial of the impact of structure and processes of change and reimagination in Asian identities. Black Caribbean identities – particularly youth identities – are then synonymous with hybridity and creativity, while Asian identities remain largely correlates of 'community', perhaps newly formulated but nevertheless bounded and impenetrable.[6] At the same time, a suspicion of 'old' ethnicity has led 'new' ethnicity to designate any expression of solidarity or 'community' as 'ethnic absolutism' or dangerous fantasy, the breeding ground of essentialist, fundamentalist, nationalist and potentially racist ideologies.

This version of 'new ethnicities' is, however, a watered-down and one-sided account, one that has ripped out the power and the politics of its original formulation in the search for a post-modern reclamation of the margins as a source of knowledge and profit. Leaving aside the popularization of concepts like hybridity,[7] Hall's conception of 'new ethnicities' is fraught with contradiction, with tension and with ambiguity – it is a narrative that acknowledges the encounter of the old and the new, history and its reinvention, continuity and change, memory and fantasy (Hall, 1990; 1992). It is in and between these encounters that identities are formed and performed; 'culture' is not a free-floating commodity enterprise but bound up with, inseparable from and constitutive of, structure (Hall, 1992; West, 1992). It is not a denial of 'community' but of its ossification:

> Cultural identities are the points of identification, the unstable points of identification or suture, which are made within the discourses of history and culture. Not an essence but a positioning ... Difference, therefore persists – in and alongside continuity. (Hall, 1990: 226–7)

'New ethnicities' in this stronger form resist categorization and knowing, they resist reclamation and they disrupt attempts at management (Hesse, forthcoming): if they did not, they would not be dangerous and there would be no need for folk devils.

Masculinities

As I argued in Chapter 1, one of the central shifts in the imagination of Asian communities in Britain has been in the regendering of identity. This has been an integral, but often unstated, element in the shift of concern from private to public spheres of concern and the recent focus on youth. It is also inseparable from the racialization of Muslim communities, and particularly their reinvention as 'the Underclass', the embodiment of social and cultural dysfunction and danger. A recurrent thread in the imagination of 'the Gang' has been the race-ing of Muslim youth, particularly through associations with African-American youth culture and ghetto subculture. The gendering of this discourse is often implicit; 'race' comes to stand for masculinity (Gilroy, 1993), but also to subsume it and to 'speak for it', rendering it effectively 'invisible' (West, 1993). Although studies of 'race' have been criticised for focusing on men and ignoring women (Wallace, 1979; Hull, Scott and Smith, 1982), it is also true that in the privileging of 'race', black masculinity has also been erased. It is significant, for example, that accounts of 'race' and gender focus exclusively on black women (Anthias and Yuval Davis, 1992; Mirza, 1997), while black masculinity has been left unscrutinized and marginalized in its assumed patriarchal dominance.

While the growth of masculinity studies in the academy has focused increased attention on male subjectivities, and concerns about identity crises amongst men, particularly in the previously 'male' arenas of education and employment, have proliferated in the media, it remains the case that black masculinities have been largely ignored empirically and underdeveloped theoretically. While (white) masculinities have been made visible in all its conflicts, ambiguities, changes and reimaginations, the primary axis for division in male identity formation has been sexuality rather than 'race' (Connell, 1987). 'Race' is significantly absent, or present only as the transparent reflection of the white hegemonic gaze – 'symbols' through which white gender categories are created and performed. In *Masculinities*, Connell argues, 'hegemonic masculinity among whites sustains the institutional oppression and physical terror that have *framed the making of masculinity in black communities*' (1995: 80, my emphasis). Where black men appear, then, the privileging of 'race' has denied agency and constructed black masculinities as subordinated and marginalized, as the living through of the dominant white imagination. Ironically, as white masculinities have been thrown increasingly into crisis and fragmented, black masculinity has been transfixed through 'race' as the new certainty – the 'authentic' masculinity against which white masculinities are defined and performed – often violently (Messerschmidt, 1998).

Masculinity in its blackness, then, serves to naturalize and essentialize male identifications, suppressing more complex representations and denying black male subjectivities (hooks, 1992). Crucially, this unidimensional portrait defines black masculinity as lacking in relation to dominant (white) patriarchal norms, 'tormented by their inability to fulfil the phallocentric masculine ideal' (hooks, 1992: 89). Black masculinity is thus imagined as not only as 'in conflict with the normative definition of masculinity' (hooks, 1992: 96), but as a failing rather than alternative formulation. Unable to fulfil their patriarchal responsibilities as providers, heads of household and authority figures, the argument continues, black men retreat to a compensatory hyper-masculinity, centred on sexuality and violence, living through 'Black Macho' fantasies, often at the expense of black women (Wallace, 1979; hooks, 1992; Mac an Ghaill, 1994).

Accounts of black masculinity have focused primarily on black youth, adding the elements of generational crisis and public presence to the incipient sense of danger. Recent work on black expressive cult notably in cinema and music, have argued against the hyper-visibility of black macho stances, and the commodification of black anger (Dyson, 1993; Giroux, 1996; Mercer, 1994). Such accounts have importantly challenged the naturalization of black masculine identities and the erasure of alternative formulations (hooks, 1992; Blount and Cunningham, 1996). As Mercer and Julien have argued, black masculinity can only be understood as part of a wider and more complex dialectics of power, in which racialized masculinities are imagined, policed, lived out and contested in specific and often contradictory ways (Mercer and Julien, 1994; Alexander, 1996). However, it remains the case that the construction of black masculinity within the social sciences has rarely been informed by critical theory and continues to occupy a position of 'Knowledge' or 'Truth-giving' (Blount and Cunningham, 1996). Thus, the vast majority of empirical work on black youth, notably in Britain,[8] continues to reinscribe common-sense images of deviance and particularly of gendered cultural pathology (Pryce, 1979; Cashmore and Troyna, 1982; Mac An Ghaill, 1994).

As mentioned in Chapter 1, Asian masculinities have been invisible in discussions of racialized male identities until very recently (Goody, 1999; Macey, 1999). Where black youth identities have been visioned as primarily male (but cf. Mirza, 1992), Asian communities have been imagined as female, with the focus on gender oppression, runaway girls and arranged marriage systems (Carby, 1982; Jacobson, 1997; Hennink, Diamond and Cooper, 1999). While some important critical work has been done on Asian women (Brah, 1996), Asian men have been largely overlooked *as* men; in the very few accounts of Asian youth, for example, masculinity is subsumed into an emphasis on 'race' (Bains, 1988; Westwood, 1991) or ethnicity (Macey, 1999).

The recent imagination of Muslim masculinities has drawn on a legacy of racialized pathologies; witness, for example, Macey's (1999) account of the gender oppression underscoring (and undermining) the Bradford 'riots'. While the term 'Muslim', like 'black', is imagined as primarily a male identity, at the same time, masculinity has become synonymous with a racialized ethnicity, which precludes the possibility of agency and transfixes Muslim men as the new dangerous 'Other'. This has particularly equated Muslim youth with a failing masculine identity that takes both women and other Asian young men as the primary targets of its lack of self esteem and frustration (Macey, 1999; Goodey, 1999). The similarities with ideas of African-American 'nihilism' (West, 1994) are palpable and hardly accidental, providing a legitimating symbol that lies at the centre of the imagination of 'the Gang'. Muslim masculinities are then positioned as outside, and in opposition to, hegemonic norms of male behaviour, defined through deviance and subject to increasingly stringent forms of social control. There is, of course, the added specificity of an assumed religio-cultural anachronism which underscores the attribution of misogyny and patriarchal oppression, and which marks out rigid boundaries for the performance of male identities. The racialization of black young men, on the one hand, and the religio-ethnicization of Asian young men on the other, leaves Muslim youth visioned as twice disadvantaged and doubly dysfunctional, with apparently no space for difference, contestation or reimagination.

Youth

The third element in the imagination of 'the Asian Gang' is generation, and the problematization of youth identities. As argued in Chapter 1, 'youth' as a category is almost inseparable conceptually from gender and, over the past twenty years, has also become closely associated with 'race'. The positioning of youth-as-problem has further associations with the urban landscape, with class status and particularly with the control of public space, i.e. with *visibility*. In *Gender and Power*, for example, Connell argues that 'concentrations of adult young men are the most intimidating and dangerous' (Connell, 1987: 133), continuing that this is particularly (or perhaps exclusively) the case in areas of 'high unemployment and *ethnic exclusion*' (Connell, 1987, my emphasis). The image of 'the Gang' has come increasingly to symbolize this nexus of crisis, the intersection of raced, gendered and socio-economic exclusion of volatile youth set against the landscape of 'the Street'. In *Masculinities*, Connell elaborates:

> *Youth gang violence of inner-city streets* is a striking example of the assertion of *marginalised masculinities* against other men. (Connell, 1995: 82, my emphasis)

The trope of 'the Street' is deeply encoded as a metaphor for gender and for 'race'; it is black men who are seen to own 'the Street'; more specifically, it is *young* black men, who are seen to imbue this space with a subculture of violence and criminality. It is 'the Street' that defines this presence as a public problem, and a locus for social control; it is 'the Street' that defines the presence of black young men as 'a Gang' (Keith, 1995a).

It is certainly true that research on 'gangs' in the US has conflated issues of race, gender and generation in the construction of 'the Gang'.

Klein (1995), for example, defines *The American Street Gang* as predominantly black male youth; self-identified groups of racially/ethnically
homogeneous men with an average age of twenty years. The gendering
of the gang is an unstated assumption – work on 'girl gangs' (Campbell,
1984) by default defines the norm as male – as Hagedorn's work on gang
masculinities makes clear, 'gender, like water for fish, is often taken for
granted in gang research' (Hagedorn,1998: 154). What is ubiquitous, but
invisible, in the construction of the American 'gang' is, of course 'race' –
Hagedorn's article does not even mention it, despite the fact that all the
young men he interviews are either African-American or Hispanic, while
Klein's work places 'race' as a defining factor but fails to unpack it, leaving
it as a self-explanatory marker of alienation and exclusion. What is also
left silent is the significance of 'youth' in marking out the sense of threat,
although it is clear from the concerns over black youth cultural forms,
such as 'gangsta rap' in the 1990s, that generation was crucial in defining
mainstream America's deepest fears.[9]

I would argue that, like the term 'mugging' before it (Hall et al., 1978),
the label of 'the Gang' has been re-imported into Britain in its already
deeply raced and gendered American formulation and used to provide a
set of common-sense associations and understandings in redefining and
refining 'the problem' of black youth. In particular, it has worked, as in
the US (Giroux, 1996), to impose a conservative culturalist perspective
on black youth identifications, which has focused on cultural pathology
at the expense of structural inequality, naturalizing 'the Gang' as the
inevitable outcome of a damaged masculine identity and absence of self-
esteem. This has focused attention on 'intra-group' or 'inter-racial'
violence, erasing the wider place of racial violence in the policing of
black communities in Britain or, indeed, placing black young people as
the new perpetrators of 'racist' violence (Goodey, 1999).

There is, of course, an alternative account of youth identities, which
draws on the cultural studies approach, and which places youth at the
forefront of social and political change, particularly in Britain, since 1945
(Brake, 1985; Osgerby, 1998). These accounts focus on youth subcultural
style, and on the role of youth identities in challenging hegemonic
structures, notably from a class perspective (Willis, 1977). The role of
black youth cultural expression within this schema has, however, always
been ambivalent; on the one hand, denying the possibility of creativity
through the imposition of racial constraint (Brake, 1985), and on the other,
representing the epitome of cultural resistance (Brake, 1985; Hebdige,
1976). This latter version carries with it, of course, the criminalization of
black youth expression (Gilroy, 1987), which marks the intersection of

the early cultural studies approach with the sociological pathologization of black youth (Cashmore and Troyna, 1982; Cohen, 1993). The expansion of the commercial youth market and the commodification of 'style' has largely undermined a simplistic 'resistance through rituals' celebration of youth (CCCS, 1975), but the resurgent interest in representation and the 'politics of difference' has given new life to those theorists seeking political potential in cultural expression.[10]

The celebration of youth culture as the cutting edge of postmodern identity formation has resonance with the 'new ethnicities' debates outlined above, most obviously in the assertion of new 'hybrid' forms, particularly in popular music, in the wake of media globalization and new patterns of cultural consumption (Osgerby, 1998; Miller, 1997; DuGay et al., 1997). The destabilising of identity positions has focused attention on the proliferation of identifications inscribed in youth culture and on the processes of 'cut-and-mix' (Hall, 1990) and of 'translation' (Bhabha, 1990), which blend together diverse cultural forms into new 'hybrid' forms – commodified, marketed and consumed as a form of progressive politics; the *coca-cola-ization* of identity politics (Gillespie, 1995). This has led to the reification of 'hybridity' as positive and progressive, in and of itself, and obscured the wider processes of power relations, appropriation and exploitation that occur in the production and consumption of youth culture (Sharma, Hutnyk and Sharma, 1996; Banerjea, forthcoming). In addition, little exploration is made of the relationship between consumption of youth styles and the living out, or not, of 'hybridity' amongst young people. At the same time, the search for exclusive space by black young people is perceived as at once 'inauthentic' and as politically regressive, usually demonized around the issue of gender and sexuality.

The place of Asian youth within these approaches is one of a traditional Absence and of an increasingly ambivalent Presence. Where Asian young men were, until the last decade, invisible in the discussion around youth, subsumed either into the comfortable patriarchal holism of 'the Asian community', or into the political category 'black', in which the struggles of Asian communities have been largely forgotten, their current hyper-visibility has congealed around these two opposing ideological imaginations of youth. The first places Asian youth as 'problem', drawing on both the longer history of 'identity crisis' (usually for young women) and the contemporary pathologization of Muslim communities. Brake, for example, notes, 'Asian youth has been stereotyped either as passive, withdrawing into its own culture, or else suffering from generational conflict' (Brake, 1985: 139). 'The Gang', in particular, places Asian youth within the conventions of a compensatory peer group identity created in response to the rejection of a failing parental culture and wider social exclusion. This has built on the culturalist, 'old ethnicities' approach to Asian communities, which has largely ignored the presence of youth altogether (Werbner, 1990; Shaw, 1988) or characterized change as loss. Where more recent studies have attempted to adopt a more fluid approach to Asian youth identities (Gardner and Shukur, 1994; Baumann, 1996; Anwar, 1998), most have perpetuated a 'traditional/ non-traditional' dualism that reifies parental cultures in some imagined originary moment and measures youth transitions in relation to – and usually against – this yardstick. Alternatively, Asian youth (usually young men) are demonized as the carriers of a dysfunctional and absolutist cultural heritage, increasingly epitomized by external aggression and internal oppression of other Asian young men and Asian women (Goodey, 1999). The emergence of new Islamicized identities amongst Muslim youth, in particular, has created an analytical crisis; the growth of a 'new' identity that denies parental culture but also actively rejects inclusion within wider British society. It is no accident, I think, that these 'new' but defiantly 'unhybrid' identities have been placed within the history of compensatory black cultural reaction (such as Rastafari), defined against the white norm and opposed to it. Modood et al. thus argue of second generation South Asians:

> For many, the strength of their ethnic identity was owed to a group pride in response to perceptions of racial exclusion and ethnic stereotyping by the white majority. The consequent sense of rejection and insecurity was instrumental in assertions of ethnic identities. (Modood et al., 1997: 337)

By the same token, it is hardly coincidental that it is emergent Muslim identities that have become synonymous with 'gang' activity, and with associations of marginality, alienation and threat.

The second approach seeks to celebrate Asian youth cultural style and expression as part of a new identity politics. The over-culturalization of Asian youth has placed them as relative latecomers to the youth cultural scene: Brake, for example, comments '*Distinct* youth cultural forms have not as yet shown themselves in any style *recognisable to outsiders*' (Brake, 1985: 139, my emphasis). Brake's unwitting othering of Asian cultural forms reveals the conceptual dilemma in approaching Asian youth, seen at once as indistinct from parental Asian cultural forms, and as impenetrable to 'outsiders'– as doubly invisible. This has mired the question of Asian youth cultures in issues of 'authenticity', which has carried over into the more recent concern with emergent youth cultures. Sanjay Sharma has thus argued that academic understandings of Bhangra have reified it as *the* symbol of a new British Asian identity, silencing other dialogues with black cultural forms (Banerjea and Banerjea, 1996) and essentializing and privileging 'Asian' identity (Sharma, 1996). The term 'British Asian' captures the central paradox in the theorization of Asian youth identities – the hyphenated, hybrid form which itself distinguishes and delimits this new 'authentic' youth identity. It is, in fact, this new 'authentic' hybrid identity that has attracted so much attention in the past two or three years, celebrating Asian identities as 'the new black', the new voice of 'the underground' (Banerjea, forthcoming), the 'new Asian cool'. It is the acceptable, commercial face of 'the Other'; marginal but not alienated, different but not dangerously so, 'authentic', but not too close to 'the real thing'.

A recent critical perspective has emerged around the idea of cultural politics, which seeks to challenge this latter perspective in its too-easy celebration of youth expression as inherently political. As Sharma, Hutnyk and Sharma (1996) have argued, the cultural studies fixation with marginal sites of cultural expression serves to obscure wider processes of exclusion and inequality, the continuance of racial violence, and the implication of the academy in the construction and control of 'the Other'. Importantly, *DisOrienting Rhythms* has an explicit agenda aimed at undermining the exoticization of Asian youth cultures and exploding authenticist myths of Asian identities, in either their essentialist or hybrid formulations, and in reintroducing politics into the increasing anti-politics of cultural studies consumption of 'difference'. By so doing, it is perhaps inescapable that the narrative risks being made to stand for, or speak for, the 'authentic Other', for taking a position that may proclaim its own instability and partiality but nevertheless inhabits the arena of 'truth giving'[11] – a bit like ethnography, in fact, but at least on the side of the angels.

* * *

In tracing the theoretical backgrounds above, the aim has been twofold. Firstly, to re-examine the theoretical assumptions which provide the foundation for the imagination of 'the Asian Gang' – in particular, the triumvirate of ethnicity, masculinity and youth. Secondly, to explore within each category the possibility of new theoretical pathways which challenge dominant versions and point the way to the re-imagination of 'the Asian Gang', and which can help frame the present discussion. Although these three elements have been considered largely separately, there are obvious overlaps and intersections; there are, in addition, a recurrence of arguments across categories, which work, in the case of 'the Asian Gang' to reinforce and reinscribe the other, so each term becomes effectively synonymous with, and substitutable for, the other. While I have tried to make these intersections explicit where possible, the common theoretical themes bear repeating here. Firstly, in the imagination of 'the Asian Gang' the most obvious commonality is the predominantly problem-oriented understanding of identity, in which crisis is assumed and works across each element to deepen the sense of impending doom. Thus, ideas of ethnic exclusion and threat feed into and exacerbate the sense of damaged masculinities and, in turn, of the public fear of young (working class) men with nothing to do and nowhere but the street to go. Secondly, the positioning of black male youth identities as problem also reinscribes the position as 'the Other', the deviant, the abnormal and plays into the ascription of criminal and pathologized identities. Thirdly, the racialization of ethnicity, masculinity and youth works to transfix and naturalize identities at the margins and to deny the idea of agency, change and subjectivity – that is, that 'the Asian Gang' exists simply as it is imagined to be, a mirror image and product of structural constraint and cultural atrophy. This assumes further that the representation of 'the Asian Gang' is a straightforward reflection of 'reality' and buys into notions of objectivity and authenticity – that black youth identities exist as an object of study and can be 'explained', understood and hence controlled. Fourthly, contemporary developments in identity theory, under the influence of postmodernism, have sought to challenge traditional approaches to ethnicity, masculinity and youth, and have drawn attention to the social constructedness of these categories. These developments have been crucial in signalling the embeddedness of these categories in relations of power and inequality, and opened the theoretical space for the recognition of change, of agency and of subjectivity; acknowledging the performative and situational nature of identity construction and allowing for ambiguity, translation and re-imagination. These approaches have highlighted the contested nature of identity and argued for the multi-faceted nature of identity formation, for example the intersection and contradictions of 'race' and masculinity. They have also championed the potential of these new syncretic forms of identity construction for political action, for challenging hegemonic represent-ations of marginalized identities and for contesting the nature of the hegemonic centre itself. However, in the rush to celebrate diversity, it is also true that the role of structure in the formation of these identities has been overlooked in favour of an inclusive multi-culture, in which politics becomes a feature of style and is put aside.

Conclusion

While the present project fairly obviously disavows the conventional problem-oriented account of Asian youth identities, I have rehearsed them here because of their centrality in the construction of popular perceptions of 'the Gang'. They provide then the theoretical and conceptual baseline that the present work has sought to deconstruct. The aim has not been, however, to simply cast them aside in favour of the more fashionable 'new' approach to identities, with its too easy reification of agency and difference, but to explore the intersection of these two approaches, recognizing the continued power of the old and the constrained impact of the new.

In seeking to reintroduce the centrality of power relations into the discussion of 'the Asian Gang', the study proposes no new or earth-shattering insights; it is rather a reclamation of the stronger version of 'new ethnicities', discussed above, which asserts the inseparability of structure and culture, which acknowledges the fraught and contradictory nature of identity construction and which recognizes processes of representation and (re)imagination in the inscription and contestation of Asian youth identities.

A central concern of the present work has been to trace the intersection of structure and culture in the representations of 'the Asian Gang', and the impact of these common-sense understandings on the lives of the young men of the SAYO project. As argued in Chapter 1, the perceived triple disadvantage of ethnicity, gender and generation has worked to position Asian young men as a 'new' threat to British society, the latest incarnation of the black youth folk devil. Representations of 'the Asian Gang' in the media have rehearsed these understandings, reinforcing the pathologization and criminalization of Asian youth identities and, in turn, feeding back into academic concerns over particularly Pakistani and Bangladeshi youth (Modood et al., 1997). It was argued, moreover, that the reification of 'culture' has precluded a more fluid understanding of Asian identities, a situation entrenched by the concerns over so-called 'Muslim Fundamentalism'. As explored in Chapters 3 and 4, these representations do not remain at the level of media mythmaking and what a friend of mine (a novelist) calls academic 'fact-faking'. Indeed, as Chapter 3 argues, the construction of the 'Muslim underclass' at a national level feeds into local pathologies structured around 'need' and 'threat'; the SAYO project itself had its roots in these convictions and a correspronding desire for control and containment, and its fortunes have waxed and waned largely in accordance with the growth or diminution of these perceptions. Similarly, as was argued in Chapter 4, the perception of the local Bengali young men as 'a gang' was partly legitimated by these wider representations and the belief in absolute, and antipathetic, ethnic identities. This served to label the conflicts discussed as 'racial' in nature and to deny alternative – usually more banal – explanations; it also framed the institutional responses to these events, which too swiftly turned them into a concrete and uncomfortable reality. By contrast, 'gang' folklore worked to position a history of concerted racial hostility towards the Stoneleigh Bengali community as 'gang' warfare, obscuring the wider structural dynamics of racial violence.

Of course, such definitions do not go uncontested, and these chapters also explore the alternative formulations offered by the young men of the SAYO project. These reformulations should not, however, be understood as either independent from, or in simple opposition to, dominant representations; indeed, the young men were aware of such representations and engaged with them in redefining their space – with greater or lesser success. These processes were often ambiguous – for example, the contestation around 'need', 'rights' and 'empowerment' within the project's history, or the use of the 'gang' mythology by the young men to provide an illusion of strength under fire and the involvement with the 'Triads'. Indeed, these external factors were often crucial in defining a sense of communal identity and mobilizing strong affective alliances, particularly in the too present shadow of the threat of violence. Chapters 4 and 5 have explored the role of external labelling and threat in the formation of peer group identifications, in the defining of boundaries and the motivation to action. However, as the chapters make clear, a reductive racialized or ethnicized account of these encounters serves to naturalize violence and obscure its more complex manifestations and motivations. While the fact of violence was often inescapable, what is important to recognize is the shifting meanings that were attached to such acts, that undermine dominant definitions and that point to a more complex set of dynamics around community and belonging. As these chapters have demonstrated, boundaries of the peer group and community were more fluid and permeable than a focus on ethnicity allows for, particularly in interaction with gender and age factors, defined, expanded and contracted according to each situation, local history and personality.

The present study aims to challenge conventional accounts of 'the Asian community' which focus on holistic and bounded, internally homogeneous cultural formations. In choosing to explore 'youth', the study makes claims for the intersection of ethnicity with gender and age formations, and marks processes of division and change in the reimagination of community and identity. Chapter 3 explores the construction of ethnicity through its association with deprivation and threat in the evocation of 'the inner city' and 'the underclass'; it also explores the contestation of these ethnicized pathologies in the history of the SAYO project. Chapter 4 seeks to challenge the racialization of Asian identities implicit in the notion of 'the gang', in particular the belief in 'inter/intra-ethnic' violence as an easy, ready-to-serve explanation for conflict. Chapters 5 and 6 are concerned with unpacking the conflation of ethnicity, gender and culture in the reification of Asian patriarchy, and exploring the processes of continuity and change in the relationship of youth to the wider community. The study thus understands ethnicity not as a culturally bounded, autonomous and internally homogeneous entity, but as insep-arable from, constructed through and disrupted by formulations of gender and sexuality, age, class and caste. This is not simply to replace 'old' with 'new' ethnicity in the creation of Asian youth identities, but to argue for a more nuanced, shifting and contextual account of identity formation, that recognises both structural constraint and cultural (re)imagination.

The performance of community that lies at the heart of these imagin-ations of identity similarly cannot be understood without reference to both these dynamics – the role of external constraint and of internal support. However, rather than privileging ethnicity as the dimension around which boundaries are enacted, the present work shows that 'community' is a contested identification in which ethnicity intersects with, is displaced or subsumed by, or contradicted through age, gender, locality, class and family. At the same time, however, acknowledging the processual nature of identity formation does not preclude the presence of strong, occasionally rigid and exclusive imaginations of communal identity and its demands. Chapters 5 and 6, in particular, have explored the intersection of ethnicity, age and masculinity in the construction of hierarchies of peer group identities that were fluid and contested but also clearly recognized and enacted in everyday interaction. Where versions of the 'new ethnicities' debate have tended to demonize these reifications as wholly negative and illusory, the present work would argue that the positive role of solidarity and support has been lost in these theoretical formulations; that it is possible – and usual – to imagine community identity in a way that makes space for solidarity without subsuming difference and without denying its shifting manifestations.

It is worth noting here that religion did not play a major role in the formation of the aspects of the identities explored here – at least not in any autonomous sense. Although the young men of the SAYO project were all Muslim, and the representations of Muslims in Britain had a significant impact in the framing of their identities as 'problem' (for example in the discussion around 'the underclass' in Chapter 3), and in the imagination of 'gang' identity, religion was more usually articulated by the young men in terms of 'culture'. Chapter 6, for example, noted that religion was a crucial part of the young men's perception of 'community' in relation to marriage and family, but it was also inseparable from the construction of 'the Bengali community'. All the young men described themselves first as Bengali and then as Muslim, but tended to see the two as interchangeable terms. There was little evidence of the emergence of a more inclusive 'British Muslim' identity (Modood, 1992), and although all the young men asserted the importance of religion in their lives, this was usually bound up with notions of family and locality, and an often-expressed – but also fleeting – guilt at not being 'better Muslims'. A number of the young men had earlier flirted with Islamicist youth groups such as the Young Muslim Organization, particularly during Hassan's leadership of the SAYO project, but had become quickly disillusioned and sceptical of their stance. There was, however, an enduring legacy of a critical and informed engagement with the construction of Islam in Bengali communities, and more widely (for example, in the media), amongst some of the young men, such as Shahin, Humzah and Hanif. This could not be understood, however, as a defensive or reactive affiliation as described elsewhere (Gardner and Shakur, 1994), nor as the assertion of a new religious identity or politics (Modood, 1992); it was rather another facet of identity and of community, one that waxed and waned in significance throughout the week or year and throughout their lives – '*a* mode of being', perhaps, but not *the* mode of being.

The same arguments can be made in relation to the performance of gender identities; in focusing on the creation of Asian masculinities, the present work has aimed to challenge hegemonic accounts of pathologized black male identity, making visible the contours and contradictions of these gendered formulations. In Chapters 5 and 6 in particular, the study has moved away from both the 'masculinities-in-crisis' thesis and the culturalist assertion of Asian homogeneous patriarchal oppression to explore the complex performance of masculine identity, hierarchy and authority, and to situate the peer group in relation to wider notions of community. Chapter 5 considers the role of friendship and support in facing situations of conflict, and points to some of the changing dynamics of peer group identities. Chapter 6 explores the role of age hierarchies and respect in the formation of Bengali masculinity, acknowledging both the power of culturally specific notions of the bounds of respect and its performance, and its contextual and contested nature. Chapter 6 also challenges simplistic notions of Asian patriarchy in the performance of gender relations, examining the complex web of hierarchy around age and family that cuts across gender. In addition, this chapter explores the role of gender and the policing of sexuality in creating or transgressing notions of community. While acknowledging 'race' and indeed culture as constitutive elements in the creation of masculine identities, the present work argues also for an account of masculine subjectivities that allow for change, contradiction, division and ambiguity, but also for solidarity and friendship, loyalty and love.

By the same token, the study has aimed to move away from simply considering 'youth' as an autonomous and criminalized social category, or, by contrast, as the vanguard of incipient social protest and resistance. As Chapters 3 and 4 have argued, the young men of the SAYO project were constrained by the perception of youth as a problem and were subject to increased surveillance and control. This was as true of the local Bengali community (Chapter 5) as of the wider community and local institutions (Chapter 3), all of which viewed the youth project itself as a 'problem' facility and its members as, by default, a 'problem' element. However, it is also true that the young men viewed themselves as part of their local community and as defending it, both from outside attack (Chapters 3, 4 and 5) and from internal division, particularly around the issue of gender relations (Chapter 6). As Chapter 4 makes clear, it is not always possible to read youth activities and alliances as 'resistance', being often bound up with more mundane, sometimes ignoble, causes and conflicts. While the present study has been particularly concerned with conflict, it is also imperative to move away from the action-centred, crisis-focused accounts of youth activity – especially black youth activity – which feed into and sustain the criminalization of black youth. The vast majority of time was spent doing nothing, hanging out with friends (Chapter 5) or at home, school or work. Chapters 5 and 6 have sought to place peer group formation against this wider, more ordinary backdrop, while more generally I have tried to de-sensationalize and contextualize the moments of conflict. I have consciously chosen also to move away from the association of youth with crisis by not exploring the more controversial issues of drug use or criminal activity – not because there was not any, but because it was mainly unexceptional and unrevealing. The everyday formation of peer group and community boundaries point to the import-ance of internal bonds that function apart from a more outward looking or defensive construction, with divisions and alliances within and between peer groups, working along and across lines of ethnicity, gender and age. It would be misleading, then, to define peer group identifications as simply oppositional and relational; they were also subject to internal changes, fissures and fusions, and incorporated a strong affective sense

of loyalty, of friendship and of community which should not be underestimated.

What the present study has attempted to do is make explicit the
strengths, ambivalences and contradictions of Asian youth identities; in
part to separate them out from the web of pathologies in which the triple
whammy of 'race', gender and generation enmesh them, and rescue them
from the benign and colourless valorizations of a toothless politics of
difference-without-difference. The study argues neither for the primacy
of structure over agency nor for subjectivity without constraint, but for
the complex and shifting intersection of image, context and individual.
Identities are always situated in time and space, too often in the encounter
between self and 'Other', the power to objectify and the desire and
determination to become Subject. Almost against my will, I have been
forced to confront the power of 'the Asian Gang', to acknowledge the
complex ways in which these representations are lived through in the
experiences of the young men who people these pages, and yet who are
not defined or delimited by them. In some ways, then, the work is a call
for the theoretical promises of the 'new ethnicities' approach to be
fulfilled; for an honest and unflinching acknowledgement and exploration
of the complexity and specificity – and the broader import – of these
encounters, which defy closure and deny a final knowing.

The present work has been very much a labour of love, but at its heart
is a belief in the need to both dismantle the common-sense demonologies
of 'race', gender and youth, and to refuse the easy one-world solutions
of universal difference and acquisitive marginality. There is a need to
reassert the constitutive nature of structure in the formation of cultural
identities, the play of power and history, but also to recognize the only
partial circumscription of marginal identities, the potential for disruption
and the imagination of 'Other' sensibilities and alliances. There is also a
need to explore the intersection of processes of racialization with the
dynamics of cultural specificity, the ways in which 'difference' is used,
perhaps most often, as a weapon of exclusion and attack rather than a
gesture towards inclusion in a post-modern hybrid multi-culture. Recognizing the complex and shifting nature of identity also demands the
recognition of solidarity and belonging; not the stasis of stagnant absolutes
but the necessary emotional touchstone of family, friends and community.
Difference matters – not always in expected ways. Identities form and
re-form. Contexts shift. Meanings change – or sometimes, perhaps too
often, they do not, even in spite of alternative realities. Alliances are made
and are dismantled. Friends and family matter, perhaps most of all. People
love and hate and fight and are reconciled – maybe. Asserting these as

truths and then ignoring them is not enough; there is a need to explore the contours and texture of each encounter, the similarities and specificities, the boundaries drawn and redrawn, the clash of authority and understandings – what my friend Wendy Bottero evocatively described to me as '3-D theorization'. Perhaps, after all, fiction is the only way.

Update: October 1999

In the two-and-a-half years it has taken me to write this book a number of changes have taken place with the SAYO project and its members. Some of these have been incorporated into the preceding chapters; still others are in the process of unfolding at the time of writing – this section is an attempt to capture some of these transformations.

The last year has seen structural changes in the local Youth Service that have profoundly altered the position of the SAYO project. The project now forms part of a borough-wide minorities youth project that has faced some administrative and budgeting teething troubles. The project itself was without staff for some months and has had its annual finances cut to preclude any holiday provisions or residential work. The senior member's committee ran a successful local football league last year, but the problems with the project's provision and the call of work and college duties resulted in a lack of interest to the point where the committee has effectively folded. During the recent restructuring a number of staff, including Sher Khan and Shahin (who had been working for the project for the previous twelve months) moved to area-based youth projects, and although new staff have been recruited, including Khalid, the majority of members have moved away from the project, making way for the next – much smaller and quieter – generation of young men. Of the original staff team, only Farhan still remains, working Saturday mornings. In the next few weeks, Yasmin herself is to move to a new project in the borough to set up a Youth Parliament.

There have been other changes: Sher Khan, Farhan and Hashim have all married. Silver made an escape bid to a youth project in a neighbouring borough but has recently returned to the SEPA project on the Stoneleigh Estate; although he no longer works with the SAYO project, he has set up a senior football team with some of the senior members who play in a Sunday Asian League. Sher Khan works for the local play service and youth service and continues to run his families' two restaurants. Shopna has been moved from Asian youth work to provide Outreach support on the Amersham Estate; she too has married. Amitabh has taken up a post in Race Equalities in Birmingham.

The senior group effectively no longer exists as it did, divided by the demands of work and college and only rarely meeting up. Shahin has just entered his final year of a law degree and is hoping to take the legal practice course to become a solicitor. He also works for the local Youth Service. Zohar has started a degree in computer science and works for the local playservice; he is still with his girlfriend Humaira. S. Ahmed has drifted through several jobs but is about to start working for a building society. Humzah has also gone through several changes of work, and is currently working for a local Argos. Liaquot is mini-cabbing for a firm in South London, Salman remains unemployed (and it is rumoured he is about to return to Bangladesh to get married) and Mustafa is still in prison, where he has apparently undergone a religious conversion; he is expected to be released sometime next year. Shakiel is currently in his second year of a degree in computer science and works part time in a local clothes shop. Khalid is working for the local play and youth service and also works as a teaching assistant in a nearby primary school. Mehraj works for Sainsburys supermarket. Ashraf is still unemployed and spends most of his time with Salman, looking for girls.

It is the junior members, the little ones, who have seen the most profound changes, moving from school through college to university and work. They have also splintered into two distinct groups, apparently permanently. The first consists of Hanif, Jamal, Sayeed, Mohammed, Ismat and several other young men; the second of Ifti, Shafiq, Faruk, Enam and a number of individuals from the Amersham Estate, friends of Malik. Hanif has recently completed his A-levels and started a degree in law; he also works for the play service. Jamal failed to sit his A-level exams last year and, along with Mohammed, is taking two one-year intensive A-levels in sociology and psychology at a local college. Ismat has also returned to college to do a B.Tec in leisure and tourism and works part-time as a playworker. Sayeed has started a course in mechanical engineering, and works in MacDonalds. Since leaving school, Ifti has worked at a local MacDonalds; he is currently on a trip to India and Bangladesh with his father. Faruk has recently returned from a long visit 'home' and is planning to retake his GCSE's. Shafiq and Enam are both unemployed.

The changes outlined above have inevitably altered my own relationship with the SAYO project and its members. Almost in spite of my own intentions and desires, I have moved away from the project in recent months, although I still pass by most weeks and am in regular contact with the area youth workers. The young men have also moved on with their lives, although I still see most of them around from time to time and I am asked to write references, appear on occasion as character witness in court and drop them to and from airports. They, in their turn, have given me lifts to and from the airport, bring me souvenirs from holidays and I still get to hear most of the gossip – and I get to answer questions about how the book is going. When I tell them it is nearly finished, they stare in disbelief. I recently told Khalid that once the book was finished, I would be happy to never think about them again, and that I would probably leave the country – but we both knew that was never likely to be an option. Although there is a sense of distance in my relationship with the project and that period of our lives, there is no sense of closure. On the contrary, I am looking forward to weddings and successes at college and work, and while the book turned out to be perhaps more gloomy than I had expected, I think the future looks mainly pretty positive. Though I am not so naïve as to suggest a 'Happy Ever After . . .'

Finishing the book is, then, a necessary but arbitrary disruption in an ongoing story. Concluding, in both senses of finishing and interpreting, providing neatly bounded, digestible insights, seems almost as impossible (and undesirable) a task as starting out. While not wishing to end on a series of disclaimers or self-defensive fudges, I would offer the following remarks on *The Asian Gang*. Firstly, the young men described in this book do not, in any way, constitute 'a gang'. They should not be seen as representative of other Asian youth, of other black youth, of other areas, of other times. Nor should they be held hostage to the events and remarks contained herein, which are the product of a particular time and space and of my own 'fiction writing'. Which is not to deny the relevance of these experiences or of the study as a whole; rather, the young men and the events contained in the preceding chapters have been used as a story through which to examine the theoretical and common-sense assumptions of black/Asian youth identities as embodied in the myth of 'the gang', to make space for re-imagination and to bid for the place of politics and of love in the research process. If the title of the work seems like false advertising then, perhaps this says more about these assumptions and the expectations imposed on black youth, about the desire for the dangerous 'Other' and the marketability of marginality, about the need for folk devils and the power of fantasy. If the contents of the book seem, by contrast, rather mundane and ordinary then I think that is not such a bad thing – perhaps, indeed, it is the most important thing.

Notes

1 They, as individuals rather than as 'representatives' cannot, of course, stand or speak for their friends or peer groups, and in some cases learned almost as much about each other as I did – this raises questions about the provision of knowledge even amongst the groups, as discussed in Chapter 6.

2 The study partly originated in a challenge to me by Professor Terence Ranger at the *Culture, Identity and Politics* workshop in Oxford in 1992 to try to make the study of Asian youth more interesting!

3 Keith (1995b) talks about the importance of 'radical contextualization' in the formation of academic knowledge and political action – the acknowledgement of the historical and geographical spaces within which 'truths' are asserted, action taken and knowledges produced.

4 As Ko Banerjea has pointed out to me, the invention of the gang is a reformulation of longer established ideas of Asian deviance and incipient criminality, particularly around issues of immigration, marriage and sexuality. Asian, particularly Muslim, identities have increasingly been used as the yardstick against which ideas of cultural compatibility, citizenship and the nation are defined.

5 Witness Madonna's flirtation with 'the East', TLC's latest video, *Unpretty*, Whitney Houston's Top of the Pops appearance with oddly positioned bindi, as well as Talvin Singh's catapult to megastardom culminating in the Mercury Music Award and (somewhat bemused) appearance on the MOBO's.

6 see Sanjay Sharma's critique of Baumann's work on *Bhangra* in *DisOrienting Rhythms* (Sharma, Hutnyk and Sharma, 1996: 35).

7 But see Banerjea's recent scalding critique of hybridity in relation to the 'Asian Underground' in *Theory, Culture and Society* (forthcoming).

8 There is a long history of ethnographic work on black men in the United States (Liebow, 1967 to Duneier, 1992) which explores the multi-faceted nature of black male identities. However, these tend not to place black identities within wider contexts of structural constraint, inequality and hegemonic representation. There is also, of course, the conventional problem-oriented accounts, such as Taylor and Wilkinson, 1982; Anderson, 1978, 1990).

9 Channel 4's recent series, *The Hip-Hop Years* makes the point that it was the consumption of hip-hop by white youth which triggered moral panics over its content and fuelled attempts at censorship.

Conclusion

10 It is interesting that most work in cultural studies in recent years has tended to reject its ethnographic roots in favour of a more textual bias for the artefacts of 'cultural production'. It has thus tended to read politics into production and ignore the complex and contradictory ways these styles are lived through.

11 While the *DisOrienting Rhythms* collection is an avowedly multi-vocal, sometimes discordant, vari-linear narrative, it has been taken up by the academic establishment, particularly in cultural studies, as 'the' voice of a new generation of black British academics, thereby producing a reductive monochrome version of its more disruptive politics.

Bibliography

Alabhai Brown, Y. (1995), 'An Islam of Slogans fed the Riots, so did White Islamophobia', *Independent*, 13 June 1995.

Alexander, C. (1996), *The Art of Being Black*, Oxford: Oxford University Press.

—— (1998), "Reimagining the Muslim Community", in *Innovations*, 11(4): 439–50.

—— (forthcoming 2000), "Dis-Entangling the Asian Gang: ethnicities, identities, masculinities, in B. Hesse (ed.), *Un/Settled Multiculturalisms*, London: Zed Press.

Anderson, B. (1993), *Imagined Communities*, London: Verso.

Anderson, E. (1978), *A Place on the Corner*, Chicago: University of Chicago.

—— (1990), *Streetwise: Race, Class and Change in an Urban Community*, Chicago: University of Chicago.

Anthias, F. and Yuval-Davis, N. (1992), *Racialised Boundaries*, London: Routledge.

Anwar, M. (1994), *Young Muslims in Britain*, Leicester: Islamic Foundation.

—— (1998), *Between Cultures: Continuity and change in the lives of young Asians*, London: Routledge.

Back, L. (1996), *New Ethnicities and Urban Culture*, London: UCL Press.

Bains, H. (1988), 'Southall Youth: an old-fashioned story', in P. Cohen and H. Bains (eds.), *Multi-Racist Britain*, London: Macmillan.

Ballard, R. (ed.) (1994), *Desh Pardesh*, London: Christopher Hurst.

Banerjea, K. (forthcoming 2000), 'Sounds of whose underground?', *Theory, Culture and Society.*

Banerjea K. and Banerjea P. (1996), 'Psyche and Soul: a view from the "South"', in A. Sharma, J. Hutnyk and S. Sharma (eds.), *Dis-Orienting Rhythms: the politics of the new Asian dance music*, London: Zed Press.

Banks, M. (1996), *Ethnicity: Anthropological Constructions*, London: Routledge.

Barth, F. (1969), *Ethnic Groups and Boundaries*, Bergen: Universitetsforlaget.

Baumann, G. (1996), *Contested Cultures: Discourses of Identity in Multi-ethnic London*, Cambridge: Cambridge University Press.

Bennetto, J. (1995), 'Research warns of Asian crime "timebomb"', *Independent,* 22 July 1995.

Benson, S. (1996), 'Asians have culture, West Indians have problems: discourses in race inside and outside anthropology', in T. Ranger, Y. Samad and O. Stuart (eds.), *Culture, Identity and Politics*, Aldershot: Avebury.

Bhabha, H. (1990), 'The Third Space' in J. Rutherford (ed.), *Identity: Community, Culture, Difference*, London: Lawrence & Wishart.

Blount, M. and Cunningham, G. (eds.)(1996), *Representing Black Men*, New York and London: Routledge.

Body-Gendrot, S. (1995), 'Urban Violence: A Quest for Meaning', *New Community*, 21,4: 525–36.

Bose, M. (1994), 'Youths combine the worst of both worlds', *Daily Mail*, 16 August 1994.

Brah, A. (1996), *Cartographies of Diaspora*, London: Routledge.

Brake, M. (1985), *Comparative Youth Culture*, New York and London: Routledge.

Campbell, A. (1984), *Girls in the Gang*, New York: Basil Blackwell.

Carby, H. (1982), 'White woman listen!', in CCCS Collective, *The Empire Strikes Back*, London: Hutchinson.

Cashmore, E. (1979), *Rastaman: the Rastafarian Movement in England*, London: Allen & Unwin.

Cashmore E. and Troyna B. (eds.)(1982), *Black Youth in Crisis*, London: Allen & Unwin.

CCCS Collective (1982), *The Empire Strikes Back*, London: Hutchinson.

Clifford, J. (1986), 'Partial Truths', in J. Clifford and G. Marcus (eds.), *Writing Culture: the Poetics and Politics of Ethnography,* Berkeley & Los Angeles: University of California.

—— (1988), *The Predicament of Culture*, Cambridge, Mass.: Harvard. University Press

Chapman, R. and Rutherford J. (eds.) (1988), *Male Order: Unwrapping Masculinity*, London: Lawrence & Wishart.

Chaudhuri, V. (1993), 'When Asian youths hit back', *Guardian*, 16 September 1993.

Cohen, A. (1993), *Masquerade Politics*, Oxford: Berg.

Cohen, A.K. (1955), *Delinquent Boys*, Chicago: Free Press.

Connell, R. (1987), *Gender and Power*, London: Polity.

—— (1995), *Masculinities*, London: Polity.

Daniels, A. (1993), 'Can Asians Recivilise our Inner Cities?' *Daily Mail*, 28 July 1993.

Downes, D. (1966), *The Delinquent Solution*, London: Routledge & Kegan Paul.

DuGay, P., Hall, S., Janes, L., Mackay, H., and Negus, K., (1997), *Doing Cultural Studies*, London: Sage.

Duneier, M. (1992), *Slim's Table*, Chicago: University of Chicago.

Dyson, M. (1993), *Reflecting Black: African-American Cultural Criticism*, Minneapolis: University of Minnesota.

Eade, J. (1996), 'Ethnicity and the Politics of Cultural Difference: an agenda for the 1990s?' in T. Ranger, Y. Samad and O. Stuart (eds.), *Culture, Identity and Politics*, Aldershot: Avebury.

Gardner, K. and Shakur, A. (1994), 'I'm Bengali, I'm Asian and I'm living here: the changing identity of British Bengalis', in R. Ballard, (ed.), *Desh Pardesh*, London: Christopher Hurst.

Gates, H. L. (1992), *Loose Canons: Notes on the Culture Wars*, New York: Oxford University Press.

Geertz, C. (1983), *Local Knowledge*, New York: Basic Books.

Gillespie, M. (1995), *Television, Ethnicity and Cultural Change*, London: Routledge.

Gilroy, P. (1987), *There Ain't No Black in the Union Jack*, London: Hutchinson.

—— (1992), 'The End of Anti-Racism', in J. Donald and A. Rattansi (eds), *'Race', Culture and Difference*, London: Sage.

—— (1993), *Small Acts*, London: Serpent's Tail.

Giroux, H. (1996), *Fugitive Cultures*, London & New York: Routledge.

Glavanis, P. (1998), 'Political Islam within Europe: a contribution to the analytical framework', in *Innovations*, 11(4): 391–410.

Goodey, J. (1999), 'Victims of Racism and Racial Violence: experiences among boys and young men', *International Review of Victimology*, 5(3).

Hagedorn, J.M. (1998), 'Frat Boys, Bossmen, Studs and Gentlemen: a typology of gang masculinities', in L. Bowker (ed.), *Masculinities and Violence*, London: Sage.

Hall, S. (1990), 'Cultural Identity and Diaspora' in J. Rutherford (ed.), *Identity: Community, Culture, Difference,* London: Lawrence & Wishart.

—— (1992), "New Ethnicities", in J. Donald and A. Rattansi (eds.), *'Race', Culture and Difference*, London: Sage.

Hall, S. and Jefferson, T. (eds.)(1976), *Resistance Through Rituals*, London: Hutchinson.

Hall, S., Critcher, C., Jefferson, T., Clarke, J. and Roberts, B. (1978), *Policing the Crisis*, London: Hutchinson.

Halliday, F. (1999), 'Islamophobia Reconsidered', *Ethnic and Racial Studies*, 22(5): 892–902.

Hebdige, D. (1976), 'Reggae, Rastas and Rudies' in S. Hall and T. Jefferson (eds.), *Resistance Through Rituals*, London: Hutchinson.

—— (1979), *Subculture: The Meaning of Style*, London: Methuen.

Hennink, M, Diamond, I, and Cooper, P. (1999), 'Young Asian Women and Relationships: traditional or transitional?' *Ethnic and Racial Studies*, 22 (5): 867–91.

Hesse, B. (ed.) (2000), *Un/Settled Multiculturalisms*, London: Zed Press.

hooks, b. (1992), *Black Looks: Race and Representation*, London: Turnaround.

Hull, G.P., Scott, B. and Smith, B. (eds.) (1982), *All the Women are White . . .* New York: Feminist Press.

Jackson, M. and Taylor, D. (1996), 'Asian Teenage Gangs Terrorising London', *Evening Standard*, 13 November 1996.

Jacobson, J. (1997), 'Religion and ethnicity: dual and alternative sources of identity among young British Pakistanis', *Ethnic and Racial Studies*, 20 (2): 238–56.

Kalra, V.S., Hutnyk, J. and Sharma, S. (1996), 'Re-sounding (Anti)Racism or Concordant Politics? Revolutionary Antecedents', in A. Sharma, J. Hutnyk and S. Sharma (eds.), *Dis-Orienting Rhythms*, London: Zed Press.

Keith, M. (1995a), 'Making the Street Visible: Placing Racial Violence in Context', *New Community*, 21 (4): 551–65.

—— (1995b), 'Shouts of the Street: Identity and the Spaces of Authenticity', *Social Identities*, 1 (2): 297–315.

Kelsey, T. (1992), 'New Rivalries divide the East End', *Independent*, 22 April 1992.

Klein, M. (1995), *The American Street Gang: its Nature, Prevalence and Control*, New York: Oxford University Press.

Lewis, P. (1994*), Islamic Britain: Religion, Politics and Identity among British Muslims,* London: I.B. Taurus.

Liebow, E. (1967), *Tally's Corner: a Study of Negro Street-corner Men*, Boston: Little, Brown & Co.

Mac An Ghaill, M. (1994), 'The Making of Black English Masculinities', in H. Brod and M. Kaufman (eds.), *Theorising Masculinity*, London: Sage.

Macey, M. (1999), 'Gender, Class and Religious Influences on changing patterns of Pakistani Muslim male violence in Bradford', *Ethnic and Racial Studies*, 22 (5): 845–66.

Malone, A. and Foster, H. (1994), 'Asian youths rebel against good image', *Sunday Times*, 21 August 1994.

Mercer, K. (1994), *Welcome to the Jungle*, London: Routledge.

Messerschmidt, J.W. (1998), 'Men Victimizing Men: the Case of Lynching, 1865– 1900', in L. Bowker (ed.), *Masculinities and Violence*, London: Sage.

Miles, R. (1993), *Racism after Race Relations*, London: Routledge.

Miller, D. (1997), 'Consumption and its Consequences', in H. MacKay (ed.), *Consumption and Everyday Life*, London: Sage.

Mirza, H. (ed.) (1997), *Black British Feminism: a Reader*, London: Routledge.

Modood, T. (1992), *Not Easy Being British: Colour, Culture & Citizenship*, Stoke-on- Trent: Trentham.

Modood, T., Berthoud, R., Lakey, J., Nazroo, J., Smith, P., Virdee, S. and Beishon, S. (1997*), Ethnic Minorities in Britain: Diversity and Disadvantage*, London: Policy Studies Institute.

Moyes, J. and Cusick, J. (1995), 'Asian Generation Gap blamed for Riot', *Independent,* 12 June 1995.

Osgerby, B. (1998), *Youth in Britain since 1945*, Oxford: Blackwell.

Petre, J. (1994), 'Knife Gangs Shatter School Life', *Sunday Telegraph*, 20 March 1994.

Phillips, M. (1991), 'Alienation runs Riot', *Guardian,* 13 September 1991.

Pryce, K. (1979), *Endless Pressure,* Harmondsworth: Penguin.

Rosaldo, R. (1993), *Culture and Truth: the Remaking of Social Analysis*, London: Routledge.

Roy, A. (1994), 'Asian Victims Learn to Strike Back', *Telegraph,* 21 August 1994.

Runnymede Trust (1997), *Islamophobia – a Challenge for Us All,* London: Runnymede Trust.

Saeed, A., Blain, N. and Forbes, D. (1999), 'New ethnic and national questions in Scotland: post-British identities among Glasgow Pakistani teenagers', *Ethnic and Racial Studies*, 22 (5): 821–44.

Sahgal G. and Yuval-Davis, N. (eds.) (1992), *Refusing Holy Orders: Women and Fundamentalism in Britain*, London: Virago.

Samad, Y. (1992), 'Book Burning and Race Relations: the Political Mobilisation of Bradford Muslims', *New Community*, 18 (4): 507– 19.

—— (1996), 'The Politics of Islamic Identity among Bangladeshis and Pakistanis in Britain', in T. Ranger, Y. Samad and O. Stuart (eds.), *Culture, Identity and Politics*, Aldershot: Avebury.

Sayyid, S. (1997), *A Fundamental Fear*, London: Zed Press.

Scantlebury, E. (1995), 'Muslims in Manchester: the Depiction of a Religious Community', *New Community*, 21 (3): 425–35.

Sharma, A., Hutnyk, J. and Sharma, S. (eds.)(1996), *Dis-Orienting Rhythms: the Politics of the New Asian Dance Music*, London: Zed Press.

Sharma, A. (1996), 'Sounds Oriental: the (Im)possibility of Theorizing Asian Musical Cultures', in A. Sharma, J. Hutnyk and S. Sharma (eds.), *Dis -Orienting Rhythms*, London: Zed Press.

Sharma, S. (1996), 'Noisy Asians or "Asian Noise"?' in A. Sharma, J. Hutnyk and S. Sharma (eds.), *Dis-Orienting Rhythms*, London: Zed Press.

Shaw, A. (1988), *A Pakistani Community in Oxford*, Oxford: Basil Blackwell.

—— (1994), 'The Pakistani Community in Oxford', in R. Ballard (ed.), *Desh Pardesh*, London: Christopher Hurst.

Sivanandan, A. (1981/2), 'From Resistance to Rebellion: Asian and Afro-Caribbean Struggles in Britain', *Race and Class*, 23 (2–3): 111–51.

Solomos, J. (1993), *Race and Racism in Britain*, Basingstoke: Macmillan.

Stanley, J. (1994), 'Breaking the Cycle of Violence', (letter), *Observer,* 19 August 1994.

Taylor, R. and Wilkinson, D.Y. (eds.)(1982), *The Black Male in America*, Chicago: Nelson Hall.

Van Maanen T. (1995), 'An End to Innocence: the Ethnography of Ethnography', in T. Van Maanen (ed.), *Representations in Ethnography,* London: Sage.

Wallace, M. (1990), *Black Macho and the Myth of the Superwoman*, London: Verso.

Webster, C. (1997), 'The construction of British "Asian" criminality', *International Journal of the Sociology of Law*, 25: 65–86.

Werbner, P. (1990*), The Migration Process: Capital, Gifts and Offerings among British Pakistanis*, Oxford: Berg.

Werbner, P. and Anwar, M. (eds.) (1991), *Black and Ethnic Leaderships in Britain*, London: Routledge.

West, C. (1993), 'The New Cultural Politics of Difference', in S. During (ed.), *The Cultural Studies Reader*, London: Routledge.

—— (1994), *Race Matters*, New York: Vintage.

Westwood, S. (1991), 'Red Star of Leicester: Racism, the Politics of Identity and Black Youth in Britain', in P. Werbner and M. Anwar (eds.), *Black and Ethnic Leaderships in Britain*, London: Routledge.

Wilson, A. (1978), *Finding a Voice: Asian Women in Britain*, London: Virago.

Index

Index

Hesse, Barnor, 119n15
hooks, bell, 17, 235
Hull, G.P., Scott, B. and Smith, B., 234

Independent, 7, 10, 11, 25n5

Jacobson, Jessica, 14, 230, 236

Kalra, Virinder, Hutnyk, John and
  Sharma, Sanjay, 229
Keith, Michael, 7, 21, 237, 252n3
Klein, Malcolm, 20, 238

Lawrence, Philip, 92, 111
Lawrence, Stephen, 25n4, 158
Lewis, Philip, 230
Liebow, Elliott, 252n8

Mac An Ghaill, Mairtin, 19–20, 25n10,
  235
Macey, Marie, 12, 14, 18, 20, 236
Marland, Michael, 3
Marriage, 212–215
Masculinities, 15–18, 234–7, 242
  Asian Masculinities, 16–18, 236–7
  Black Masculinities, 17, 234–6
  Brothers, 171–197
  see also women
Mercer, Kobena, 236
  and Julien, Isaac, 236
Messerschmidt, James, 235
Miah, Badrul, 9, 24n4, 25n5
Miller, Daniel, 239
Mirza, Heidi, 235, 236
Modood, Tariq
  Muslim identity, 13–14, 25n7, 230,
    231, 246
  Muslim underclass, 6, 15, 58
Modood, Tariq et al,
  Muslim identity, 87n4, 231, 240, 243
  Statistics, 58–9, 87n3

Observor, 9
Osgerby, Bill, 238

Panorama, 6, 57
Patten, John, 6
Pryce, Ken, 17

Religion, 14–15, 245–6
Rosaldo, Renato, 28, 225
Runnymede Trust, 14
Rushdie, Salman, *see Satanic Verses*
Rutherford, Jonathan, 19

Saeed, Amir, Blain, Neil and Forbes,
  Douglas, 15
Sahgal, Gita and Yuval-Davis, Nira, 16
Samad, Yunas, 6
Satanic Verses, 6, 7, 10, 13, 231, 233
Sayyid, Bobby, 230, 231
Sharma, Ashwin, Hutnyk, John, and
  Sharma, Sanjay, 19, 24n2, 225–30,
    233, 239, 241
Sharma, Ashwin, 232
Sharma, Sanjay, 240–1, 242n6
Shaw, Alison, 13, 20, 240
Sivanandan, A., 15
Solomos, John, 6
Stanley, Jonathan, 9
Sunday Telegraph, 9
Sunday Times, 8

Taylor, R. and Wilkinson, D., 252n8
Times, 6, 11

Underclass, 14–15, 57–60, 229, 243

Van Maanen, T., 28

Wallace, Michelle, 234–5
Webster, Colin, 15, 17
Werbner, Pnina, 13, 20, 240
  and Muhammed Anwar, 14
West, Cornell, 17, 21, 234, 236
Westwood, Sally, 236
Willis, Paul, 238
Wilson, Amrit, 15
Women, 197–215
  sisters, 197–212
  wives, 212–15

Youth, 18–21, 237–41, 242
  Asian youth, 18–19, 238–41
  Black youth, 18–20, 237–9